CONFLICT AND INTERVENTION IN AFRICA

Conflict and Intervention in Africa

Nigeria, Angola, Zaïre

Herbert Ekwe-Ekwe

Visiting Lecturer in Politics, Goldsmiths' College and Birkbeck College, University of London

St. Martin's Press   New York

© Herbert Ekwe-Ekwe 1990

All rights reserved. For information, write:
Scholarly and Reference Division,
St. Martin's Press, Inc., 175 Fifth Avenue,
New York, N.Y. 10010

First published in the United States of America in 1990

Printed in Hong Kong

ISBN 0-312-04617-0

Library of Congress Cataloging-in-Publication Data
Ekwe-Ekwe, Herbert, 1953–
  Conflict and intervention in Africa: Nigeria, Angola, Zaïre/
Herbert Ekwe-Ekwe.
    p.   cm.
  Includes bibliographical references.
  ISBN 0-312-04617-0
  1. Nigeria—Foreign relations. 2. Angola—Foreign relations.
3. Zaire—Foreign relations. I. Title.
DT515.62.E38 1990
967—dc20   90-30356
                                                     CIP

To my parents, Gladys Nwaoyiri Ekwe-Ekwe
and Humphrey Akpa Ekwe-Ekwe

Truth, one would have thought, is not a simple, once-given, God-ordained, immutable entity but more like a combination of sense perception with our scientific concepts, others' testimony and traditional knowledge and custom. As an account of reality which exists independently of our consciousness of it, the truth does not depend on the status or authority of the person rendering it or on the elegance or beauty of our description, but on the extent to which our account conforms with reality, that is, what is the case, and coheres with all existing knowledge. We attain the truth – if and when we ever do – not by confining ourselves to the narrow circle of received or immediate experience only, but through a comprehensive view of interpretation and correlation.

> Mokwugo Okoye, 'A Little Heresy', 1975

Contents

Acknowledgements		ix
1	Conflict and Intervention in Africa: An Overview	1
	I Introduction	1
	II General Features of Conflict and Intervention in Africa and the Rest of the Southern World	3
2	Nigeria	11
	I Introduction	11
	II Western Europe and the United States	22
	III Africa: The Debates on 'Self Determination', 'Territorial Integrity', and the 'Inviolability' of Post-Colonial Borders	51
	IV The Soviet Union	59
	V A Concluding Note	66
3	Angola	69
	I Introduction	69
	II The Western Response: The United States and Others	72
	III The Soviet Union, Cuba and China	89
	IV Africa: South Africa and the Contiguous States	102
	V Conclusions	110
4	Zaïre	112
	I Introduction	112
	II Western Evaluations and Reactions	115
	III African Attitudes	125
	IV Cuba, The Soviet Union and Conclusions	129
5	The Dynamics of Intervention: A Comparative Survey	131
6	Conclusions: Conflict, Intervention and the Future	151

viii   *Contents*

Notes   159
Select Bibliography   178
Index   188

Acknowledgements

This study has developed from my PhD thesis in politics in Lancaster University. I wish to express my profound gratitude to Christopher Clapham who supervised the initial research for his invaluable advice and criticism throughout the various phases of the enterprise. I should also like to thank Ian Bellany, Martin Edmonds, Reginald Harrison and Laura Summers, all of the Politics Department, Lancaster University, for the useful discussions I had with them while working on the thesis.

I owe an intellectual debt to Billy Dudley, late professor of political science, University of Ibadan, for his part in stimulating my initial interest to pursue research in conflict studies while I was an undergraduate at Ibadan University. I also acknowledge the following teachers and friends at Ibadan for the various ways they have contributed towards my academic career: Peter Ekeh, Richard Joseph, Sam Nolutshungu, Elone Nwabuzor, Omafume Onoge, Emmanuel Osuji and Osita Uwalaka.

Stimulating discussions on several aspects of African politics with the following intellectuals, many during fleeting moments, helped to sharpen the focus of this book: Sully Abu, Jide Adeniyi-Jones, Akuma Aja, Sam Ajeleti, Tade Akin Aina, Joe 'Poju Akinyanju, Mitchell Alamina, Ifi Amadiume, Iyorchia Ayu, Abdulrahaman Mohamed Babu, Celestine Bassey, Nii K. Bentsi-Enchill, Ines Caravia, Chinweizu, Merle Collins, Paul Diakite, Aame Abakpa Diga, Elom ('Chief of Staff') Dovlo, Egwu U. Egwu, Michael Ejieh, Ndubisi Eke, Edem Edem Ekwo, Mohamed El-Doufani, John Fernandes, Rosemary Galli, Joe Gaydecki, Cal Giles, Emmanuel Hansen, Eddie Iroh, Winston James, Onwuchekwa Jemie, David Johnson, Yiu-Chung Leung, Stanley Macebuh, Aaron Makondo, Edris Makward, Bene Madunagu, Eddie Madunagu, Xolani Mkhwanazi, Sam Moyo, Tony Nnokam, Pitika Ntuli, Odi Nwabiani, John Nnia Nwodo, Joe Obi Jr, Victor Obichere, Chike Obidigbo, Odia Ofeimun, Amma Ogan, Bisi Ogunbadejo, Yemi Ogunbiyi, Gabriel Ojegbile, Chuba Okadigbo, Aja Okorie, Peter Okoronkwo,

Sonala Olumhense, Kalu E. Kalu Onwunta, Lemmy Owugah, Tony Phido, Ed Scott, Ahmed Sheikh, Sunmi Smart-Cole, Henderson Tapela, Tesfachew, Tunde Thompson, Eskor Toyo, Sonni Tyoden, Onyema Ugochukwu, Amrit Wilson and Zaya Yeebo. I am particularly grateful to Lemmy Owugah for his role in creating the rigorous scholarly environment at Calabar University which put to the test a series of 'contending' methodologies in the social sciences.

Annie Martin and I have spent several hours debating a number of the issues raised in this book. Her ever-critical insights have contributed enormously to the final outcome. I wish to thank Annie for translating the German and French background texts used in the study.

Finally, my immense thanks and appreciation to Helen, Ngozi, JacMoses, Victor, Chima, Chinyere, and Esther for their unrelenting work for the family during this time of my absence from home.

Herbert Ekwe-Ekwe

1 Conflict and Intervention in Africa: An Overview

INTRODUCTION

The aim of this book is to investigate the nature of civil conflict and intervention in Africa with special reference to Nigeria, Angola and Zaïre. We shall concentrate on five main features associated with the subject in each of the three study areas: (a) the determinant of the extent of intervention in the conflict[1]; (b) the type of intervention the contending power groups or factions (in each conflict) are prepared to accept during hostilities[2]; (c) the motive for intervention[3]; (d) the mode of intervention,[4] and (e) the consequences of intervention (or outcomes of intervention).

The study consists of six chapters. This chapter is an overview of the occurrence of conflicts and interventions in Africa, and the rest of the Southern World, since the end of the Second World War in 1945. Chapters 2–4 form the core of the book. Each gives a detailed analysis of the conflict and intervention in the three case studies – Nigeria (chapter 2), Angola (chapter 3) and Zaïre (chapter 4). This is also the chronological order of the occurrence of these conflicts.

Each of the 'core' chapters is preceded by an introductory section which provides the background information leading to the outbreak of the conflict and the intervention by external powers. In this regard, we shall particularly assess the nature or features of pre-war relationships (or linkages) between the rival domestic parties in the various conflicts and the external actors involved in them.[5] This will be essential in helping us to answer some of the questions raised by the dominant themes under investigation, especially those dealing with the determinant of the extent of intervention and its consequences.

Also in each of these three chapters, the major external participants in the conflicts are isolated and their roles are analysed under specified sections. On Nigeria, this entails a detailed analysis of the intervention of Britain, France, the Soviet Union and the Organisation of African Unity. In the Angola chapter, our focus will be on the United States, the Soviet Union, Cuba, South Africa and the Organisation of African Unity, while on Zaïre, the external powers examined will be France, the United States, Morocco and the OAU.

In discussing the activities of each of these outside powers in any of the conflicts, the five dominant themes we mentioned earlier will be the focus of our enquiry. We shall attempt to establish the principal forms of intervention. In doing this, we will explore what existing (or potential) interests these foreign participants have had in any of the conflict states or could have been expected to exploit in the circumstances[6]: in other words, determining the factors motivating intervention. We will also try to find out any cases of rivalry among foreign powers with respect to their interests in the crisis state and examine what effects such a factor has had on the nature and impact of intervention.

It will be important to identify the time or phase in each of these conflicts at which intervention becomes evident, and then assess critically the effect or impact this has on the conduct, progress and outcome of the war. We should note that while we are trying to establish the role of a *particular* external power in a given conflict, we are also involved in comparing the features and effects of this role with other participants (in the same conflict). This is essential in answering the questions raised by the fifth dominant theme in this study: the consequences of intervention.

Chapter 5 is a detailed comparative analysis of the case studies. Using the five dominant themes of discourse as a reference to our understanding of intervention in these conflicts and others that have occurred in Africa in the past 30 years, we shall formulate some propositions which we hope will contribute to a greater understanding of external intervention in conflicts in Africa. Finally, chapter 6 extends the schematic preoccupation of the previous chapter by focusing on the nature of conflicts, and interventions, that will become more pronounced on the African political scene as we approach the next century.

This work is not supposed to be a historical account of the Nigerian, Angolan and Zaïrean civil wars, but we will find that during the course of our discussion, we may need to discern certain events in the military or diplomatic aspects of the conflicts in order to evaluate (or re-evaluate, as the case might be) the subsequent action (or reaction) of the external actors.

II GENERAL FEATURES OF CONFLICT AND INTERVENTION IN AFRICA AND THE REST OF THE SOUTHERN WORLD

Since the end of the Second World War in 1945, more than a hundred wars have been fought in Africa, the Middle East, Asia, Latin America and the Caribbean resulting in the deaths of 30 million people, over one-half of the total deaths recorded during the Second World War. In Europe and North America, during the same period, there has been no major war despite the ever intensifying nuclear (and conventional) arms race between East and West. While Western statespersons recently celebrated 40 years of peace in Europe in style and pomp, there was no loss of irony that their regimes, military, intelligence, financial and economic institutions promote and perpetuate the very conditions of conflict and deprivation in the Southern World. Emmanuel Hansen has observed:

> We appreciate that it is easier to get agreement on limiting nuclear weapons or to seek their abolition than to obtain a consensus on appropriate social and political systems; but this is a position which, if adopted, still leaves the victims of oppression where they are. We support, and we shall continue to support efforts to destroy, limit and abolish the use of nuclear weapons. But we are also painfully aware that before nuclear weapons were invented, we were dominated by Europeans through slavery, colonialism and now neocolonialism. For us this is a painful reality. If all the nuclear weapons in the world were destroyed we would still be dominated until the social system which oppresses us and which gave rise to the creation of nuclear weapons were eliminated. So long as people are oppressed the basis of serious conflict exists.[7]

Debts, Deteriorating Exchange Relations, and the Current Crisis

The ever-skyrocketing level of Southern World debt, owed to Western banks and other financial institutions has recently exacerbated the general crisis situation in this geographical region with the frequent occurrence of so-called IMF riots as the examples of Peru, Panama, Mexico, Tunisia, Egypt, Sudan, Senegal, Nigeria, Zambia and Bangladesh acutely illustrate. The fact is that the debt has afforded the West another means of extracting even more surplus from the South, as recent studies show.[8] Since 1981, the South has become a net exporter of capital to the West, amounting to a total of US$7 billion that year.[9] This figure increased to US$56 billion two years later, and by 1985 it had shot up to US$74 billion.[10] This was the same year that total new Southern-World borrowing and debt rescheduling was US$41 billion, while debt servicing was nearly three times as much at US$114 billion.[11] The sub-regional trends are particularly revealing: between 1981 and 1985, Latin America and the Caribbean's net capital transfer to the West rose from US$0.2 billion to US$42.4 billion; Asia's increased from US$1.7 billion to US$9.7 billion, while figures from Africa are US$5.3 billion for 1981 and US$21.5 billion in 1985.[12]

It is very important to emphasise Africa's 1985 net capital transfer to the West because this was the same year that the pop musician, Bob Geldof launched his 'Live Aid' Africa famine charity programme. Geldof's globally-televised pop fiesta raised £50 million, but as John Clark poignantly demonstrates in a special report for the charity organisation, Oxfam, 'for every £1 given in famine relief to Africa in 1985, the West reclaimed some £2 in debt payments'.[13]

The figures on the export of capital, given above, do not include profits repatriated from the Southern World to the West, during the same period, through the operations of Western-owned transnational corporations, nor do they include the amount represented by other forms of 'capital flight', nor indeed statistics from the Middle East. If the latter are included, the total outflow of capital from the South to the West between 1981 and 1985 would hardly be less than US$230–240 billion.[14] This figure is four times larger than the United States' Marshall Recovery Plan Programme for Europe after the Second World War.[15] Unlike Marshall, which Europe paid back, in addition to interest, 'this tribute from the poor to the rich countries will not be repaid'.[16] This uninterrupted export of critical resources from the Southern World has grave implications for human survival in the region. It will inevitably reinforce the overall dynamics of the politics of national liberation whose objective has fundamentally been the control and the utilisation of the resources of society by the local population.

Civil Conflicts as National Liberation Struggles

Most of the wars in the Southern World have been 'internal' or civil conflicts except the following inter–state confrontations: the Korean War (1950–53); the Sino–Indian border fighting (1962); the Algeria–Morocco border war (1964); the Arab–Israeli wars (1948, 1956, 1967, 1973, 1982); the Honduras–El Salvador War (1969); the Indo–Pakistani War; the Ethiopia–Somalia War (1974); the Sino–Vietnamese border war (1978); the 1979 Tanzania–Uganda fighting which led to the overthrow of the Idi Amin regime in Kampala; the Iran–Iraq War; the Libya–Chad border clashes (occasionally in the past 15 years); the Burkina Faso–Mali border war (1986), and the two-cornered border fighting between Thailand and Kampuchea, and Thailand and Laos (intermittently over the past decade). Even in the examples just cited, the origins of most of the wars are in fact located within the context of crisis in the political economy of a *specific* state (Korea, Israel, Pakistan, Ethiopia, Uganda, Chad, Kampuchea), thus emphasising the prevalence of civil conflicts in the region.[17]

These civil conflicts are essentially national liberation struggles, and while the features of their occurrence and results have been multifaceted, their overall trajectory have been fundamentally anti-imperialist. These have included direct struggles against classical colonialism (Vietnam, Kenya, Angola, Algeria, Mozambique, Eritrea, Western Sahara, Palestine, Namibia, South Africa, Zimbabwe), quasi-colonialism (China, Iran), neo-colonialism (Cuba, Grenada,

Nicaragua, Zaïre – particularly the Shaba uprisings discussed in this study) and liberation insurgencies organised by constituent nations and nationalities in the post-colonial state (Bangladesh in Pakistan, Biafra in Nigeria, Tamil Eelam in Sri Lanka).

The success of the Chinese Revolution (1949), the defeat of French colonialism in Indo–China (1954) and Algeria (1962), and the Cuban Revolution (1959) radically altered the correlation of social forces in the Southern World in the first two decades after the end of the Second World War. The age-long hegemony of Western imperialism in the region was so effectively challenged that these victories were to herald even more successes in the 1970s when a total of 14 revolutions occurred.[18] As Fred Halliday has shown,[19] these latest revolutionary successes have been a contributory factor to the effervescence of counter-revolutionary politics in the West in the 1980s, and the resultant Cold War.

The Interventionist Regime

The attitude and response of the superpowers, and their allies, to the national liberation struggle in the Southern World is pointedly contradictory. The Soviet Union has generally been a supporter of this process of liberation which it views as an integral corpus in the general struggle of the world's progressive forces against imperialism.[20] But Soviet support for Southern-World national liberation is far from being consistent, especially in the non-classical colonial categories, as the example of Nicaragua during the course of the Sandinista insurgency against the Somoza dictatorship typically illustrates. Tomas Borge, the Nicaraguan Minister of the Interior and the only surviving founder member of the Sandinista Front for National Liberation, recalls:

> We did not receive support during the war from any of the socialist countries, except Cuba. The Soviet Union and the others did not support us because they believed that only the Latin American Communist parties were the representatives of revolutionary changes, and it was not possible for them to think otherwise at that time. They had been

through a whole series of experiences, developing ideas in distant countries that divorced them from particular realities ... It cannot be said – in that idiotic language that is sometimes used – that Nicaragua's revolution was the fruit of Moscow gold. Not even the Soviets, the Soviet revolutionaries, believed in revolutionary change in Nicaragua. So how were they going to help us!'[21]

Even in the classical colonial type of liberation struggle, the Soviet Union has been known to switch sides, thus displaying a 'crass opportunism' as exemplified in the Eritrean case.[22]

It is, however, in the United States, the other superpower, that there exists a clearer consistency in approach to Southern-World national liberation. The US is opposed to it. Neil MacFarlane has succinctly described the US position: 'There is no real attempt in American literature to give substance to and to employ in analysis the term national liberation. Where it appears, usually in the phrases national liberation movements or wars of national liberation, it refers to left-wing, *pro-Soviet*, often *terroristic*, and usually *illegitimate* (that is, in US eyes) anti-American non-governmental actors. Its evaluative content is generally negative'.[23] (emphasis added). It is against this background of virtual hostility to the liberation movement in the South that the US has since 1945 pursued an unrelenting policy to oppose these struggles through 'surgical' military interventions or protracted counter-insurgency operations as the cases of the Philippines, Iran, Vietnam, Dominican Republic, El Salvador, Lebanon and Grenada indicate.

It is this US detection of the 'Hand of Moscow' in most of the national liberation upheavals in the Southern World that not only underscores the very simplistic analysis that successive governments in Washington make of events in the region, but also the *raison d'être* for interventionism. Ronald Reagan's administration was no exception. Its interventionist strategy in this region was encapsulated in the Reagan Doctrine.[24] Apart from the usual direct US military intervention (Lebanon, Libya, Grenada), the Reagan Doctrine also expanded the role of the United States in supporting the so-called low-intensity conflicts in the region (Afghanistan, Nicaragua).[25]

When Ronald Reagan came to power in 1981, the South was going through another phase of the national liberation struggle. Reagan had campaigned actively against the incumbent president, Jimmy Carter, and was committed to halt these revolutionary projects if elected.[26] And while campaigning for re-election in 1984, Reagan announced with glee that in the previous four years of his presidency, no national liberation victory had occurred anywhere in the Southern World.[27]

Predictably, President Reagan chose the Middle East as the arena to mount his 'roll back' of Southern World revolutions. After all, the 1979 Iran hostage crisis, with all its attendant humiliation for the United States, had overshadowed his ascendence to power. In 1982, Reagan supported the Israeli invasion of Lebanon. Two objectives were earmarked for this aggression: (a) the permanent displacement of the Palestinian conflict from its central geographical axis (in Palestine) to another Arab state – Lebanon, and (b) the destruction of Palestinian forces then deployed in Lebanon. But both ended disastrously. Israel was forced to withdraw from most of the Lebanese territory that it had initially occupied by the sustained counter-action of the Lebanese National Patriotic Forces (LNPF). In 1983, the LNPF achieved another success when it forced the United States military contingent stationed in Lebanon out of the country after bombing the latter's main base in Beirut. The US suffered heavy casualties in personnel, and losses of millions of dollars worth of military equipment in Lebanon before its expulsion.

The United States' invasion of Grenada, soon after the débâcle in Lebanon, was partly aimed at minimising the dramatic impact of the latter both in the US and internationally. Even here, it was highly unlikely that the US would have embarked on the invasion of such a small country as Grenada with the impunity displayed at the time if the tragic split within the governing New Jewel Movement, and the murder of Premier Maurice Bishop, had not occurred. The US success in Grenada was in essence a 'Pyrrhic military victory'.[28]

While President Reagan is right that no revolutionary breakthrough occurred in the Southern World between 1980 and 1984, his counter-revolutionary strategy had hardly achieved any decisive victory either. Besides Grenada, all national liberation movements in the region generally held out against the onslaught of the forces of the *ancien regime*. It was at worst a period of strategic stalemate. In a place like South Africa where the savagery of state oppression has been most vehement, resistance took a much more complex organisational character. Black people here have converted their wretched townships into sanctuaries of multiform resistance not seen in recent human history.

The superpowers, for obvious reasons, presently play a dominant role in the array of forces that make up the interventionist regime in many a Southern World conflict, but their allies, particularly in Europe, have retained a considerable leverage of action to intervene to defend *their own interests* in a conflict state, especially when such a state is a former colony. This is usually the case in Africa where Europe wields a much greater influence than it does in other sub-regions of the South.

Yet, as this study shows, our understanding of interventions in African (and Southern World) conflicts, would be incomplete if we were to restrict the focus of our enquiry or concentrate only upon extra-continental or extra-regional forces as has often been the practice in a number of works on the subject. While these forces have tended to play a hegemonic role in the interventionist process, a more comprehensive appraisal nonetheless must incorporate the role of contiguous state(s), sub-regional/regional and other local interest groups. Indeed, as we demonstrate later, the ultimate determination of which sectors of the interventionist forces emerge hegemonic in a given conflict does depend on the complex interplay of the interests and roles of regional powers.

Case Studies

This book concentrates on the conflicts and interventions in Nigeria, Angola and Zaïre because they represent the most politicised in Africa since the 1960–63 Congo War. The importance of the three states cannot be overstressed. Nigeria, with a current population of about 100 million, is Africa's most populous country. Apart from South Africa and possibly Namibia, Nigeria with Angola and Zaïre are sub-Sahara Africa's potentially wealthiest countries. Each of the three has a greater territorial area than any other sub-Saharan African state except Sudan, Chad, Mali and South Africa. Finally, each of the conflicts represents one of the three dominant *genres* of the national liberation movement in contemporary Africa: the anti-classical colonial (Angola), the anti-neocolonial (Zaïre), and struggles by constituent nations and nationalities in the post-colonial state (Biafra in Nigeria).

2 Nigeria

I INTRODUCTION

On 15 January 1966 mutinuous middle-ranking officers of the Nigerian army led by Major Chukwuma Nzeogwu overthrew the first post-independence civilian government headed by Abubakar Tafawa Balewa. With the subsequent defeat of these rebel forces by federal loyalist troops led by the army commander, General Johnson Aguyi-Ironsi, a military junta was set up with him at its head to administer the country.

Aguyi-Ironsi's regime lasted only six months. As with the Balewa administration, this government failed because it could not effectively tackle the pressing socio-political problems inherent in the Nigerian federation. These problems had acquired an additional, immensely complicated dimension resulting from the circumstances surrounding the Aguyi-Ironsi take-over. A number of political (and military) leaders had died during the coup, including the Prime Minister himself, and Ahmadu Bello (the premier of the northern region), both influential leaders of the predominantly Hausa-Fulani northern Nigeria. There was growing dissension in this part of the country over the political implications of the coup which was principally planned and executed by Igbo military officers. One fear was that these officers intended to inaugurate an Igbo domination of the country.[1]

On 24 May 1966 Aguyi-Ironsi enacted a decree (Decree No. 34) which abolished the existing four-region federal administrative structure. In its place, a unitary state was proclaimed, converting the regions into groups of administrative provinces. Essentially, this new constitutional order drastically curtailed the extensive sphere of political, economic and juridical authority hitherto exercised by the regions *vis-à-vis* the central government in Lagos. Significantly, the notorious regional police auxiliaries were abolished by this decree.[2]

The northern response to Decree No. 34 was immediate

and was directed to the attainment of three objectives: (a) it aimed to expel the Igbo and other eastern Nigerians who worked in the region's civil service, business and industrial enterprises from their posts; (b) it wanted to destroy the Aguyi-Ironsi regime and neutralise the Igbo influence in the military; and (c) it called for northern secession from the Nigerian federation.

The move to drive out the Igbo living in the north began with a wave of effectively coordinated civil disturbances in the principal towns and cities of the region on 29 May 1966. These continued to occur intermittently throughout June and became intensified after the overthrow of the Aguyi-Ironsi government on 29 July and the coming to power of General Yakubu Gowon.

These northern riots took the form of direct attacks on Igbo individuals, families, homes and property, and assumed the massive proportion of a pogrom in late September 1966.[3] This was when attacks were carried out on trains, aircraft and coaches carrying survivors fleeing to eastern Nigeria. These massacres took a toll of 80 000–100 000 killed, with thousands of others injured and permanently disabled. The effect of these killings was the mass exodus of hundreds of thousands of Igbo from the north, and other parts of the federation (Lagos, mid-west, west) to their eastern homeland.

The brutality of these events, and their harrowing consequences, soon gave popular credence to the eastern (and later Biafran) charges of genocide unleashed on its people. It was the aftermath of the massacres which was the underlying reason why eastern leaders, led by General Odumegwu Ojukwu, the military governor appointed by Aguyi-Ironsi, decided on secession from Nigeria with the proclamation of the Republic of Biafra on 30 May 1967.

External Reaction

The crisis that led to the declaration of Biafran independence was viewed with anxiety abroad. Chad and Niger, two land-locked states north of Nigeria, relied on the Nigerian ports of Port Harcourt and Calabar for access to the Atlantic

Ocean. Most of their import and export trade went through Nigeria.

As the Nigerian internal situation deteriorated in the summer of 1966, these states were increasingly apprehensive of the consequences on their trade. The disruption of rail links between the eastern region and the rest of the country meant that Chadian and Nigeri import commodities were beginning to pile up in Port Harcourt and Calabar, two ports which had in the meantime come under eastern administrative control.

As a result, Chad sent a ministerial delegation to Lagos in November 1966 to discuss the issue with the Gowon regime. Gowon himself later held talks on the subject with President Hamani Diori of Niger in Kano. During the meetings Nigeria promised these neighbours that the port of Lagos would be made available to them until the crisis was resolved. In addition, Nigeria committed itself to offset the extra freight expenses that the new route (longer than the one from the east) would entail. In return, Chad and Niger reaffirmed their support for the Nigerian federation.

In pursuance of these early diplomatic contacts with contiguous states, Nigeria soon persuaded Cameroon, to the east, to deny eastern officials the use of Cameroon airports of Buea and Douala. These airports were often used by eastern envoys travelling to other African states and Europe, particularly after Lagos imposed an economic and diplomatic blockade on the east in March 1967. Furthermore, President Ahmadu Ahidjo of Cameroon repeatedly threatened to deport any easterners domiciled in Cameroon who campaigned publicly for the political objectives of the dissenting eastern region.

These contacts between Lagos and three of its neighbours, firmly established at least four months before the outbreak of the civil war, were to be of profound importance to the federal government. Cameroon's support was particularly crucial, considering that it is the only country that shares a border with eastern Nigeria. In effect, Niger, Chad and Cameroon emerged as Nigeria's closest allies within the Organisation of African Unity (the OAU). In the Organisation Commune Africaine et Malgache (OCAM), the 'francophone' Africa political organisation, Presidents Ahidjo and

Diori were firm in resisting the pressure from Côte d'Ivoire (a state that recognised the Biafran secession) for official OCAM support of Biafra. The two presidents, who also had close ties with President Charles de Gaulle of France, continuously lobbied de Gaulle and other French government leaders during the conflict against French diplomatic support of the secession.

Aburi Initiative

West African concern towards the Nigerian crisis was not only restricted to the contiguous states. Ghana, about 80 miles to the west, arranged a two-day conference of Nigerian leaders at Aburi (Ghana) in January 1967. The meeting was chaired by Ghana's military leader, General Joseph Ankrah, with Ojukwu and Gowon in attendance. This was the first conference of Nigeria's principal leaders since the overthrow of the Aguyi-Ironsi administration, and the massacres in northern Nigeria.

The Aburi summit resolved on a confederal constitutional solution to the Nigerian crisis,[4] but the federal government later reneged on this agreement due to fierce opposition from the civil service in Lagos, some sections of the military and the Hausa-Fulani political 'establishment'.

For Ghana, the Aburi meeting was a diplomatic success. It was therefore disappointed when the agreement was not implemented. The Ghana government held Lagos responsible for this development, and thereafter began to show greater sympathy for the east. While Accra did not accord diplomatic recognition to Biafra, it remained lukewarm in its support for the federal government. The Ghanaians allowed Biafran citizens resident in the country to establish an Information and Publicity Office in Accra, and to organise solidarity campaigns unrestricted.

In neighbouring Cotê d'Ivoire, which emerged as Biafra's staunchest ally in the region, eastern officials began to campaign actively for sympathy in the country immediately after the Gowon regime abandoned the implementation of the Aburi Accord in February 1967. In the following month, two eastern delegations visited Abidjan, the capital, for talks with Ivorien leaders, including President Houphouet-Boigny, on the political situation. Eastern leaders counted very much on Ivorien support because of the long-standing business relationship between Houphouet-Boigny and Igbo industrialists, including Louis Odumegwu Ojukwu (General Ojukwu's father). It was therefore not surprising that after the Nigerian civil war began, Houphouet-Boigny became a firm supporter of the Biafran independence movement. He was particularly instrumental in helping Biafra secure 'limited' diplomatic recognition from France in July 1968.[5]

There was also a keen interest shown in the Nigerian crisis by the rest of Africa, particularly after the collapse of the Aburi Accord. Eastern government envoys who had been travelling around other African countries to state their case, had been impressed by the general sympathy expressed by several African leaders over the massacres of easterners a year before.[6] Prompted by this, General Ojukwu called on Ethiopia, Egypt and Liberia in April 1967 to mediate in the crisis. Essentially, Ojukwu was looking forward to converting this overall African sympathy to some form of continental pressure on the federal government, especially in restraining the latter from resorting to a military solution of the crisis.

But Lagos quickly rejected any African mediation because the conflict was an 'internal affair'. Gowon stressed this in a briefing of the Lagos diplomatic corps on 24 April 1967. He enumerated five reasons why his government could not accept any mediation from Africa:[7]

(a) the current situation in Nigeria is an internal affair;
(b) the invitation, emanating from Lt. Col. Ojukwu as it does, has the undertone of seeking *de facto* recognition by these African Heads of State. It also implies that there is a dispute between two sovereign and equal states;
(c) to avoid possible division in the ranks of the OAU, and especially among those who would be genuinely interested in assisting Nigeria;
(d) the fact that Lt. Col. Ojukwu refuses to recognise the existence of the Federal Government and myself as the Head; and
(e) the invitation of any Head of State must, as a matter of protocol, emanate from me as Head of the Federal Military

Government. In reaching such a decision I would of course, consult my colleagues on the Supreme Military Council.

In the previous month, Gowon had told an exclusive meeting of African ambassadors assigned to Lagos that his regime would employ force to crush any secessionist move by the eastern region.[8] Gowon compared the situation in Nigeria then with Congo-Leopoldville (Zaïre) in 1960 when the eastern province of Katanga declared its independence from the central government, and a civil war followed. He argued that most independent African countries had problems related to their minority peoples, but did not feel that secession was a solution. He declared: 'Africa desires unity; all our countries are struggling to achieve this goal. Each African nation must therefore maintain and consolidate its integrity to contribute effectively to this common struggle'.[9]

It was quite clear that for both sides of the Nigerian conflict, a high premium was placed in seeking the goodwill of the other African states as civil war became increasingly likely. While several African states sympathised with the east in its ordeal, following the massacres that precipitated the crisis, very few were orientated towards supporting an eastern secession from Nigeria as a result. The main thrust of the federal argument presented to the rest of Africa during a flurry of diplomatic campaigns, undertaken by Lagos in May-June 1967 was straightforward and concise: a successful Biafran secession would encourage separatist movements elsewhere on the continent. Added to the existing OAU Charter provisions which emphasised the 'inviolability of post-colonial boundaries', the overwhelming majority of African states, as expected, endorsed the political position of the federal faction to maintain the existence of the Nigerian federation when the civil war began on 6 July 1967.

Non-African Responses

Outside Africa, Britain followed events in Nigeria with great concern. Britain was the former colonial power, and had created the Nigerian federation in 1914 after its conquest, which began effectively in the 1850s, of a constellation of feudal kingdoms, city states, village democracies, cantons and principalities in this south-eastern stretch of West Africa. After independence in 1960, the Nigerian government, headed by Abubakar Tafawa Balewa (the deputy leader of Northern People's Congress – the NPC), continued to maintain exceptionally close political and economic ties with Britain. The majority of Nigerian military officers received their training in Britain (with the rest going to the United States of America, India and Pakistan). Soon after independence, the Balewa government secretly entered into a defence pact with London.[10] This provided for British military assistance in exchange for the provision of bases for the Royal Air Force in Nigeria. The pact was only abandoned in 1962 as a result of concerted opposition from university students, trade union organisations, the Action Group (the official opposition party), and critics from the National Council of Nigerian Citizens (the NCNC – the junior partners of the ruling national coalition).

On the major contentious diplomatic and political subject affecting Africa and the West in the early 1960s, namely decolonisation in Southern Africa, the Balewa regime was often keen to identify with British (and Western) positions. Despite widespread protests from democratic and popular circles in Nigeria, South Africa was invited to attend the Nigerian independence celebrations. Balewa followed this by recognising the British-created Central African Federation (which then linked the territories of Northern Rhodesia-Zambia, Southern Rhodesia-Zimbabwe, and Nyasaland-Malawi) in spite of the vehement opposition to this political union by African nationalists in the region.

In April 1962 the Nigerian government turned down the request of the Movimento Popular de Liberação de Angola (the MPLA – the main African nationalist resistance organisation in Portuguese-occupied Angola) to establish military training facilities in Nigeria. In 1963, Lagos embarrassed African liberation movements, and popular African opinion at the United Nations when it supported the creation of a South African federation made up of separate black and white states. The government was only forced to retract from this stand after internal opposition. In 1965, after Ian

Smith's unilateral declaration of independence in Southern Rhodesia, the OAU called for member states to break diplomatic relations with Britain. Balewa rejected this call, and instead launched a diplomatic effort in Africa to discourage such a move.[11] In consultation with the British Prime Minister, Harold Wilson, Balewa organised a summit of Commonwealth leaders in Lagos in the first week of January 1966 to discuss the Rhodesian crisis. This summit, which ended a day before the coup d'état that toppled Balewa, helped considerably to quell international criticism of the Wilson administration's handling of the Rhodesian conflict.[12]

In Nigeria's economic life, Britain maintained a dominant position in both the ownership of capital and trade.[13] Before the start of the civil war, British capital investment in Nigeria was £1 billion (mainly in the country's principal extractive industries – petroleum, oil, coal and tin – banking and insurance) and British companies were in control of 41.3 per cent of Nigeria's total imports and external trade. Through Britain's principal initiative, Nigeria received about $273 million in technical and capital assistance from the Organisation for Economic Cooperation and Development (OECD) countries in its first eight years of independence.[14] Given the large size of its population and the hospitality of its government, Nigeria offered British industries (and those of Britain's trading partners in the OECD), their largest consumer market in Africa.

It was against this background of close friendship in Anglo-Nigerian relations, that the Balewa government was overthrown – a regime which, according to the perceptive Nigerian political theorist, Billy Dudley, 'though sovereign, behaved as if it were still a colonial state'.[15] Predictably, the British government was worried over the loss of such a close ally. As soon as it was learned that Balewa had died in the coup, London offered military assistance to General Aguyi-Ironsi to overcome the rebel officers, especially after Major Nzeogwu threatened to march on Lagos from his bases in Kaduna.[16]

After Aguyi-Ironsi's success in suppressing the rebellion, Britain was quickly reassured of continuing Nigerian goodwill when the new government promised to honour all financial and economic agreements entered into by the previous regime. After the 29 July 1966 coup that brought General Gowon to power, the intervention of the British High Commissioner in Lagos, Francis Cumming-Bruce (and the US Ambassador, Elbert Matthews) was important in persuading an influential segment of the rebel forces in control of Lagos (led by Col. Murtala Muhammed who was later head of state in 1975) from declaring the secession of northern Nigeria from the federation.[17]

In March 1967, following the federal government decision not to implement the Aburi confederal settlement agreed earlier on in January, the new British High Commissioner in Lagos, David Hunt, visited Enugu for talks with General Ojukwu. Hunt strongly advised Ojukwu not to push the grievance of the Igbo people to the point of secession.[18] He made it clear that Britain would not support such a development and added that several countries would share that view. It was a stormy encounter between the two men, with Ojukwu accusing the British government of favouring the federal government in the crisis. A year later, London officially confirmed that Ojukwu had been advised against secession two months before the proclamation of the Republic of Biafra.[19]

Considering the nature of the close ties and influence that Britain still retained in Nigeria prior to the outbreak of the 1967 civil war, British intervention in that conflict in some way was inevitable. Its preference for the continued existence of the Nigerian federation, at every critical phase of the crisis, was obvious and this meant potential sympathy for the federal government. The only thing that was not completely certain when the war started was what form British intervention would take.

Turning finally to the Soviet Union, which became involved early in the war on the side of the federals, it is significant to recall that unlike Britain, Soviet influence in Nigeria was minimal before the war. The Balewa regime was very suspicious of the Soviet Union and its intentions in Africa. It took two years after independence for Nigeria to establish a diplomatic mission in Moscow, and this was only as a result of pressure from the opposition parties and students' pressure groups. Before then, all Nigeria's business with the Soviet Union, and the rest of Eastern Europe, including the minimal trade relationship (barely 3 per cent of Nigeria's exports went to these countries) was handled by British embassies in the states concerned.

Travels between the Soviet Union and Nigeria were restricted by Lagos. It also discouraged Nigerians taking up Soviet scholarships tenable for study in the Soviet Union. A statement once made by Balewa typified his government's attitude to the Soviet Union and Eastern Europe: 'I and my colleagues are determined that while we are responsible for the government of the federation of Nigeria and for the welfare of its people, we shall use every means in our power to prevent the infiltration of Communism and Communist ideas into Nigeria'.[20] In all, meaningful contacts between the Soviet Union and the Nigerian people were restricted to radical trade unions, left-leaning political parties and politicians, and student organisations.

The January 1966 coup opened up opportunities for the Soviet Union to improve its relations with Nigeria. Official Soviet commentators generally welcomed the coup which 'marked the end of feudal and bourgeois domination'.[21] Ironsi's unification decree was regarded as 'progressive',[22] and the Soviet media were broadly critical of the Igbo massacres in the north.[23]

In April 1967, just a month before the eastern secession, a Soviet trade and technical delegation visited Nigeria. The group went to both Lagos and Enugu (the eastern capital), giving it the opportunity to assess the deteriorating political situation in the country. While members of the mission made no public comments on the politics of the country before returning to Moscow, it was highly likely that the Soviet officials would have viewed the situation as conducive to encourage an increase in Soviet influence in a country that had remained unfriendly for many years. Already, Moscow had been allowed by the federal government to send a trade mission to Nigeria. This was a gesture that had been unthinkable just 16 months before.

Up to November 1967, that is four months after the beginning of the civil war and six months after the Biafran secession, the Soviet Union continued to maintain its 'even-handed' attitude to both sides of the conflict. This was particularly reflected in the coverage of the crisis in the Soviet media. Oye Ogunbadejo aptly sums up the situation: '... Moscow treaded warily. Striving to keep open as many options as possible, it endorsed national unity in Nigeria but did not publicly condemn the drift towards secession. Carefully choosing its political stance, the Soviet Union sympathised with the plight of the eastern region's Ibos and called on the federal military government to take cognisance of Ibo grievances and aspirations. But Moscow never advocated eastern secession...'[24]

It was Nigeria's request for arms supplies from the Soviet Union during the previous month that radically changed Moscow's position. It agreed to supply Lagos with sophisticated aircraft in the war against Biafra. The Soviet Union now had an historic opportunity to improve its ties with Nigeria. It was a major breakthrough for Moscow, especially as it came soon after Britain and the United States had turned down a similar request from Nigeria.

Phases of Conflict

The Nigerian civil war lasted for 30 months (longer than either of the other two conflicts that we shall be examining). We should, however, see the military perspective of the conflict in two main phases. The first was from 6 July 1967 to mid-October 1967. The second phase was from mid-October 1967 to 12 January 1970 when Biafra surrendered. The first phase displayed the initial Biafran opportunity to repulse and contain federal military assaults on the northern fronts. This was followed by the Biafran breakthrough on the western front which resulted in the successful capture of the mid-west region from the federal army. The federal counter-attack on this front which drove the Biafrans out of the mid-west and the losses of their capital (Enugu) and the southeast port of Calabar by mid-October 1967, undermined all other significant military offensives that the Biafrans initiated throughout the rest of the war. Most war-time observers were even signalling the end of the secession after these early October 1967 victories of the federal army.

The second phase featured the period of the war of attrition that was fought out in central Biafra or the so-called Igbo heartland. As from this time, the reliance of both sides on the international environment for critical resources to continue the struggle became more pronounced. This was particularly true of the encircled Biafrans. Concomitantly, this second phase of the war signified a greater internationalisation of the conflict.

II WESTERN EUROPE AND THE UNITED STATES

Britain

The initial British response to the Biafran declaration of independence was equivocal and non-commital. While London ruled out any early recognition of the Ojukwu government, it did not, however, condemn the secession. Official British thinking on the Nigerian crisis only became clearer a month later after the outbreak, and in the aftermath of the Six-Day Arab-Israeli War. The fighting in the Middle East which had led to the closure of the Suez Canal, had severely disrupted British oil imports from the region. The adverse effects of this on the British economy were potentially enormous. Another possible dislocation of British oil supplies, this time from Nigeria, could not have come at a worse moment.

In the first quarter of 1967, British oil imports from Nigeria accounted for 10 per cent of British needs (or about one-third of total Nigerian petroleum export) and this was a source that would easily offset the losses being incurred from the Middle East. The beginning of the Nigerian military offensive on Biafra on 6 July 1967, with grave threats to the oil installations, most of which were located in Biafra, was therefore viewed with great apprehension in London.

At this time, Shell-BP, in which the British government held a 49 per cent share, was Nigeria's largest oil-producing company. Shell-BP and other oil companies operating in Nigeria had made contingency plans to get oil tankers in and out of the Biafran oil terminal of Bonny, in the event of the outbreak of hostilities. Shell-BP also decided to pay the forthcoming autumn oil royalties cheque into a 'suspense account' instead of paying it to the federal government, or indeed to the Biafrans who were in *de facto* control of most of the oil fields of the Nigerian federation. This shrewd move from Shell-BP no doubt reflected this early British government ambivalence toward the crisis. But this position did not go down well in Lagos which felt that as the 'legitimate' central government, all revenues from the country, *including the east*, must be paid into its own coffers.

Quite clearly, the British government chose to weigh its options carefully in the first two months of the Biafran War, even though there were some indications already that its ultimate attitude would be support for the federal government position.[25] This early British vacillation was dictated by the following factors: (1) The impreciseness of the military situation after one month of fighting. While the federals had captured the Biafran towns of Nsukka, Ogoja and Obudu during this period, their optimism for a '48 hour overrun' of Biafra did not materialise. The Biafrans were still in control of their capital Enugu to the north, and the river and market port of Onitsha to the west, in addition to the vital oil exporting southern sea ports of Port Harcourt and Calabar. In such a situation, Britain would have felt that there was nothing to be gained by openly antagonising the Biafrans, who could ultimately repulse the federal attack, by declaring support for Lagos. Even though the Nigerians themselves would have preferred unambiguous British support at that time, they were relieved that London had assured them (especially through a number of parliamentary statements made by British ministers[26]) that it would not recognise Biafra[27]; (2) The main British priority at this time was to ensure that the flow of Nigerian oil to the United Kingdom should not be interrupted by the war. In the first month of fighting, the vital oil facilities, including the strategic oil terminal at Bonny and the refineries in and around Port Harcourt, were still in Biafran hands. This meant that unless the military situation changed more favourably to the federals, Biafra rather than Nigeria was the *de facto* authority to decide to whom to sell the eastern oil. The British had anticipated this when they devised the scheme to pay the next royalties to a 'suspense account'. As events showed later (in August 1967), Shell-BP endorsed a plan to pay a part of these royalties to Biafra (£250 000), but were overtaken by federal military successes in the southern front which secured parts of the oil installations. The deal was called off and no money was paid to Biafra; (3) Britain was concerned with its extensive economic and financial interests in Nigeria which totalled over £1 billion in invested capital. It was only natural that it would avoid any precipitate decisions at this stage; (4) Twenty thousand British subjects were resident in the country, the majority of them in the non-Biafran regions. Most of the Britons who were in Biafra worked in the oil industry – again important in British considerations; (5) Since the 1966 killings of easterners living in northern Nigeria, there had been a lot of public sympathy shown for the east in Britain and elsewhere overseas. The British government was aware of this. While not prepared to support the eastern secession, London did not wish to identify with the federal regime, which was responsible for some of the killings and had now embarked on military operations in the Biafran homeland; (6) After a month of inconclusive fighting, there was still to evolve some concerted African diplomatic initiative to mediate in the conflict. Britain, as the ex-colonial power, was very cautious to avoid identifying too closely with either of the conflicting parties, so as not to prejudice an African mediation.

Support for the Federal Government

On 25 July 1967 the military situation changed dramatically. A federal naval task force stormed and captured the Bonny oil terminal. Port Harcourt, just 40 miles north of the creeks, was now under threat from a possible federal amphibian attack. Thus, the federal government was in control of Biafra's major petroleum outlet, and this also meant that it was in a strong position to bargain with both Shell-BP and the British government over the entire question of oil deliveries. Furthermore, the federals requested arms supplies from Britain, particularly aircraft, to continue their military campaign.

In August 1967 the British High Commissioner in Lagos, David Hunt, was called home for consultations. In his talks with Prime Minister Harold Wilson, Hunt asked the British government to back Nigeria officially in the conflict, in addition to furnishing it with military equipment. Britain's unequivocal support for the 'united Nigeria' political objective emerged after these meetings, as Hunt recalled later:

> The crunch came only about a month after the war started ... The Federal Government had placed orders for arms with manufacturers in the United Kingdom and these had applied for the necessary export licences ... Mr Wilson listened carefully to our arguments but to him the nub of the matter was that Nigeria was a fellow Commonwealth country in difficulties, that we had equipped her in the first place and she could therefore expect a continuity of supply and, on the other side, that a refusal would be equivalent to intervention in favour of the rebels. He saw very quickly and attached great importance to the point that such an act (not supplying arms to the Federals) would damage our interests not only in Nigeria but also in the rest of Africa.[28]

Hunt later emerged in the conflict as one of the most fanatical supporters of the Nigerian cause, 'a Federal "super hawk" ... (who) was both consistent and candid in his views that Britain's national interest lay with the whole-hearted support of the Federal side'.[29] Hunt had regular consultations with General Gowon. This role followed closely that of his predecessor, Francis Cumming-Bruce.

In the meantime, Biafra accused Shell-BP of complicity in the Nigerian attack on Bonny. It alleged that the oil company's vessels had escorted the federal navy through the treacherous mangrove of the Bonny estuary. Two other British companies were similarly accused by Biafra for aiding the Bonny attack – the United African Company and John Holt (both long-term British business establishments in the federation).

Some British complicity in the Bonny take-over was implied in a speech made by David Hunt to a Nigerian audience in November 1967: '... (T)he successful and expedient operation carried out by the Nigerian Navy leading to the capture of Bonny was a result of the warships supplied by Britain. Britain's support ... was also demonstrated in all battlefields by the equipment supplied by Britain in the hands of Nigerian soldiers'.[30] When it is recalled that the Bonny assault preceded Hunt's crucial consultations with the British government in August, then it was obvious that London had been in support of Lagos all along, albeit unofficially. The importance of the Wilson-Hunt talks was that this pro-federal British position was now official.

The first strong indication that the British government had declared its support for Nigeria, however, emerged in mid-August. The British dispatched a consignment of Bofor anti-aircraft guns, small arms and ammunition.[31] More of these were sent later in the month and by September supplies had become systematised and regularised, but London withheld a Nigerian request for the dispatch of a squadron of fighter aircraft. It had been part of a standing British policy not to sell sophisticated military aircraft to African states,[32] apart, of course, from South Africa.

Before long, Britain came under renewed pressure from the Nigerian government for the supply of more advanced weapons. This followed a Biafran lightening infantry thrust into the mid-west/western regions of Nigeria which began on 9 August. On 17 August the Biafran army captured the town of Ore, a strategic western regional junction 160 miles from Lagos. This was a very serious military reversal for the federals, who until then were making appreciable progress on the northern and southern fronts (the Biafran thrust into Nigerian territory was through the western front).

Britain responded favourably this time: armoured vehicles (including Ferret armoured cars), artillery weapons, rocket launchers and assorted ammunition were dispatched to Lagos. Britain agreed to deliver immediately two Seward Defence boats (the 'Bonny' and 'Sapele') which had been contracted to the Nigerians before the war. The third boat, 'Ibadan II', would be supplied in 1968 (the cost of the three boats was £4.5 million). Britain's share of federal military equipment continued to escalate as the war went on. In figures published for 1967 (including the last six months, which incorporated the period of the war), British arms supplies (excluding aircraft and accessories), represented 48 per cent of the federals' total. In 1968 this reached 80 per cent and by December 1969 (one month before the collapse of Biafra), Britain accounted for 97 per cent of Nigeria's total arms imports (excluding aircraft).[33]

A principal factor responsible for Britain's dominance in the Nigerian war effort between 1968 and 1970 was the arms embargoes declared by the other 'traditional' arms suppliers to Nigeria (the Federal Republic of Germany, the Netherlands, Italy, Belgium and the United States) on both sides of the conflict. There is no attempt in this presentation to ignore the Soviet arms supplies to the federals. These were mostly aircraft and accessories, and did not play a critical part in the federal prosecution of the war. This was because the Nigerian fighting was primarily a ground war, and the federal use of its airforce was militarily insignificant (we shall return to this theme later).

British Interests in the Nigerian Federation

It is now appropriate to explore the reasons why Britain played this dominant role in supporting the federal cause to destroy the Biafran independence movement. Apart from South Africa, the capacity of British economic and industrial investments in Africa was highest in the Nigerian federation. Besides the near-50 per cent shares which the British government had in Shell-BP (the predominant oil prospecting company in the federation, as we have already mentioned), it also had 60 per cent shares in the Amalgamated Tin Mining (Nigerian) Ltd., a major prospecting tin, cobalt and iron ore mining company.[34] In the non-mining sector of the economy, John Holt and Company Ltd. was one of the two largest in the country.[35] At this time (1967), this company, owned by a British family, had branches throughout the major towns of the federation.

The United Africa Company (UAC), another British business group, was responsible for about 41.3 per cent of Nigeria's entire import and external trade. The UAC is the major African subsidiary of the British transnational corporation, Unilever. It evolved from the Royal Niger Company which, in cooperation with the businessman Tauban Goldie and the administrator Frederick Lugard, laid the foundations of what later became the Nigerian federation between 1886 and 1914.[36] The UAC had large wholesalers and retailing establishments run chiefly by its own subsidiaries which included the ubiquitous G. B. Ollivant Ltd., Kingsway Chemist Ltd., and African Timber and Plywood (Nig.) Ltd. in major towns and cities across Nigeria.[37] UAC also had part interests in these other important companies in Nigeria: Nigerian Breweries Ltd; Nigelec Ltd; Taylor Woodrow (Nig.) Ltd; Gulf Oil of Nigeria Ltd. and Nigerian Prestressed Concrete Ltd. Ikenna Nzimiro's famous aphorism, 'UAC was Nigeria and Nigeria was UAC'[38] was surely not overstating UAC's stranglehold on the Nigerian economy during this period.

As for finance, Barclays Nigeria (a subsidiary of Barclays Bank Ltd. of England) and the Standard Bank (Nigeria), owned largely by Lloyds Bank and the Westminster Bank, predominated in Nigeria's banking service sector. These institutions had branches throughout the regions of the country. A total of 20 000 British subjects living in Nigeria were involved in these businesses and other services in the economy.

Considering the spread of these British capital investments and other economic interests across the entire federation (totalled over £1.5 billion), it was highly conceivable that any threat to the territorial character of Nigeria would disrupt their growth and operations. There were statements made by some highly-placed officials of the British government before and during the war which raised this fear. Lord Walston (Parliamentary Secretary, Board of Trade) said in June 1967:

> We have been watching carefully – indeed – what has been happening in Nigeria, and we have done so for many reasons ... We have a vast trade with Nigeria ... There are, of course, the relatively newly discovered oil deposits which are being exploited now with such enormous success ...[39]

In a speech to engineering students of the Ahmadu Bello

University, Zaria (northern Nigeria) in November 1967, David Hunt (British High Commissioner to Nigeria) expressed his government's desire for the continuing growth of the existing Anglo-Nigerian economic ties:

> I can take pleasure in the prospect of greater industrialisation in Nigeria, not merely because we are pleased by the prosperity of our friends but also because I look forward to an industrialised Nigeria as an increasingly better customer for those sophisticated and expensive goods by whose export Britain now lives.[40]

In these circumstances, the British government clearly reasoned that it was rational to support the party in the Nigerian civil war which was fighting to maintain the political status quo. Foreign Secretary Michael Stewart underscored this proposition when he told parliament at the height of the war that 'Britain was probably the only country in the world that could not, in fact or in honour, be neutral about this [the Nigerian civil war]'.[41]

Escalation of Federal Offensive

So, having firmly secured British military backing for its political position in the conflict in mid-August, Nigeria was poised for an all-out offensive on the Biafrans on all of the war fronts, in addition to counterattacks on the secessionist forces occupying the mid-west/western regions.

These offensives were launched in the first week of September (1967) and they quickly paid off. Within a month, the Nigerian 2nd infantry division terminated the Biafran occupation of Ore (western Nigeria), and the entire mid-west region. Also in October, the Biafrans lost their capital, Enugu, when the federal 1st division broke through the secessionists' defences south of the university town of Nsukka, which had fallen in July. In the southern front, the Biafrans were routed from Calabar by the 3rd federal marine division which soon began a drive overland to attack the Biafran towns of Aba and Port Harcourt. On 1 January 1968, General Gowon announced that 31 March 1968 was now the new deadline to overrun Biafra. This looked highly possible to attain, given the obvious military superiority of the Nigerian army, and the now diminished size of the Biafran Republic. The fact was that seven months after the outbreak of the war, Biafra had lost two-thirds of its territory to the federals.

But Biafra did not collapse by 31 March 1968. This was principally because it had improved its arms importations from abroad (especially through French sources – see below). Most of these weapons were basically defensive – anti-tank weapons, anti-aircraft pieces and ammunition for the few Howitzers and mortars that it possessed, in addition to small arms and ammunition. The Biafrans began to fight a defensive war which was aimed at slowing down the federal advance on all fronts. Simultaneously, newly-trained Biafran commando groups and militias (especially the Biafran Organisation of Freedom Fighters – BOFF), launched guerrilla operations behind federal lines, with the objectives of disrupting Nigerian communications facilities, reinforcements and military bases.

Between March and September 1968 this strategy was an impressive success, but for the loss of the oil port of Port Harcourt to the federals. Given this improved military situation, and some major diplomatic gains abroad (the recognition of Biafran independence by some African states), the Biafrans became highly optimistic that they could now enter into a negotiated settlement of the conflict from an improved bargaining situation (we shall elaborate on this later).

In the meantime, British arms deliveries continued to reach the Federal government without any let-up. As from May 1968, until the end of the war (January 1970), at least a hundred tons of arms and ammunition were leaving the United Kingdom for Nigeria every week. It was very clear that the British government was prepared to support the federals until they achieved their political goal in the conflict – the restoration of the Nigerian federation. As Premier Harold Wilson told parliament in October 1968, his government had persistently pressed for an end to the war 'on the basis of the recognition of the Federal system in Nigeria....'.[42]

In view of the ferocious level of the fighting so far,

including Biafra's continued insistance on a separate independent state, it was quite clear that federal Nigeria's strategic objective was either the unconditional surrender of Biafra, or its military overrun. Either of the two was going to be dictated inextricably by the military situation. Thus the British government preference for a settlement based on the 'recognition of the federal system' could only be pursued successfully by ensuring that Lagos had the military capability to achieve its strategic goal.

This vital factor (the continuing military support for Nigeria) was the main reason for the persistent criticism of the British policy in the conflict by some British parliamentarians and other pressure groups in the country. During the 30-month-old war, six emergency debates on British arms deliveries to Lagos were held in the House of Commons. The main criticism of government policy always came from the Labour back-bench parliamentarians, who called for the termination of arms support for the Nigerian government, so as to enable Britain to play a 'constructive' mediating role in the conflict. Government critics were not, however, able to mobilise sufficient votes to force the government to change its position. Their most impressive attempt in parliament to alter the government's policy came during a very heated debate in March 1969, when 62 members (mostly Labour) voted against the government-tabled resolution to continue arms supplies. Another 160 Labour parliamentarians abstained from the voting, and support for the government (232) had to be bolstered by Conservative MPs.[43]

The Wilson administration always insisted that by supplying arms to the federals, it was guided by four main considerations[44]: (1) that Britain was Nigeria's pre-war 'traditional' military supplier; (2) that Nigeria was a Commonwealth country and that by supporting the federal government, London was aiding a legal, friendly government fighting an insurrection; (3) that by continuing to supply arms to Lagos, Britain would be able to exercise leverage within the federal government, especially in relation to the conduct of military operations in Biafra; and (4) that Britain was trying to restrain or check growing Soviet military cooperation with the federal government by maintaining British arms deliveries to Lagos. But parliamentary critics were not impressed by these arguments. Britain was not a sole 'traditional' arms exporter to Nigeria. Immediately after independence in 1960, one of the main policies of the new Nigerian army had been to diversity its arms procurement sources to include the Federal Republic of Germany, Italy, Israel, the United States, Switzerland, Sweden, the Netherlands and Belgium, as well as Britain.[45] Between 1964 and 1966 the only supplies of British military equipment to Nigeria were 12 Ferret armoured cars and two Saladin armoured vehicles with a further four Saladins pending.[46] Nigeria had stopped importing rifles and machine guns from Britain in 1964, when it signed a contract with the West German firm, Fritz Werner, for these imports, and a construction of a munitions factory in Kaduna. Nigeria also bought sub-machine guns and 105 mm Howitzers from Italy and 81 mm mortars from Israel. To illustrate the success of this diversification, Britain's share of Nigeria's total arms import for 1966 (the last pre-war year) was 38 per cent.[47]

This share progressively increased during the war, as we have stated elsewhere (from 48 per cent after the first six months of the war to 97 per cent on the eve of the defeat of Biafra), because the other exporters (enumerated above) placed embargoes on Nigeria which the British filled up.

The Wilson government's reference to the Commonwealth association as a reason for arms supplies to Lagos was equally contestable. The Commonwealth is a politico-cultural organisation which has no military obligations binding on its members. If Britain felt it should support Lagos due to the Commonwealth links, then the other 38 member states should have equally reacted in the same way. But apart from Britain, no other Commonwealth country sent military equipment to the federals (Canada and India, which had some areas of military cooperation with Nigeria before the war, severed these at the outbreak of hostilities).

Even in bilateral relations, there was no existing Anglo-Nigerian defence or military treaty which the British government could have invoked to justify its pro-federal arms policy.

It should also be stated that the British government's continuous reference to the Gowon regime as the 'legal federal government' was highly contentious. In the Nigerian context, there was nothing more legal about the Gowon government than about the Ojukwu administration, as both came into existence at various stages after the military overthrow of a constitutional government on 15 January 1966. It was true that after the July 1966 coup in Lagos, Gowon was in *de facto* control of all the federation but for the eastern region, which was under the *de facto* administration of Ojukwu. In fact, one of the factors that led to the civil war was the non-resolution of the central government's leadership question between Gowon and Ojukwu. In the meantime, recognition for the Gowon federal government or the eastern government for that matter, was essentially a political choice for foreign governments which had nothing to do with the legalities of the conflicting claims.

The other reason given by the British government for maintaining its arms supplies to the federals was that through this relationship, London would be able to influence Lagos to show some 'moderation' during military operations in Biafra. This was particularly after the spring of 1968 when federal air raids on Biafran civilian populations were attracting a lot of criticism in the international press.

The extent of British influence on the federals as regards the latter's conduct in its military operations is still debatable. The Defence Advisor in the British High Commission in Lagos, Colonel Robert Scott, maintains that British influence was considerable, especially in ensuring that the federal army observed 'internationally-accepted' standards of behaviour during actual combat. Scott, however, concedes that while British influence and 'pressure' were aimed at the federal High Command in Lagos, the actual behaviour of troops in the field could differ. In a report he prepared on federal tactics in combat, Scott stressed the indiscriminate firing by federal troops as they approached their target (especially villages or towns), comparing it to the 'best defoliant agent known'.[48]

This view is also shared by Brigadier Benjamin Adekunle, a highly controversial federal field commander who often acknowledged the severity and excesses of his troops when they overran Biafran villages in interviews he gave to the press during the war. On one such occasion, Adekunle said:

> I want to prevent even one Ibo having even one piece to eat before their capitulation. We shoot at everything that moves, and when our forces march into the centre of Ibo territory, we shoot at everything, even at things that do not move.[49]

In August 1968 the British government was responsible for suggesting to the federals the setting up of a six-nation international committee to 'monitor' the behaviour of the federal military as it pursued its operations into the Biafran heartland.[50] This initiative came at a time of widespread international criticism of the atrocities committed by federal troops in overrun Biafran territories. The move to set up this committee could be cited as an example of British policy, aimed at influencing Lagos, to which ministers referred during the debates mentioned earlier. But there were no indications of London employing its close relationship with Lagos to reduce the level of military operations. To the contrary, the Nigerian Civil War continued to intensify in every dimension until the federals achieved total victory in January 1970.

The final point raised by the British government to justify its arms supplies to Lagos was to check the growth of Soviet military cooperation with the federal government. As we have already stated, the Soviet Union became involved in the Nigerian conflict in early August 1967, after Britain (and the United States) refused to sell a squadron of fighter aircraft to the Nigerian airforce. We noted the reasons for the British refusal. One of the most important factors in this regard was that it was not British policy to sell military aircraft to independent Africa. The other point, of course, was that London calculated that what the federals needed in their confrontation against Biafra were ground weapons – artillery, armoured vehicles, small arms and ammunition.

In retrospect, this British calculation was borne out. The Nigerian Civil War was principally a ground war. The Soviet Union supplied Nigeria mostly with aircraft, anti-aircraft and support equipment, and these played a marginal *military* role in the war. On the contrary, the planes were often used to bomb Biafran civilian centres indiscriminately, which brought the Nigerians adverse international publicity.

What the federals needed to prosecute the war were largely ground weapons, and these were the equipment that the British supplied without let-up throughout the war so that by 1969 these accounted for 97 per cent of Nigeria's total imported stocks. In view of this, the question that arises is: who was *really* restraining the other – Britain or the Soviet Union? In this situation, it was clearly the federal Nigerian government that enjoyed the advantage of being in a position where two powerful allies, albeit of contradictory ideological orientations, were prepared to supply it with an assortment of weaponry it felt it needed to wage the war. As another observer of the conflict has argued, the federal government was always able to invoke the threat of turning completely to the Soviet Union after 1968, whenever it required more British weaponry.[51] This was one of the reasons for the ultimate dominance of British military support.

We should add that in practical terms, there was no pressure for the Nigerian government to switch completely from British to Soviet ground weapons after the British government firmly promised to supply these in August 1967. For instance, the standard infantry rifle for the Nigerian army was the 7.62 mm NATO rifle. It has been estimated that for a planned offensive for any of the three Nigerian infantry divisions, the federal military allocated at least five million rounds of 7.62 mm ammunition with another five million rounds in reserve in Lagos.[52] The main source for the supply of this ammunition was, of course, Britain. If Nigeria had contemplated switching to Soviet ammunition, it would have sought the 7.62 mm equivalent. There could have been an immediate problem because the Soviet 7.62 mm did not fit the breech of the standard NATO rifle.[53] So, if Britain were to have cut off weapons deliveries to Lagos at any time after January 1968 and the Nigerians had reacted by switching to the Soviet Union, the federal army would have been forced to re-equip its entire infantry (at least 150 000 men) with Soviet rifles to overcome the difficulties that a drop in ammunition would cause. This would have been extremely costly (in terms of money) and militarily dangerous, except for the fact that there was a prolonged ceasefire.[54] This underlines the crucial role of Britain's support for the Nigerian war effort and the very marginal effect of Soviet military cooperation with the Lagos authorities during the period. It does seem that one of the most important effects of the Soviet 'factor' in the Wilson administration's reasons for backing Nigeria was that this policy was always supported by the Conservative opposition during the parliamentary debates on the war.

In all, the British government was the principal foreign backer of the Nigerian federal military. Its four main stated reasons for this support are open to several criticisms, as we have shown. What was certain was that the British favoured the continuation of the Nigerian federation which they created in 1914, when a civil war which threatened its existence broke out in 1967. The Nigerian federation contained very important British economic and financial interests which could have been seriously disrupted in the event of its disintegration. In the Nigerian situation after July 1967, it was only logical that London would favour the party that sought to uphold the territorial character of the federation. This was the determining factor for support of the federal government in Lagos. Given the depth of this British military involvement, we can add that this singularly demonstrated the pressing desire of the British government to offset the forces of Biafran independence at all cost.

Non-governmental British Involvement

It is now in order to examine the role of non-governmental British agencies in supplying arms to the parties in the Nigerian conflict. This is particularly essential in the case of Biafra which did not receive any military support from the British government, but which bought British weapons through private sources in the United Kingdom. It is also important (as we shall show shortly) because the federals also bought weapons from non-governmental circles in Britain.

A month before the outbreak of the Nigerian war, a press report in the United States claimed that Biafra had been smuggling in British weapons from private sources in the United Kingdom, in anticipation of a federal military attack on the territory.[55] On 4 December 1967 a British mercenary officer arrived in Britain from France to purchase arms worth about £250 000 for Biafra.[56] This consignment included 40 heavy machine guns, ten 22 mm anti-aircraft cannons, 40 recoilless rifles, 50 bazookas and quantities of ammunition. A senior Biafran diplomat in Europe then, Raph Uwechue, has acknowledged that these early Biafran arms purchases from Britain were part of stocks bought from European private arms dealers, which also included Czech, Swiss and West German arms.[57]

In December 1967 Biafra began to recruit mercenaries in Britain.[58] Veteran mercenary Alistair Wicks established an office in London to hire mercenary officers for the Biafran army. The impact of mercenaries in this war, if any, will be assessed later. One comment we can make, however, at this stage is that a large proportion of mercenaries recruited by both sides were killed in the pitched battles that were fought in all the theatres of war in the summer of 1968.

Turning to Nigerian arms purchases from private British sources, *The Times* (London) reported six weeks after the outbreak of hostilities[59] that Nigeria had chartered planes from two British airlines (Dan Air and Laker Airways) to fly 'commercially purchased' arms from Britain to Nigeria. Nigeria was offering up to £5500 per flight to the airlines. The consignment of arms purchased included artillery pieces, machine guns, mortars and bazookas. Crown Agents in London were actively involved in buying arms for the federals.[60] Throughout the war, they acted as a reliable source for the purchase of small arms ammunition for the federal army.

As for mercenary fighters, another veteran, John Peters, who was a one-time British army sergeant, began to recruit mercenaries in London to fight for the federal army in July 1967.[61] Soon, British-born pilots and naval training personnel (all mercenaries) were actively fighting for the Nigerian government. Some of these were former RAF pilots. They flew British jet provost-trainers of the Nigerian Airforce, which were equipped as ground attack aircraft. Ex-RAF ground technicians who were recruited at this time also helped to guard NAF ground facilities at the Ikeja, Makurdi and Benin air bases.

It is relevant to explain why Nigeria embarked on this high level of arms purchases from British private sources (and elsewhere in Europe) in spite of the steady military deliveries which it was receiving from the British government.

Basically, right from the beginning of the war, Nigeria had grossly underrated the Biafran determination to defend itself from the obvious preponderant military might of the federal army. Lagos had also calculated that as the internationally-recognised government of the federation, it enjoyed an obvious diplomatic leverage which the Biafrans lacked. Relying on this, the federals were confident that they could put their case across to the world community with less difficulty, and acquire the resources (essentially military equipment) needed to prosecute the war. These factors prompted the Nigerian high optimism of a 'quick police action' and the various rash deadlines to crush the Biafran secession – 48 hours . . . two weeks . . . 30 September 1967 . . . 31 December 1967 . . . 31 March 1968 . . . 25 May 1968 . . .

With the failure of the particularly highly-publicised 31 March 1968 deadline to defeat Biafra, there was a serious mood of frustration in federal circles. The embarrassment caused, in addition to the growing dissension within the armed forces over the slow progress of the war, reinforced the Nigerian government's resolve to step up military operations against Biafra.

To effectively support renewed offensives on Biafra, Nigeria had to utilise all available arms procurement sources, including private ones. Writing later on the extent of this frustration in the Nigerian High Command, Robert Scott (Defence Advisor, British High Commission, Lagos) said that there was the greatest urge within the federal military to diversify arms purchase sources and end the war immediately.[62] This desperate mood was equally confirmed by General Henry Alexander, a British member of the six-nation International Observer team that was set up in 1968 to monitor the activities of the federal army during combat. In May 1969, Alexander, who had personal business interests in Nigeria,[63] advocated the intervention of the Royal Air Force to bomb the (Biafran) strategic airport at Uli in order to break the deadlock of continuing Biafran resistance.[64] The London-based International Institute for

Strategic Studies (IISS) did not lose sight of the predicament of the Nigerian army in the Biafran campaign. In its annual review of the global military situation, the IISS notes:

> Within the last decade, no such country (in the Southern World) has conducted a successful invasion against a neighbour of remotely comparable strength. At least two problems appear to prove insuperable. First, logistics – supply, communications and maintenance – make enormous demands on a modern army and in a hostile environment they seem to be too much ... Second, few such armies have developed a sufficient number of leaders in the field to stand up to casualties without a breakdown of the command system. Both considerations applied with special force to the Nigerian army in its war with the Biafran secessionists.[65]

British Diplomatic Initiative

Before we end the British section of this study, let us examine the diplomatic role played by the British government in arranging the Kampala peace conference of the warring sides of the Nigerian conflict in May 1968. The conference was convened under the auspices of the Commonwealth Secretariat in London, but with the active cooperation of the British Foreign Office. Initially, the British suggested London as the venue for the conference, but the Biafrans rejected this in protest at the British government's support of federal Nigeria. A compromise venue, Kampala, Uganda was agreed by all the parties and the meeting was chaired by Arnold Smith, the Commonwealth Secretary General, from 23–31 May 1968.

The conference ended in failure because the two sides rigidly maintained their conflicting political positions.[66] But Britain was quick to single out Biafra for criticism, again demonstrating its unflinching support for the federal cause. Lord Shepherd of the Foreign Office told the Lords:

> I do not think it unreasonable for the Federal Government to have sought some assurance that a ceasefire would lead to the maintenance of the territorial integrity of Nigeria,

which is precisely what they have been fighting for.[67]

Foreign Secretary Michael Stewart also spoke in the same vein: 'We must understand that a solution to this problem must rest on the position of one Nigeria, not two Nigerias'.[68]

This form of diplomatic support from Britain was very helpful to Nigeria in its political campaign to limit international sympathy for the Biafran cause. This was particularly successful within the Commonwealth countries. According to Prime Minister Wilson, the British government campaigned actively within the Commonwealth (and among Britain's other allies) to discourage any recognition of Biafran independence.[69]

On the whole, Britain's active military (and diplomatic) support for Nigeria played a crucial role in ensuring the ultimate federal victory over Biafra. Militarily, London supplied the Nigerians with most of the weapons they requested. In addition to military equipment acquired elsewhere, the federal army maintained an effective offensive capability throughout most of the 30-month-old war. Britain's consistent insistence throughout the war that the crisis should be settled on the basis of a 'United Nigeria' framework was very helpful to the federal political position. This meant that Britain effectively used its position within the Commonwealth Association of Nations and the Atlantic alliance to discourage member states from supporting the Biafran secession.

France

Yet Britain's ability to influence a number of leading states of the international community to support its pro-federal policy on the Nigerian conflict had its limitations. France, a historical rival in both Europe and Africa, adopted a different position. In an official statement issued in July 1968 the French government argued that the 'bloodshed and suffering that the Biafran people have endured for more than a year demonstrates their determination to affirm themselves as a people ... [the conflict should be settled on the] basis of the rights of peoples to self determination'.[70] Further pro-Biafran statements made later in the year by President de

Gaulle himself increased speculation in Europe and elsewhere that France was about to accord diplomatic recognition to Biafran independence. The Biafrans themselves were overjoyed by this development, especially as it came at a time of very low morale caused by the military reverses of the previous year including the May 1968 loss of the vital oil refinery town of Port Harcourt. While these French statements of exhortation ultimately fell short of a formal diplomatic recognition from Paris, Biafra was nonetheless convinced that it had made a breakthrough in Europe. Biafra felt that given the powerful diplomatic position that the French commanded in the European Economic Community at this time, the de Gaulle administration could raise the issue of the civil war in Community discussions. This would give the conflict a greater European focus which the Biafrans reasoned was essential in checking the ever-increasing British support for the federal government.

Aware that the French government had very close political ties with the 'francophone' African states (nine out of the 15 West African states are 'francophone'), the Biafrans were also optimistic that Paris would influence the latter to show more diplomatic sympathy for their cause. Lastly, and this was the most important consideration, Biafra hoped that French support would afford it a much more assured source for arms supplies to continue its struggle, especially at a time of very grim military setbacks.[71]

Belated, Limited and Circumscribed Support

But why the belated French support for Biafra? A number of students of this conflict have dealt with this question[72] and the majority stress that the French attitude to the Nigerian war was essentially part of a Gaullist foreign policy trajectory aimed at asserting France's own independent judgement from those of Britain and the United States.

Yet in declaring support for the Biafran secession in July 1968, France risked considerable financial losses in the Nigerian federation.[73] When Biafra seceded in May 1967, France had a total of £35 million worth of investments in

Nigeria and only 28 per cent (or about £10 million) was in Biafran territory.[74] In fact by July 1968, when France first declared its support for Biafra, the entire French investments in Biafra, including those owned by the French oil company, SAFRAP (a subsidiary of the state-owned Entreprises de Recherches et d'Activités Pétrolières – ERAP), were already in territory overrun by the Nigerian army (this included especially the Ogwaza, Azumini and Ebocha oilfields).[75]

So it appeared imprudent, especially in economic terms, for France to wish to support Biafra at a time when the secession faced imminent collapse. As for the Biafrans, it was doubtful that French support would radically alter their deteriorating military situation, unless, of course, Paris airlifted massive military supplies to them. But this was exactly what the French government did not do, and we need to examine the reasons for its reluctance.

There was a continuing disagreement within the French government over the Nigerian Civil War. This was between the President's Secretariat for African Affairs (headed by the influential Gaullist Jacques Foccart) and the Quai d'Orsay itself (the Foreign Ministry). Foccart's office was actively pro-Biafra and wanted outright full French diplomatic recognition of the new republic, and President de Gaulle lent support to this position.

Foccart had met several Biafran roving envoys, such as Michael Okpara, Kenneth Dike and Godwin Onyegbulam, since the outbreak of hostilities. He was also in regular contact with Raph Uwechue, Biafra's Chief Representative in Paris. The French official became convinced of the Biafran cause, and soon emerged as the leading advocate in the French government for an active Biafran policy.

The Quai d'Orsay, which institutionally was responsible for foreign policy, did not share Foccart's appraisals of the Nigerian conflict nor those of President de Gaulle. It was much more conscious of French economic interests in Nigeria that might be jeopardised if a pro-Biafran policy were adopted.[76] Furthermore, the Quai d'Orsay was more responsive to the pressure from pro-Nigerian influential North African countries such as Algeria, Morocco and Egypt (as well as the West African states of Cameroon and Niger), which lobbied intensively against French support for Biafran independence in Paris.[77] In these circumstances, the Quai d'Orsay was able to delay by at least a year the French government's announcement of its definitive position on the conflict, and even when this was made it was essentially cautious. The Quai d'Orsay succeeded in denying the Biafrans both the full diplomatic support they required, and the massive military supplies which could have helped to stem the Nigerian offensive.

Raph Uwechue has recalled that it was quite clear to the Biafra Office in Paris in the summer of 1968 that the Quai d'Orsay's views would prevail in the French intra-governmental disagreement over the Nigerian war. He said that 'the reality of the situation' was duly communicated back home to the Biafran leadership 'which already had an exaggerated feeling of expectation of French goodwill'.[78] Uwechue's summation of the effect of French aid on the Biafran struggle was:

> The French policy and aid would at best save Biafra from total destruction, but not make it strong enough to challenge Nigeria as effectively as total independence would demand.[79]

The Biafran government for its part then, felt that Uwechue's evaluation of the developments within the French government was 'indicative of a hasty judgement'. This unsympathetic reaction led to Uwechue's resignation from the Paris appointment in December 1968.

De St. Jorre, another observer of French policy towards the Nigerian conflict, however, agrees with Uwechue's conclusions: 'The effect of France's Biafran policy was like that of drugs on cancer: it kept the recipient alive but ensured – barring a miracle – a lingering death'.[80] General Philip Effiong, Chief of Biafra's General Staff, was later to reflect on the impact of French support on the Biafran struggle: 'the bastards did more harm than good by raising false hopes and by providing the British with an excuse to reinforce Nigeria'.[81]

Nature of Arms Supplies

From September 1968 until the end of the war in January 1970, the French government was involved in supplying arms to Biafra. The whole operation was handled and supervised by Foccart's Africa Division Office of the French presidency, and the French secret service – the Service de Documentation Extérieure et Contre-Espionage. The process of arms transfer itself was intricate and highly convoluted, involving certain banks in Paris, and the West African 'francophone' states of Côte d'Ivoire and Gabon, which had recognised the Biafran secession.[82]

In this deal, Côte d'Ivoire and Gabon advanced loans to Biafra in French CFA francs (convertible to French francs) to use in purchasing French arms in Paris, while the French government was committed to back up these loans. An important proviso was that France must determine the amount of any loans granted. Both Côte d'Ivoire and Gabon were also required to supply Biafra with some weapons from their own stocks, and these in turn were later replenished by the French.

Through this arrangement small arms and ammunition (these included Ceteme rifles and ammunition, some 7.62 mm NATO-standard rifles and ammunition and a few M-16 American rifles), mortars (81 mm and 4.2 in.), anti-aircraft equipment, radio gear, light machine guns, and some bazookas were airlifted to Biafra from staging bases in Libreville and Abidjan. The total quantity of this French supply source accounted for about 50 per cent of Biafra's entire arms imports in this last year of the war, and it cost the Biafrans $5 million.[83]

By using Côte d'Ivoire and Gabonese territories in this network of delivery, the French government was able to avoid sending any weapons directly to Biafra from France throughout the war. This was the basis of French government's continuous assertions during the conflict that it was not aiding Biafra militarily. It was therefore able to maintain publicly that Paris was keeping to the arms embargo it had declared on both sides of the conflict in June 1968.[84] On the other hand, the French government was able to employ this tortuous arms delivery system to its advantage in its relationship with Biafra. As General Ojukwu told John Stremlau after the war: 'I was never happy with French arms supplies or any system I could not control. The French were always trying to exert controls with their arms. There were a couple of slow-downs once they began supplying us that were intended to force us to change our policies... The French would have liked to control my entire regime... There could be no question of our becoming totally dependent on the French'.[85] But given the very depressed nature of Biafra's military position before the French-directed airlift began in September 1968, there was no doubt that the sudden infusion of French weaponry helped the Biafrans to stem the pressing federal offensive on all fronts of the war. Yet Biafra never stood the remotest chance to turn the scale in the battles due to the defensive characteristics of the weapons delivered, nor to contemplate emerging victorious from the war.

The Biafrans, however, utilised the limited diplomatic status they had in France to improve their arms purchases from private sources in Europe. Well-known arms merchants such as Pierre Lorez, Paul Favier and Roger Faulques handled most of these purchases, including transportation to Biafra by way of Lisbon and the Island of São Tomé, off the Biafran coast.[86] These merchants helped the Biafrans to open up contacts with other European dealers who were marketing Soviet weapons which came from Israeli sources (these weapons were part of the consignment captured by the Israelis from the Arab armies during the 1967 Middle East War). These Soviet arms were among the cheapest the Biafrans bought in this business, which cost them a lot in foreign exchange.[87]

Arms to Lagos

French arms were also reaching Nigeria from both government and private sources in spite of the declared embargo of June 1968. In August 1968, several Panhard armoured cars (with 90 mm guns and 60 mm anti-tank cannon) were delivered to the federal army.[88] Earlier on in the year, federal military technicians visited France to take 'specialised courses' on the handling and maintenance of advanced French weaponry. The federals also brought French arms through private interest groups in France which had business interests in Nigeria.

Altogether, the French military supplies to Biafra, which amounted to $5 million, was small when compared to the enormous sums of money that the Nigerian government derived from the sale of its export products to France, which went on without interruption throughout the war. Nigeria was therefore in a position where it was able to purchase most of its military equipment from revenue that accrued from these exports.[89] Such was Nigeria's advantage in this trade relation that in 1969 it had a trade surplus with the French of at least $66 million.[90]

Little wonder the Biafrans themselves were ultimately frustrated with the limited French support. In retrospect, all that the French arms deliveries did for Biafra was to postpone what already looked like an inevitable collapse of the secession in the summer of 1968. Apart from the sheer valour and determination to continue the struggle, the Biafran resistance was already cracking at this time.[91] The Biafrans were in fast retreat, having lost about three-quarters of their territory. French support for Biafra obviously was responsible for a sudden upsurge in morale within the ranks of the secessionist forces, followed by an improvement in defensive capabilities across all theatres of the war. The limited nature of this support was, however, clearly evident when the Biafrans could not withstand a renewed onslaught on their positions by the federal army 18 months later.

Portugal

The Biafrans had a very useful relationship with Portugal. Lisbon's airport and the airport in the then Portuguese-occupied territory of São Tomé were made available to the Biafran government as staging bases for its arms flights into Biafra. Biafran emissaries travelling to Europe and elsewhere also used these Portuguese facilities, which were run from a Biafra Office in Lisbon. The Portuguese capital soon became the major centre of the Biafran private arms purchasing business in Europe, with the establishment of the 'Africa Operations Bureau' headed by the French arms merchant, Pierre Lorez. By providing support to Biafra, Portugal was primarily motivated by the heavy financial returns which it derived from Biafra's payments for the airfields and other facilities provided.[92] Portugal did not supply Biafra with any arms. In December 1967 Nigeria's Foreign Minister, Okoi Arikpo, visited Lisbon in efforts to persuade the Salazar regime to close down the Biafra Office in the town, and revoke the landing rights granted to Biafran planes at São Tomé. Arikpo failed to get a Portuguese commitment to this effect, but was assured that Lisbon would not accord recognition to Biafra.[93]

For Portugal therefore, support of Biafra meant an additional financial source to buttress its war commitments in the African occupied territories. The Salazar regime was absolutely cautious in avoiding being seen by the rest of the international community in the obvious contradictory role of aiding, albeit indirectly, Biafran national liberation, while fighting desperately to destroy similar aspirations in Angola, Guinea Bissau and Mozambique.

The United States of America

The United States imposed an arms embargo on both sides of the conflict as its immediate response to the outbreak of the Nigerian Civil War. The US embassy in Lagos had viewed the deteriorating political situation in Nigeria, especially after the 29 July 1966 coup with great apprehension. The Ambassador, Elbert Matthews, as well as the then British High Commissioner to Nigeria (Francis Cumming-Bruce), intervened in the delicate talks that went on among the officers who overthrew the Aguyi-Ironsi regime, especially with respect to the future of the federation. Their initiative played an important role in dissuading the northern officers in control of Lagos from declaring the secession of the northern region from the federation.

Against this background, US support for Biafran independence was out of the question. Matthews made his government's position clear[94]:

> My government recognised the Federal Military Government of Nigeria. We have repeatedly made known our complete support of the political integrity of Nigeria. Many times we have expressed our hopes that Nigeria would continue to remain a united country. This is not only an official view, but one that is also felt by American businessmen engaged in the rapidly growing trade between our two countries.

The US concern for the political developments in Nigeria at this time requires elaboration. Before the Biafran secession, the United States imported 2.5 million barrels of oil per day from Nigeria. This accounted for 20 per cent of total US imports, and it came principally from eastern oil fields operated by Gulf (second to Shell-BP in Nigeria's oil operations). In 1962, two years after Nigeria's independence, US total investment in Nigeria was $54 million. It tripled in two years to $162 million and at the outbreak of war, in 1967, it stood at $200.[95] Before the end of the war, this figure doubled, especially due to costs incurred in reconstructing oil installations that were damaged during the 1968 fighting in the southern front. There were 7500 US citizens who worked in Nigeria, making them the largest number of foreigners after Britons.

A few weeks after the outbreak of the war, Nigeria asked for military aircraft from the US but this was rejected on grounds of Washington's arms embargo. It was a disappointment to Lagos, which expected that US diplomatic sympathies would be matched with military support. The federals were, however, relieved that Washington would maintain a 'discreet neutrality' in the conflict which would not lend support to the Biafrans, especially in view of the latter's extensive publicity campaigns in the United States at this time. As time went on, the reasoning in Lagos was that as the United States felt that the conflict was Britain's 'primary responsibility',[96] then they (the Americans) would not oppose their principal ally (Britain) which had declared unequivocal support (including military) for the continuing maintenance of the Nigerian federation.

While Nigeria was undoubtedly disappointed with the US

embargo on arms supplies to the belligerents, the Gowon regime, however, rightly calculated that as long as British support for its cause was guaranteed (both militarily and politically), the United States was not going to react favourably to Biafra's quest for diplomatic recognition.[97] In essence, Nigeria viewed Britain's unflinching support for it as the 'trump card' in encouraging continuing American diplomatic goodwill. Furthermore, part of the *quid pro quo* of Washington's backing for the British government's pro-Nigerian policy was London's support for the United States war in Vietnam.[98] Thus the 'subdued attitude' which characterised the federal government's reaction to US 'neutrality' in the conflict paid off very well. Nigeria generally avoided open criticism of the American position. As for the Biafrans, their robust mobilisation drive to win US public opinion fell short of getting support from official Washington. Even aspects of the Biafran publicity campaign which referred to increasing Soviet influence in Nigeria (references to Soviet arms deliveries to Lagos) did not alarm Washington. While the latter often criticised Soviet intervention, it nevertheless strongly justified Britain's arms deliveries to Lagos on the grounds that London had 'traditionally supplied Nigeria with arms'.[99] It came to the conclusion that no revolutionary situation existed in Lagos during the period which the Soviet Union or indeed any other power could have exploited.[100]

During the US presidential campaign in September 1968, presidential candidate Richard Nixon made a critical attack on the Johnson administration for not intervening to stop the Nigerian war. Nixon described the conflict as a 'terrible tragedy ... (which) has now assumed catastrophic dimensions ... (G)enocide is what is taking place right now – and starvation is the grim reaper ... Every friend of humanity should be asked to step forward to call an end to this slaughter of innocents in West Africa'.[101] He promised that if elected in November (1968), he would raise the issue of the war with the British government.

Nixon duly ordered a reappraisal of US policy on the war after he was elected president. The outcome was made known in February 1969 but it showed little change from that of the Johnson administration. The US reiterated its 'neutrality' in the conflict and called for an early negotiated settlement between the two parties. There would henceforth be greater involvement by the US in the provision of relief supplies to the war victims. In this regard, eight giant American C-97G stratofreighter cargo planes were made available to the International Red Cross and church groups.[102] As for any US diplomatic initiative on the conflict, Nixon did not appear to have tried to pressure the British government to alter its pro-Nigerian policy when he met Prime Minister Wilson in London for a summit in late February (1969).[103]

So, while the Johnson and Nixon administrations maintained a military neutrality throughout the duration of the war, the Nigerian belligerents sought to purchase US weapons through private sources in the country. Biafra acquired two United States B-26 bomber aircraft through US agents linked up with a French arms dealer, who was already in the Biafran arms traffic. The Biafrans made use of these planes in bombing federal communication lines and supply routes during fighting in the mid-west region in August 1967. Nigeria was also able to purchase some American B-26s from similar sources before the Soviet aircraft deal was concluded in mid-August 1967.

Biafra made extensive use of the sympathy it had generated in several sections of the US community in propagating its cause for independence. Leading US senators who were involved in the anti-Vietnam war movement such as Eugene McCarthy, George McGovern, Edward Kennedy, Thomas Dodd and William Proxmire often identified themselves with the humanitarian dimension of the conflict. They were very disappointed in 1969 that President Nixon did not embark on an independent US diplomatic initiative to achieve a ceasefire in the war, even though they welcomed the President's increase of American relief supplies to the area.

It is difficult to assess the extent to which domestic pressure in the United States, as well as the Biafran publicity exercise (which was the most intense abroad) were able to influence the continuing 'even-handed' policy that Washington adopted throughout the war. It does seem that while completely supporting the federal government of Nigeria, successive US administrations successfully tackled the domestic critics of their policy by meeting some of their demands (namely, more humanitarian aid to the war victims), and left the political component (settlement of the conflict) to an African diplomatic initiative. In stating the latter, Washington was implicitly reassuring Lagos. More importantly, successive United States governments were satisfied with the role and effectiveness of its principal ally, Britain, in containing the Biafran secession. This was why the administrations' spokespersons often reiterated that the solution of the conflict was a 'British responsibility'.

Quite clearly the Johnson administration would have come to the conclusion from the local assessment of its embassy in Lagos at the outbreak of the war, that the secession could not succeed, unless Biafra were to receive support from a major international ally.

Apart from the temporary dislocation in the Gulf crude oil operations in southern Biafra (1968), US economic interests were not in jeopardy throughout the war. Just as the French, most US commercial and industrial enterprises were located in the Nigerian regions undisturbed by the war. Furthermore, with the increasing escalation of the Vietnam War to contend with at this time, there was no incentive in the United States to get sucked into another civil war elsewhere on the globe.

III AFRICA: THE DEBATES ON 'SELF DETERMINATION', 'TERRITORIAL INTEGRITY', AND THE 'INVIOLABILITY' OF POST-COLONIAL BORDERS

Most African states were extremely cautious in reacting openly to the Biafran declaration of independence on 30 May 1967. The act of secession in any of the post independent African states had become the most unpopular undertaking in the continent's political development. This attitude had been reinforced by the devastating experience of Zaïre (then Congo-Leopoldville) in the early 1960s, when the province of Katanga had seceded.

As members of the Organisation of Africa Unity (OAU), African states adhere strictly to certain articles in the Organisation's charter,[104] which commits all signatories to 'safeguard the sovereignty, independence and territorial integrity of all member states'.[105] Another article stresses the sovereign equality of all member states, non-interference in the domestic affairs of states, and the inviolability of existing national borders.[106]

All these vital OAU charter articles ultimately guided the attitude and overall reaction of the majority of the 42 independent African states to the Biafran declaration of independence.

It should be recalled that when the OAU was formed in 1963 (and also when the charter was drawn up), the major consideration of the new African sovereign states was the consolidation of their new status of political independence after many years of Western colonialism. The leaders who attended the inaugural conference in Addis Ababa were all aware that most of their states (as they existed on the eve of the decolonisation process) were arbitrarily created by the respective colonial administration from hitherto disparate states and nationalities. They therefore felt that the only way to save these newly-acquired independent territories from disintegrating into their various ethno-national and pre-colonial state constituents, was to commit themselves to the concept of 'inviolability' of existing borders.

Except for Gabon, Côte d'Ivoire, Tanzania and Zambia, which recognised the Biafran secession, all other African states basically steered along this official OAU course, even though some other considerations motivated certain African states, for instance, the Arab North, in their hostility towards Biafra, as we shall elaborate later.

It was evident that the challenge of Biafra to many African states was not just that there was a major preoccupation on the part of these countries with the effect(s) that Biafran independence would have on the rest of the Nigerian federation. Rather it was that African leaders who came from equally heterogeneous states as Nigeria (such as Ethiopia, Sudan, Zaïre, Kenya and Chad, among others) viewed the sustenance and ultimate success of the Biafran secession as capable of having a 'domino effect' on their own countries.[107]

This was in effect the major argument that the Nigerian federal government pursued throughout the war in its diplomatic campaign against Biafra in Africa, and it was in the main successful.

However, President Julius Nyerere of Tanzania, a highly respected pan-Africanist and a progressive politician, introduced a new element in the OAU attitude to secession in April 1968. He felt that in the final analysis, 'unity can only be based on the general consent of the people involved ... In Nigeria this consciousness of a common citizenship was destroyed by the events of 1966, and in particular by the pogroms in which 30,000 Eastern Nigerians were murdered ... It is these pogroms, and the apparent inability or unwillingness of the authorities to protect the victims, which underlies the Easterners' conviction that they have been rejected by the Nigerians...'[108] Nyerere argued that Tanzania could not acquiesce in a situation, such as in Nigeria, where a war had to be fought to force an unwilling people to remain within a federation. He stated that if the people of Zanzibar (the offshore Indian Ocean Island which is part of Tanzania) wanted to leave the Tanzanian Union, 'I could not advocate bombing them into submission'.[109]

In effect, Nyerere's reconceptualisation of 'self determination' in the African context meant the following: that just as the principle of self determination was crucial in the decolonisation movement against European colonial powers, this concept could still be relevant in solving problems of sovereignty (or 'competing' nationalisms) in the new independent states. On this consideration,[110] Tanzania recognised the independence of Biafra, and a few days later, Zambia's Kenneth Kaunda, a long-term close associate of Nyerere in the Southern African decolonisation struggle, also accorded recognition to Biafra.

But other African, radical, leaderships, such as those in Egypt, Algeria, Guinea and Mali, did not go along with the Nyerere viewpoint. The basic reason for the distinctly anti-Biafran stance taken by these leaderships during the conflict was much more due to their respective domestic politics. These are predominantly Muslim states and it is this ideological element which chiefly dictated their sympathies for federal Nigeria, whose population had a Muslim majority.

Furthermore, Biafra had evidently antagonised these

states in a speculative radio broadcast (on the day secession was declared) which claimed that it had been recognised by Israel. This event happened just on the eve of the June 1967 Six-Day War. Another issue of discord between Biafra and Arab/Muslim states concerned the constant analogy which leading Igbo leaders often made to the Jews to characterise the plight of the Igbo in the Nigerian federation. As a result, the Igbo have always been more sympathetic to Israel in the Middle East conflict, while the people of northern Nigeria were generally pro-Arab.

The predominantly Muslim states of sub-Saharan Africa, such as Niger, Cameroon (both bordering on Nigeria), Mauritania and Senegal, equally showed the same strong inclination in their diplomatic support for the federal government even though at the same time a number of these states showed sympathy for the Eritrean independence struggle in Ethiopia. The Cameroon President, Ahmadu Ahidjo, and his Nigeri counterpart, Hamani Diori, who were both very close to important French leaders (including President de Gaulle), continuously campaigned in French government circles against a Biafran recognition by Paris.[111] Their constant advice reinforced that of influential North African leaders (especially Algeria's Houari Boumedienne) who equally pressured the French government not to recognise Biafra.[112]

Thus the reaction of African states to the Nigerian civil war was not necessarily dictated by their usually discernible ideological position in pan-African politics. The war created a situation unimaginable in the annals of post-colonial African alliances; 'radical' states like Algeria, Egypt, Guinea and Mali voted to 'Keep Nigeria One' in OAU conferences with 'conservative' states of Malagasy, Cameroon and Ethiopia. Equally surprising was the situation where 'conservative' states like Côte d'Ivoire and Gabon were found to be championing the cause of the Biafran secession with dedicated anti-imperialist Tanzania and Zambia.

It is essential to recall that before announcing Ivorien recognition of Biafra on 14 May 1968, President Houphouet-Boigny adopted an argument similar to that Nyerere had used the month before to support the Biafran secession. The Ivorien leader stressed: 'We say no to unity in war and through war ... Unity is for the living and not for the dead'.[113]

There were other reasons in any case why Houphouet-Boigny decided to recognise Biafra. The Ivorien President was a staunch Roman Catholic with a minority Muslim population, who saw the predominantly Catholic Biafrans as allies against the Islamic penetration of West Africa.[114] He also saw the Biafran episode as a good opportunity to deepen the friendship he had maintained for several years with leading Biafran entrepreneurs and industrialists, prominent among whom was Odumegwu Ojukwu Snr (General Ojukwu's father). The Ivorien President, a long time anti-communist, was also highly suspicious of Soviet support for Nigeria, coming just after the expulsion of Soviet diplomats from neighbouring Ghana.[115]

Houphouet-Boigny, who had maintained a high degree of influence among members of the Gabonese leadership, played a major role in the decision by Gabon to recognise Biafra in April 1968. Suzanne Cronje has described Houphouet-Boigny as a 'sort of super-president of Gabon',[116] and this seems appropriate in describing the prestige of the Ivorien leader in a country where his speeches are often reproduced in the Gabonese ruling party daily, *Union Gabonaise*. Also, the role of a fair number of Biafran residents in Gabon, some of who worked in the country's commerce, could have been another contributing factor in President Bongo's decision to recognise the Biafran secession.

In the main, most African states supported federal Nigeria in the conflict and this was overwhelmingly demonstrated in the three OAU heads of state summits which were held during the civil war (in Kinshasa, Addis Ababa and Algiers). In the September 1967 Kinshasa summit, the OAU appointed a six-nation 'Consultative Mission' headed by Emperor Haile Selassie of Ethiopia to visit Nigeria. Other members of the group were President Mobutu of Zaïre, President Tubman of Liberia, General Ankrah of the National Liberation Council, Ghana, President Diori of Niger and President Ahidjo of Cameroon. The OAU made it clear that the group was not going to mediate ih the conflict, but to 'assure the Head of the Federal Government of Nigeria of the Assembly's [OAU] desire for the territorial integrity, unity and peace of Nigeria'.[117]

The OAU group ultimately went to Lagos in November 1967 without Presidents Mobutu and Tubman, who were reportedly attending to urgent domestic state duties, but who indicated that they still supported the purpose of the visit. There were, however, strong indications that the reasons why Mobutu particularly did not go to Lagos were due to his doubts about the usefulness of the visit, and the effects of official press comments made in Lagos following a statement the Zaïrean leader made about the Nigerian war. On 10 October 1967 (after the Kinshasa summit and before the expected visit of the OAU mission), Mobutu publicly rejected the constant official federal Nigerian comparison between the Katanga and Biafra secessions. As the army commander who led the military campaign against the Katangese forces in Zaïre a decade before, Mobutu insisted that the 'parallel was false'.[118] There was, however, no intention by Zaïre, in spite of Mobutu's assertion, to alter its policy towards the conflict, which remained the maintenance of the Nigerian federation.

Addressing the (now) four-nation OAU mission when it called on him, General Gowon reminded the African leaders that they had not come to Nigeria to mediate in the civil war but to 'call on the rebel leaders to abandon secession'[119] and accept the unity of the Nigerian federation. Gowon once again raised the official Nigerian argument of the consequences of a successful Biafran secession for the rest of Africa: 'It was the Democratic Republic of the Congo and Tshombe yesterday, it is Nigeria and Ojukwu today. Who knows which African country will be the next victim of secessionist forces?'[120] As was expected, the mission reiterated its pro-federal position. In a statement issued the following day, before its departure, it said: 'The secessionists should renounce secession and accept the present administrative structure of a federal 12-state structure'.[121] Predictably, the Biafrans rejected the outcome of the visit. A government statement accused the OAU of 'stage-managing a conference which has flouted the established principles of natural justice to accord the right of hearing to all parties in a dispute'.[122]

Both the Algiers OAU summit in September 1968 and the Addis Ababa conference of September 1969 re-endorsed the official OAU policy on the war. Each conference resolution on Nigeria in the official communiqué always emphasised the OAU standard position on a United Nigeria solution: 'Appeals solemnly and urgently to the two parties involved in the civil war to agree to preserve in the over-riding interests of Africa, the unity of Nigeria and accept immediately the suspension of hostilities...'[123] Only the four African states which recognised Biafra voted against the resolution in Algiers (with Rwanda and Botswana abstaining), while in Addis Ababa they (along with Sierra Leone) instead decided to abstain.

It was clear that by the time the Addis conference started, the four states had begun to doubt the possibility of Biafra's ultimate survival, especially in the light of renewed federal offensives which began on the eve of the summit. By abstaining from the OAU 'One Nigeria' resolution this time, the four were signalling to the Biafrans that they could not continue to support the Biafran position of 'total sovereignty' indefinitely. We should add that these states severely criticised the Algerian government (in a joint statement) during the 1968 Algiers summit for barring a Biafran delegation from entering the country, while allowing members of the Eritrean independence movement to attend and lobby delegates.

Military Support

Some African states, such as Egypt and Algeria, added military aid to their diplomatic support for federal Nigeria. This was in the form of arms, and the dispatch of military advisers to the federal airforce. Cairo sold three Soviet-made MIG 17 fighters to the Nigerians in one instance,[124] while Algiers transferred five MIG 17s from its airforce to Lagos in the summer of 1969.[125] Libya and Sudan sold arms to Lagos[126] and most of the Nigerian air force planes that went on bombing raids to Biafra throughout the war were piloted by Egyptians and mercenaries recruited elsewhere.[127]

In retrospect, it is clear that the overwhelming diplomatic support that the federal Nigerian government derived from the majority of African states had a tremendous impact on the ultimate political (and subsequently the military) outcome of the war. Any non-African state (especially in Europe and the Americas) which considered recognising the Biafran secession, would have cautiously watched the attitude and reactions of the majority of African states to the conflict. Africa's official position to the rest of the world, via the OAU, was that the war was an 'African affair'. In terms of intra-OAU relations, it was Nigeria's 'internal affair'. Both aspects of the OAU stand on the conflict effectively satisfied the main diplomatic tenet of the federal government throughout the war.

Having adopted the OAU articles which are unequivocally critical of secession, most independent African states were right from the outset sympathetic with the federal government's political position in the conflict. As a consequence, Biafra lost the crucial battle for African diplomatic support. The course of the conflict showed that firm African support was the vital platform for both contesting parties to launch the drive towards the extra-continental endorsement of their varying political viewpoints. The federal government's victory in securing this platform meant that its case was easily receptible to the other states of the world. As for Biafra, the problems were enormous. Having lost Africa, it could not make any effective political breakthrough outside the continent. Several countries, especially in Europe and the Americas, were often more prepared to isolate the humanitarian aspect of the war (and send relief aid) while dealing with Biafran envoys, because of their preference to endorse the official OAU stand that the political component of the conflict was an 'African affair'.

'White' Africa

Lastly, let us examine the attitudes and roles of Rhodesia (now Zimbabwe) and South Africa in the Nigerian conflict. Predictably, the conflict in Nigeria afforded welcome propaganda for the two white minority-ruled states which had continuously contended that independent Africa was unstable.

Yet both the federal government and Biafra sought and

Nigeria

employed the services of South African and Rhodesian nationals during the civil war. Nigeria recruited South African and Rhodesian pilots for its air force (in addition to ground staff) and a number of these participated in combat operations against Biafra.[128] The Biafrans, on the other hand, employed Rhodesians and South Africans to fly the arms airlift from Lisbon to their embattled territory.[129] The two sides also recruited mercenaries from the white-ruled states, especially in the early part of the war,[130] but most of these were either killed or wounded in the ferocious battles that took place in all war theatres between January and March 1968. Survivors soon abandoned their services.

South African and Rhodesian mercenaries, in addition to those recruited from elsewhere in Europe, made an insignificant impact on the war. The fighting took a large toll of them. In the Nigerian Civil War, a lot was at stake politically for both sides. The risks involved and undertaken by the military forces from both sides of the frontline were enormous and the resultant casualty figure was very high – nearly two million (including civilians). This figure represented twice as many as those killed throughout the two decades of the Vietnam war. In such a situation, it was only the very politically motivated who could take such risks – this circumstance obviously did not suit the usual financial disposition or motivation of the mercenary fighter. As soon as the high level of casualties on the battlefield increased alarmingly in the early months of 1968, the surviving bands of mercenary forces hired by both sides disbanded.

As was expected, each side in the Nigerian conflict continued to accuse the other of employing mercenary units from South Africa and Rhodesia (and Europe) as part of the propaganda war (beamed particularly in this case to their African audiences) without ever acknowledging the fact that these fighters were also in their employ.

IV THE SOVIET UNION

Before the outbreak of the Nigerian Civil War, the influence of the Soviet Union in the Nigerian federation was minimal. The first civilian government of Abubakar Tafawa Balewa was unfriendly and very suspicious of the Soviet Union. It took two years after independence (1962) to establish diplomatic ties with Moscow, and this was due mainly to the pressure of the NCNC coalition partner in the government, and the opposition Action Group. Even after that, serious travel restrictions were placed on Nigerians wishing to visit the Soviet Union, including students who planned to study there. Soviet and East European scholarships for Nigerian students were officially discouraged, and communist literature was banned from the country. Nigerian government leaders did not conceal their dislike for the socialist system even in public. Balewa once told parliament:

> I and my colleagues are determined that while we are responsible for the government of the Federation of Nigeria and for the welfare of its people, we shall use every means in our power to prevent the infiltration of communism and communist ideas into Nigeria.[131]

In 1963 when the Action Group leader, Obafemi Awolowo, was accused of plotting to overthrow the federal government, the Soviet Union was implicated.[132] The USSR were accused of sending weapons to Nigerian 'rebels' training for the operation in camps in Ghana.

In view of this official hostility, the Soviet Union was forced to limit its contacts in Nigeria with student organisations, left-leaning trade unions and parties. The Soviet Union established close links with both the radical Nigerian Youth Congress and the Marxist-oriented Nigerian Socialist Workers' and Farmers' Party (NSWAFP). During the first party congress of the NSWAFP in 1965 in Lagos, the Soviet Union sent a politburo member to represent the Soviet Communist Party. In fact Soviet commentators began to refer to the NSWAFP as a possible 'vanguard party' in a Nigerian revolution.[133] The NSWAFP, in turn reciprocated by sending a delegation to the 23rd Party Congress of the Communist Party of the Soviet Union in 1966.[134] The USSR was also in close contact with the left-wing Nigerian Trade Union Congress (leader Wahab Goodluck was the Vice-President of the NSWAFP) and often attacked the pro-Western Trade Union Congress of Nigeria in analyses of the labour movement in Nigeria.

The Soviet Union welcomed the January 1966 military take-over and felt that there was now a better opportunity to develop ties with Nigeria. A Soviet political commentator saw the coup as a blow to the reactionary feudal and bourgeois domination of the Nigerian state system, adding that it was now necessary for the new regime to embark on progressive policies to help the people.[135] Moscow also showed a keen interest in Aguyi-Ironsi's abolition of the four-region federal structure for a unitary government in May 1966. A long-term party analyst in Moscow's African Institute saw the move as 'progressive', because the 'infringement of nationality rights under the federal structure necessitated the proclamation of a unitary system of government'.[136]

The Soviet media reported the Igbo massacres in northern Nigeria with great sympathy for the victims. As the country drifted towards secession and possible civil war, Soviet commentators generally called on the federal government to take 'careful cognisance of Ibo grievances and aspirations',[137] but cautioned that Nigeria's problems could not be effectively solved by dissolution of the federation.[138]

In April 1967 a Soviet technical delegation arrived in Lagos to negotiate new agreements with the federal government on cultural and trade relations. The latter was particularly important for both sides because until then, Soviet-Nigerian trade had been minimal. Before 1962 Soviet exports to Nigeria were practically nil, while Nigerian products were sold to the USSR only by way of Britain and the Netherlands. Between 1963, when formal trade links were established, and 1966 the highest trade turn over between the two countries was in 1965 and the figure was £N3200 (Soviet exports to Nigeria were £N1200, and Soviet imports £N2000).[139] In 1966 this slumped to £N1900,[140] possibly due to the deteriorating political situation in Nigeria.

Part of the Soviet visiting mission also went to the eastern region. There it entered into an agreement to build a teaching hospital in Enugu and offered to send Soviet architects and technicians to Nsukka for the proposed expansion of the University there. The Soviet delegation finally returned to Moscow one week before the Biafran declaration of independence.

There was no doubt that the visit by this Soviet mission to

both Lagos and Enugu, prior to the eastern secession and the civil war, offered the Soviet Union a good opportunity to evaluate the intricacy of the deteriorating Nigerian political situation on the spot.

It should be recalled that by the mid-1960s there was some disillusionment in the Soviet Union over its relationship with independent Africa. This had been exacerbated in the diplomatic 'set-backs' incurred in Congo-Leopoldville earlier on in the decade due to the assassination of Patrice Lumumba, with whose government the Soviet Union had established good relations. There was also the case of Ghana in February 1966, when the Kwame Nkrumah administration was toppled in a right-wing coup d'état. In May 1966 Guinea, which had for several years maintained close ties with the USSR, suddenly expelled the Soviet mission from the country.

Given this background, the worsening political conflict in Nigeria in the spring of 1967 and the subsequent war provided a much-needed opportunity for the Soviet Union to attempt to develop some influence in a country where, hitherto, it had been forced to maintain a very low profile. The reason why Moscow decided to support the federals in the conflict in August 1967 was the combination of two inter-related developments. The first concerned the refusal of the United States and Britain to supply Nigeria with sophisticated aircraft a fortnight after hostilities began. Secondly, and more essential, was the USSR's perception of an ultimate federal victory in the war based on the report of its technical delegation that went to Nigeria in April, the Soviet embassy in Lagos, and the talks held in Moscow with a visiting Nigerian ministerial party the previous month.[141] Furthermore, it was highly unlikely that if the Soviet Union sought to improve its ties with Nigeria (which it had keenly tried to do without much success for nearly a decade), it would support secessionist political objectives in the country. For instance, while Soviet support for a Biafran secession would have been very unpopular in most official African opinion, such an act would also inevitably have resulted in a Soviet confrontation with Britain (and the West) which would view their huge economic interests in Nigeria as threatened. So, with Soviet support for Lagos, any possibility that the Nigerian civil conflict could incorporate an East-

West ideological 'colouration' receded immediately.

The Soviet Union formally informed Lagos of its support in the war in a note sent to General Gowon by Premier Kosygin in August 1967.[142] Next Moscow embarked on justifying its pro-Nigerian position ideologically. This was necessary since the USSR realised that support for Lagos meant aiding the same party in a conflict with Britain which was part of the 'imperialist West that is responsible for the Nigerian people's tragedy', as Soviet commentators were keen to stress at the time.[143] The analysis of Vladimir Kudryavtsev, a well-known Soviet scholar on Africa, is illustrative of the justification of the Soviet position.[144] Kudryavtsev acknowledged that the Igbo had 'more than other peoples of Nigeria acquired attributes which brought them near to what is understood by the word "nation" but this, in itself could not be taken as the only ground for backing their secession'.[145] He also vehemently rejected criticisms that often emanated from some Marxist circles in Europe (especially in France[146]) that by supporting Lagos, the Soviet Union was joining 'imperialists and oppressors' to subjugate the Biafran people. 'It was naïve', the Soviet commentator observed, 'for anyone to equate Soviet support [for federal Nigeria] with that of the capitalist West'.[147] He agreed that both Britain and his country supported the continuation of the Nigerian federation, but argued that this was an 'external coincidence' which did not mean that both powers supported Nigerian unity on the same premises'.[148]

Kudryavtsev contended that the premises for support were 'diametrically opposed from the class point of view and are in essence mutually exclusive'.[149] He argued that Britain supported the unity of Nigeria just as France supported the Biafran secession. This was due to 'capitalist rivalry over oil, economic assets and influence' in that part of West Africa.[150] The Soviet Union, on the other hand, Kudryavtsev maintained, backed Nigeria 'in consideration of the tasks [sic] of the African peoples' anti-imperialist struggles both for strengthening of already won independence and the complete liberation of the continent from the remnants of colonialism'.[151]

Evidently, Kudryavtsev's position on this subject is a hog wash of an analysis which sheds no light at all on the extensive economic and strategic opportunities in Nigeria, and the neighbouring region which the Soviet Union hoped to explore with the success of federal Nigeria in the war. The point at stake though, is that Soviet marxism has very scant understanding and appreciation of the contingent issues of 'nations' and 'nationalities' in the Southern World, subjects that are often dismissed as epiphenomenon within the ambience of its stultified overarching bureaucratic socialist framework of discourse. Contemporary events in the USSR *itself* (in its Asiatic Republics, and even in the (European) Baltic States, Moldavia, the Ukraine and elsewhere), and the Soviet interventions in Afghanistan, and Ethiopia to suppress Eritrean, Tigrean, and Oromo nationalisms (as well as its 1968 invasion of Czechoslovakia), underline the historic failure of Soviet marxism on this score. It is an historic irony that the Kremlin, which 20 years ago feverishly rushed aircraft, bombs and guns to federal Nigeria to crush the Biafran independence movement, has recently watched effortlessly as the East European bloc of states that it has controlled militarily and politically for 40 years crumble as a result of mass and popular uprisings. But even more specific to our subject, Moscow faces the prospects of the dissolution of the USSR due to demands for independence by several of its constituent nations and nationalities.

There were obviously other prevailing factors during this period which made Soviet support for Nigeria less controversial in Africa. By backing the federals, Moscow did not run the risk of upsetting most of its African allies and friends (especially in the Arab world) as a majority of these (also members of the OAU) supported the Nigerian cause. The USSR must also have calculated that it was not going to provoke some 'Cold War' confrontation with the West over its Nigerian policy. The Kremlin was certain that the major Western power that had had a long-term colonial (and post-colonial) influence in the area (Britain) wanted to safeguard the territorial character of the Nigerian federation. This was equally the political preference of the United States, as we have also shown. So within the context of prevailing international politics, Soviet support for federal Nigeria carried minimal risk.

Aircraft, Technicians and Guns

As soon as Soviet support became firm in August 1967, Moscow approved the immediate dispatch of a consignment of military aircraft to the federals. This involved 20 MIG 17 fighters and six Czech L-29 Delphin trainers.[152] Two hundred Soviet technicians were dispatched to Nigeria to assemble and test the aircraft, which were then flown by Egyptian pilots in the airwar against Biafra.[153] Also before the end of the year, three Soviet patrol boats were delivered to the Nigerian navy.

In the first two years of the war the USSR continued to deliver mainly aircraft, bombs and other assorted air weapons to the federals. Considerable quantities of Soviet ground armaments, such as Kalashnikov rifles (and ammunition), started reaching Lagos after September 1969. In the last month of the war (December 1969), Moscow delivered the high-precision heavy 122 mm field guns, which the federals committed to their final assault on Biafra.

So the main Soviet weapons the federals used in the war were the aircraft. These planes carried out two years of often indiscriminate bombings of Biafran towns and villages with very low impact on the military progress of the war. Michael Leapman has described the 'amazingly imprecise (targeting by the) Egyptian pilots ... (whose) main concern seemed to be drop their load as quickly as they could and then head off for home'.[154] If there was any federal action that lent credibility to Biafra's charges of genocide during the conflict, then one must isolate the features and the devastating effects that these air raids had on the Biafran civilian population. Ironically, the overall effect of the bombings was a stiffening of Biafran resistance.[155]

In the pure military sense, therefore, the Nigerian war was a ground war. In view of this, we can only objectively assess the impact of Soviet weapons in the conflict in the last four months of the war – namely, when Moscow started to deliver ground weapons to Lagos. There was a noticeable impact: the 122 mm guns (with a range of 13 miles) were deployed on the southern front and were effectively used in the attack on Uli airport, Biafra's link with the outside world, and in the final battles leading to the capture of Owerri, Biafra's temporary capital.

In essence, the precise usefulness of Soviet support for the federals in the first 26 months of the war was largely political (seen significantly when Moscow decided to supply the fighter aircraft in August 1967 after Nigeria's 'traditional' friends – Britain and the US – had refused), and this by extension incorporated the sympathies of the other states in the East European bloc. But when the USSR began to deliver the crucial ground weapons that the federals had mostly relied upon to prosecute the war, they entered into an arena that until then had witnessed the absolute dominance of the British government.

V A CONCLUDING NOTE

In the Nigerian Civil War, Britain and the Soviet Union gave the most substantial military support to the federal party. Britain, the former Western colonial power that was responsible for creating the Nigerian federation, and which had considerable economic and industrial interests in the country, felt that these interests would be threatened in the event of the disintegration of the federation.

Initially the British government was very cautious in supplying the federals with the sophisticated variety of weaponry they requested, especially aircraft, in their war against Biafra. This was due to London's embargo on the sale of advanced military aircraft to independent Africa. Secondly, the British had accepted the highly optimistic Nigerian view that the encounter with Biafra was going to be a brief 'Police Action'. Thirdly, the British government was contending with persistent criticisms in Parliament and elsewhere in the country for opting to side with the federals in the conflict.

But with the prolongation of the war as the Biafran resistance unexpectedly stiffened, the British progressively stepped up their arms deliveries to Lagos, until Britain became the main supplier of the federal army. With the immense stockpile of British military equipment, in addition to that later supplied by the Soviet Union, the federal army was able to maintain an effective offensive capability throughout the war, with the eventual enforcement of a Biafran capitulation.

The Soviet Union saw the conflict as an opportunity to increase its influence in a part of Africa where, until then, it had been forced to maintain a very low profile. Also, considering the major diplomatic setbacks that the Soviet Union had suffered in the West and Central African regions in recent years, Moscow was confident that it would achieve Nigerian goodwill by supplying the aircraft that Britain and the United States were reluctant to dispatch in August 1967. Although the federal use of the aircraft in the war achieved an insignificant military value, the Soviet decision to supply the planes immediately increased Moscow's political prestige in federal circles.

Diplomatically, Moscow and London played influential roles in sustaining the federal Nigerian cause. Soviet support for the federals implied diplomatic sympathy within the countries of Eastern Europe. As for Britain, the pro-federal policy was essential in effecting a 'restraining role' within the Commonwealth states (of which Nigeria was a member) with regard to the question of Biafran recognition.

France and Portugal chiefly aided the Biafran war effort. Although neither of these states accorded diplomatic recognition to Biafra, each played vital roles which helped to sustain the Biafran resistance until its collapse in January 1970. France's 'semi-recognition' of Biafra in the summer of 1968 followed by a step-up of arms deliveries through Ivory Coast and Gabon, were instrumental in averting the near-military defeat of the secession that year. The Portuguese allowed the Biafrans to establish transit facilities in Lisbon and the territory of São Tomé – then one of their African colonies. Even though Biafra paid heavily (financially) for these services, Lisbon ultimately became the main focus in Europe for arms and diplomatic flights associated with the Biafran war effort.

Most African states, including the official position of the OAU, were in favour of the continuing maintenance of the Nigerian federation. For them, the conflict was an 'internal war' (thus suiting a consistently-held Nigerian political position) which should be settled on the basis of existing OAU charter provisions. These emphasised the 'inviolability' of post-colonial African borders.

Having failed diplomatically to get a sympathetic endorsement of its case in Africa, Biafra stood even flimsier chances of getting this recognition elsewhere. At best, most governments' responses (especially in the West) were to view the Biafran case as a humanitarian one, the sort of human tragedy which needed urgent relief aid.

In evaluating the basic roots and conditions within which it started, the Nigerian Civil War was no doubt an internal conflict. But having started on 6 July 1967, the character, length, conduct and eventual outcome of the confrontation (30 months later) was critically dependent on the resources which the international community made available to each of the protagonists. The fact that the federal Nigerians received a preponderant chunk of these resources (especially the military component) was the decisive factor in determining their victory over Biafra.

3 Angola

I INTRODUCTION

On 25 April 1974 the Portuguese Armed Forces Movement (MFA) overthrew the right-wing dictatorship that had been in power in Portugal for almost half a century. This coup occurred 13 years after Portugal embarked upon a counter-insurgency war against African liberation movements in Angola. The movements were the FNLA, MPLA and UNITA. Inevitably, the coup in Lisbon had a major impact on the Angolan war, and those in other African countries occupied by Portuguese imperialism – Mozambique, Guinea-Bissau and Cape Verde, and São Tomé and Principe Islands. The new Portuguese government soon committed itself to the attainment of full independence by each of these states. Angola's independence date – 11 November 1975 – was chosen during a conference between the MFA and members of the three Angolan independence movements which was held in Alvor, Portugal, in January 1975.

According to the Alvor Accords,[1] Angola would be administered by a transitional government made up of the FNLA, MPLA and UNITA, as well as the Portuguese, prior to independence. The agreement also provided for the formation of an Angolan national army, in which each liberation movement would have 8000 troops, while the Portuguese provided a contingent of 24 000 soldiers. A ten-member National Defence Council was set up to supervise the gradual integration of all combatants from the three movements into a national armed forces.

MPLA

The Movimento Popular de Libertação de Angola (MPLA – the Popular Movement for the Liberation of Angola) was founded in December 1956. It emerged from the merger of the Party for the United Struggle of the Angolan Africans (predominantly a grouping of Mbundu intellectuals in the

Luanda area or the so-called assimilados) and the Movement for the National Independence of Angola, whose members were mainly drawn from 'mestico' (mixed racial parentage) intellectuals.[2]

In 1960 the MPLA began to organise armed cells in Luanda and surrounding districts as part of its strategy to terminate the Portuguese colonial occupation of Angola. On 4 February 1961 units from these armed cells successfully attacked a police patrol in Luanda. Using captured weapons, the militants forced their way to the main Luanda maximum security prison in an effort to release detained MPLA political activists.

However, MPLA operations were crushed by the Portuguese armed forces and over the following two days, the colonial regime executed 3000 Africans in Luanda. A further 5000 Africans were shot the following week as Portuguese reprisals extended to neighbouring districts of Luanda. MPLA survivors from these massacres escaped to the forests of northwest Angola to find refuge and regroup.

After three years of reorganisation, the MPLA's political and military position improved dramatically following its successful commando attacks on Portuguese positions in Cabinda, the Angolan oil principality that shared a border with Congo-Brazzaville. The new radical government in Brazzaville, led by Alphonse Massemba-Débat, had allowed the MPLA to set up bases in Congo-Brazzaville, and it was from there that the Cabinda attack was carried out.

Soon, the MPLA began to infiltrate a number of Angola's northern districts, and later Luanda itself, from its Congo-Brazzaville bases. With the reconsolidation of its support base in Luanda later, the MPLA began to broaden its guerrilla operations in the eastern districts, especially Moxico, which borders on Zambia.

FNLA

The Frente Nacional de Libertação de Angola (FNLA – the Angolan National Liberation Front) was formed in March 1962. The FNLA was principally a movement based among the Bakongo of northern Angola. Its membership was drawn principally from two earlier political organisations in the region – the Democratic Party of Angola and the Union of the People of Angola (UPA).[3] The UPA had made its mark in the anti-Portuguese liberation war in March 1961, just over a month after the MPLA attacked the army patrol, by organising an uprising involving plantation workers in the northern districts of Uige, Lunda and Zaïre.[4] During the disturbances, hundreds of thousands of acres of coffee, which then accounted for 40 per cent of Angola's foreign revenue, were destroyed, in addition to administrative and police headquarters in the region. The Portuguese colonial regime responded to these revolts with even greater ruthlessness than before. Between March and June 1961, 50 000 Africans were massacred in Portuguese reprisals across a wide geographical area, which included the districts of Cuanza Sul, Huila, Benguela and Huambo.[5] Ground troops including settler militias and the airforce, were deployed during this terror campaign. About 1.5 million Angolans were forced into exile, most of them into neighbouring Congo-Leopoldville (now Zaïre), where they formed the main support base for the newly formed FNLA.

In April 1962, the FNLA, under the leadership of Holden Roberto, formed an Angolan government in exile (GRAE – Govêrno Revolucionário de Angola no Exílo) with its headquarters in Leopoldville. It received diplomatic support from its Congolese government hosts, and later from the OAU. The FNLA continued to organise military campaigns in northern Angola and by the time of the coup in Lisbon, it had established important military bases in Uige, Lunda and Zaïre districts.

UNITA

The third liberation movement was the União Nacional para Independência Total de Angola (UNITA – the National Union for the Total Independence of Angola). UNITA had most of its support from the Ovimbundu of the central and eastern districts of Huambo, Bie and Moxico.[6] It also had some following among Angolans domiciled in the southern districts of Mocamedes, Huila and Cunene.[7]

In December 1966 UNITA carried out its first military action against the Portuguese occupation. It attacked Vila Teixeira de Sousa and the other important towns on the strategic Benguela railway.[8] This communication line was to be the main target of UNITA's operations during the period. In view of its contiguity to the MPLA's own zone of military operations, there were often clashes between these movements in the last four years of the anti-Portuguese war.

Angola's three liberation movements did not set up a united front during the war against Portugal. The absence of such a front has to be understood within the context of the enforced cleavages among the country's various nationalities which were encouraged and reinforced by the colonial political economy, the sheer size of the country and the attendant communications and logistical difficulties, and the differing ideological positions of the movements as regards the reconstruction of society after the termination of Portuguese imperialism.[9] The four-party provisional government that was formed after the Alvor Accords did not resolve these contradictions either.

II THE WESTERN RESPONSE: THE UNITED STATES AND OTHERS

The sudden dissolution of the Angolan provisional government in June 1975 and the flight of the remaining personnel of the Portuguese colonial state attracted worldwide publicity. In the United States, successive governments had completely ruled out the possibility of an African victory during the 13 years of the Angolan liberation war.

NSSM 39

Soon after his election in 1968, President Richard Nixon appointed a presidential commission to study developments in Southern Africa. The Commission, headed by Henry Kissinger (then White House Advisor on National Security Affairs), completed its study in 1969 and concluded: 'There is no likelihood in the foreseeable future that [African] liberation movements could overthrow or seriously threaten the existing white government(s)'.[10] Furthermore, '(t)he whites are here to stay and the only way that constructive change can come about is through them. There is no hope for the blacks to gain the political rights they seek through violence, which will only lead to chaos and increased opportunities for the communists'.[11] The assumptions and the conclusions of the Kissinger study, often called NSSM 39, were based fundamentally on the following: '(M)ilitary realities rule out a black victory at any stage. Moreover, there are reasons to question the depth and permanence of black resolve'.[12]

NSSM 39 stated clearly that the preservation of the huge US economic, scientific and strategic interests in the region lay in the effective control of the white-ruled states of South Africa, Namibia, Zimbabwe, Mozambique and Angola.

It was against this background that both the Portuguese coup and the collapse of the four-party provisional government in Luanda completely invalidated the strategic assumptions that underpinned NSSM 39.

Washington's immediate reaction to the April 1974 coup in Lisbon was to give support to the so-called 'Portuguese Commonwealth' solution (encompassing Portugal, and the territories of Angola, Mozambique and Guinea-Bissau which would now have 'autonomous political status') that was initially outlined by General Antonio de Spinola, the first leader of the Armed Forces Movement. Spinola envisaged that in this 'Commonwealth' arrangement, Lisbon would continue to control the foreign relations, defence and the finance ministries in the African states.[13] 'Self determination', Spinola once told reporters after the coup, 'should not be confused with independence'[14] in Portuguese-occupied Africa.

Just in case the Spinola strategy failed, the US began to seek the support of President Mobutu of Zaïre (a close US ally in the region) to ensure that the Zaïrean-backed FNLA (and UNITA) would play a major role in the unfolding political struggle among the three liberation movements for control of the Angolan state. Washington felt that the strong influence of Mobutu in the area would guarantee an FNLA-

UNITA political triumph over the more politically-radical MPLA.[15]

US Support for Portuguese Counter-insurgency Strategy

We should now consider in greater depth the range of US-Portuguese military cooperation during the 13 years of the African liberation war in Angola. It is also essential to evaluate the nature of US interests in Angola so as to establish the politico-economic and strategic reasons which consequently motivated Washington's support for the FNLA-UNITA alliance after the collapse of Portuguese colonialism.

US-Portuguese relations developed extensively in all fields in the years after the Second World War. Between 1949 and 1961, that is, prior to the beginning of the Angolan War of independence, US aid to Portugal amounted to $370 million. Well over two-thirds of this ($290 million) was for military assistance while the rest was categorised as economic.[16] Following the outbreak of the Angolan War in February 1961, the US amended existing treaty provisions with Portugal in which the latter was bound not to use US military equipment against liberation insurgents in Angola, nor indeed in the other African countries occupied by Portugal. Lisbon, of course, ignored these guarantees and continued to use US weaponry in its counter-insurgency operations in Angola.

The US often protested to the Portuguese authorities about the use of its weapons in Angola and elsewhere but these violations never led to a termination of the transfers.[17] Indeed, six months after the first phase of the African uprisings in Luanda, the US House of Representatives passed a resolution to continue military support for Portugal.

It would appear from official figures that in the subsequent six years (1962–68), US-Portuguese military cooperation showed a progressive decline as a result of US diplomatic efforts to respond positively to a series of United Nations resolutions in 1961 which condemned Portuguese imperialism and particularly the barbarity of its counter-insurgency operations in Angola. Washington suddenly cut a projected $25 million worth of military supplies due for Lisbon, during the 1961/62 fiscal year, to $3 million, and by 1968 its total arms deliveries to Portugal (that is, for the six-year period) amounted to a paltry $33.7 million.[18] This was about a sixth of the military bill estimates for Portugal from the US, during the period, which had received approval in the House of Representatives' debates on the subject in August 1961.

Yet there is evidence to show that contrary to these official figures, the United States' military supplies to Portugal during 1962–68 were much higher. In 1962, for instance, Washington authorised a credit allocation of nearly $50 million to Portugal by the US Export-Import Bank.[19] No restrictions were placed on Portugal's use of this fund. In January 1963 the US sold 30 Cessna T-37C category aircraft to Portugal.[20] While the US had been using the Cessna for *offensive* military operations in Vietnam, Washington, however, described the aircraft sale to Portugal as a 'defence support' arrangement.[21] In 1965 alone, the US sold seven Douglas B-26 bombers to Portugal.[22] Portuguese troops continued to receive their training for the African wars either in US bases in Portugal (under the auspices of the US Military Assistance Advisory Group) or in the United States itself.[23]

By mid-1963 the standard weapons that the Portuguese military used in the Angolan war were from the United States. William Minter has shown that these weapons included M-47 tanks, 105 mm and 155 mm guns, trucks and jeeps for the army, and F-84 Thunder jets, PV-2 Harpoon bombers, T-6 trainers (equipped for armed reconnaissance flights) and C-54 transports for the airforce.[24] John Marcum illustrates the situation graphically: 'By January 1962, outside observers could watch Portuguese planes bomb and strafe African villages, visit the charred remains of towns like Mbanza M'Pangu and M'Pangala, and copy the data from 750-pound napalm bomb casings from which the Portuguese had not removed the labels marked "Property US Air Force"'.[25]

The United States also pursued a parallel political support for Portugal during the period. This was typified by the outcome of an August 1963 meeting in Lisbon between the US Under-Secretary of State, George Ball, and Portuguese Premier Antonio Salazar. After the meeting, Ball declared:

'the loss of Angola and Mozambique would be catastrophic for Portugal'.[26] If the African liberation war in these states were to succeed, Ball argued, half a million expatriate Portuguese 'would debauch' into an impoverished and underdeveloped Portugal.[27]

The US expanded even further its support for the Portuguese military offensive against Angola (and other African-occupied states) between 1969 and 1974 when the Lisbon fascist regime fell. Between 1969 and 1972, US military equipment sold to Portugal was worth about $110 million. The December 1971 agreement for the extension of the US use of the mid-Atlantic Portuguese military bases of the Azores was particularly generous for the Lisbon authorities.[28] They were eligible to apply for a loan of up to $400 million from the US Export-Import Bank, and received an 'aid package' that included $30 million in 'agricultural commodities under the PL 480 programme'.[29] Given the military priority of the Portuguese regime at this time, a high proportion of these resources were, of course, transferred to its African war effort.

US Interests in Angolan Colonial Economy

A discussion of US interests in colonial Angola is now in order. In the mid-1960s Cabinda Gulf Oil, a subsidiary of Gulf, the giant US oil conglomerate, began to exploit the Cabindan oil fields. By the time of the Lisbon coup in 1974, Cabinda was producing about 10 million tons of oil a year, making Angola Africa's fourth largest oil producer (after Libya, Algeria and Nigeria).[30] Such was the magnitude of the Cabinda operations that by 1974 Gulf had invested $209 million in the project. The company's annual taxes to the Portuguese colonial administration were also an added source of revenue. In 1969 Cabinda Gulf oil tax and royalties payment to Portugal was $11 million, which amounted to about half of the latter's 1970 military budget for the Angolan War.[31] In 1972 Gulf's taxes and royalties to Portugal jumped to $61 million in addition to the sum of $90 000 being its contribution to the so-called Angolan Mining Fund.[32] Other US oil companies given exploratory rights in

Angola during the period were Exxon, Sun Oil Company, Occidental, Amerada Hess Corporation, Cities Service Company, Amoco, Challenger Oil, Gas Company, American Pacific International Inc., and Texaco Petróleo de Angola, which was predominantly US-owned. In November 1974 Texaco announced that it had found a new offshore oil field at Santo Antonio do Zaïre (close to the Zaïrean border), with reserves estimated to be ten times larger than those in Cabinda.[33] At least 60 per cent of Angolan oil was exported to the USA.

Coffee was another major Angolan product exploited and exported to the US. The 'robusta' brand of this commodity has featured high in Portuguese exports to the United States for several years. In 1973, for instance, the US imported $206 million worth of Angolan coffee.[34] The following year, Angola's total coffee production was 220 000 tons, making it Africa's second leading producer and the world's third largest.[35]

Diamonds, iron ore, titanium, manganese, phosphates, copper and other associated minerals were part of the extensive riches of Angola. The principal diamond fields in the Lunda district of northeast Angola were controlled by Companhia de Diamantes de Angola (Diamang). This was a subsidiary of De Beers Consolidated Mines Limited and the Anglo-American corporation of South Africa, together with interests from other US, Belgian and British financial and industrial conglomerates. Diamang had an exclusive mining territory of 50 000 sq. kms in this region (95 per cent of the country's total output). Its 1972 diamond output was $110 million, while in 1973 it was $150 million, making it the country's third largest foreign exchange earner after oil and coffee.[36]

As we have shown, US economic interests were entrenched in the Angolan treasure house! Mário de Andrade and Marc Ollivier have aptly summarised the political economy of the epoch: 'The spectacularly rapid headway made by foreign investments in Angola over recent years is the most important consequence of Portugal's ... policy in Angola and Mozambique, which consists in selling off the colonies' fabulous natural resources to imperialist monopolies in order that they may provide the political support and financial resources needed to withstand the national liberation struggle launched by the African peoples'.[37]

US 'fall back' Position

After the February 1961 MPLA military attack, some US government officials envisaged the possibility (albeit 'slim') that the Portuguese could lose their control of Angola and elsewhere in Africa. While it preferred to support the Portuguese government, the US began to establish contacts with some sectors of the Angolan liberation movement which were considered 'moderate'.

John Stockwell, who was the head of the Angola Task Force set up by the US Central Intelligence Agency in 1975 to support the two anti-MPLA liberation movements, the FNLA and UNITA, has confirmed that as far back as 1962 the CIA had been sending arms and funds to the FNLA as part of the US 'fall back' strategy. The FNLA in return provided the CIA with 'field intelligence about the interior of Angola'.[38] While Stockwell does not provide any details of the nature or indeed the amount of arms the US transferred to the FNLA during the period, John Marcum has described this as 'modest'.[39] As soon as the 1969 Kissinger Study reinforced US belief in the ability of Portuguese imperialism to destroy the Angolan resistance, Washington terminated its links with the FNLA but still kept the movement's leader, Roberto, on its pay-roll, for a sum estimated at $10 000 per annum.[40] In 1975 Washington reactivated its links with the FNLA in its decisive attempt to stop the MPLA from taking over the political leadership of Angola after the collapse of Portuguese imperialism.

Holden Roberto was a close friend (and brother-in-law) of Zaïre's President Mobutu Sese Seko, who in turn was the US's strongest ally in Central Africa. The US had for long been impressed by Roberto's strident anti-communism and his essentially neo-colonial views on the solution of the Angolan colonial question.[41] FNLA official economic policy for post-independent Angola had declared its intention to respect all private property and foreign investments in the country.[42] Roberto reiterated his party's policy on this subject in a widely publicised interview in 1972 during which he made a scathing attack on the MPLA's 'scientific socialism'.[43]

UNITA's political and economic orientation was similar to the FNLA's. Its leader, Jonas Savimbi, spoke at length in a February 1975 interview on the movement's thinking on post-colonial Angola: 'We want good relations with the West and particularly with the EEC ... We already have contact with some EEC countries and want to deepen these relations because we think Europe will play a moderating role in the international situation ... We must have free enterprise. If we took away the stimulus of profit then we would have stagnation ... I think we should follow the example of the great African statesman, President Houphouet Boigny of the Ivory Coast'.[44] Savimbi pursued this theme even further when he told another interviewer: '[We would] leave as much as possible of the economy to private enterprise ... We welcome any source of foreign investment, and will give the investor all facilities and guarantees'.[45]

The pro-free market economic orientation of these two movements was diametrically opposed to that of the MPLA. Marxist in its direction, the MPLA had maintained since its inception that if it came to power in Angola, it would socialise the country's means of production. 'Colonialism', notes the MPLA, 'has injected the whole social body of Angola with the microbes of ruin, hatred, backwardness, misery, obscurantism and reaction. The course it is intended to impose on us is therefore absolutely contrary to the higher interests of the Angolan people, to our survival, our freedom, our rapid and free economic progress, and our happiness, ensuring bread, land, peace and culture for all'.[46] The movement viewed the reconstruction of post-colonial Angola as follows: 'This requires the Angolan people's mobilisation and struggle, on all fronts and under all conditions, to wipe out imperialism, Portuguese colonialism, to make Angola an independent country, and to set up a democratic and popular Angolan government. This coalition government will assemble all the forces which will have fought Portuguese colonialism relentlessly and uncompromisingly to the last. The working class will head this government of all the anti-imperialist forces'.[47]

This forceful and uncompromising anti-capitalist worldview of the MPLA was viewed with serious concern by the

United States. The US was apprehensive of the consequences of the MPLA's 'democratic and popular independence tendency on its huge economic and strategic interests in Angola, if this organisation were to come to power.'[48] Washington was therefore prepared to leave open channels for some dialogue with FNLA and UNITA leaders as possible eventual African successors to Portuguese-occupied Angola, while supporting the colonial regime, but was evidently hostile to the MPLA and its ideas for the future.

Our study so far has shown that the US's primary objectives in Angola have been to protect its huge economic and long-term strategic interests. For many years, especially during the 13 years of the African liberation war, the pursuit of these objectives meant the support of the political status quo – continuing Portuguese imperialism. The immediate consequence of the April 1974 coup in Lisbon was Portugal's inability to continue to sustain its colonial war in Angola. For the United States, this development was in effect a dramatic dual blow: (1) the regime that supervised its extensive interests in Angola had fallen; and (2) the fall of the Portuguese regime was a decisive repudiation of the 'theoretical' assumptions that underpinned NSSM 39.

1975–76: The US 'In Search of Enemies'

After the breakdown of the Angolan four-party provisional government in July 1975, the US government ordered the 'Forty Committee', the sub-committee of the National Security Council (NSC), to carry out a comprehensive review of its policy in Angola. The committee was chaired by Secretary of State Henry Kissinger and was attended by CIA Director William Colby, Deputy Secretary of Defense William Clement and General Brown, Chairman of the Joint Chiefs of staff. The Forty Committee decided to send immediate military supplies worth $14 million to Angola for use by the FNLA and UNITA.[49] Clearly these deliveries were intended to be the first phase of a US plan to help these two movements to establish military superiority over the MPLA. Stockwell recalls: 'Neto's forces [the MPLA] appeared strong enough to take the Angolan capital, Luanda, and surrounding areas. Mobutu was exhausted economically and could no longer support Holden Roberto. Roberto did not have countrywide political support ... [But US] limited material support to Roberto and Savimbi could establish a military balance ... and prevent *the quick and cheap installation in Angola*' of an MPLA government (emphasis in the original).[50] Six months later, the aid package rose to $25 million. By the time the Angolan task programme was over in April 1976, the total official sum allocated to it was $31 million,[51] though Marcum reckons that the real sum was twice as much,[52] while a report in the *Los Angeles Times* even puts the final figure at $100 million.[53]

Some of the military equipment was sent directly to the FNLA-UNITA, but the substantial transfers of US military aid went to the Mobutu regime in Zaïre for subsequent relay to the client guerrilla armies. These include armoured vehicles, missiles, heavy weapons, machine guns and rifles, vehicles, ammunition and radio equipment.[54] At this stage the US did not wish to be too conspicuously identified with these two movements (against the MPLA), in view of the critical political mood in the US after the disaster of the Vietnam War and the Watergate crisis.

Washington further proposed sending $60 million in financial and military aid to Zaïre in 1976.[55] Of this amount, $20 million was designated 'Security Support Assistance', which was aimed to 'support or promote economic and political stability'.[56] It was expected that Zaïre would use part of the latter fund to support the anti-MPLA forces across the border in Angola.

Apart from supporting the FNLA and UNITA with arms and finance, the US also recruited mercenary fighters, or what the CIA euphemistically termed 'foreign military advisors',[57] for these organisations. The hundreds of mercenaries hired involved several nationalities, including British, Portuguese, French, American, Zaïrean and South African, and the gross monthly payment for a fighter was about $173 000.[58]

In the ensuing months, the US government tried to justify its military support for the FNLA-UNITA front. Kissinger repeatedly referred to the increasing Soviet support for the MPLA rival movement, emphasising that this was indicative of Soviet 'hegemonial aspirations' in Angola.[59] The Angola war, he added, was a 'grave problem', and warned Moscow that its policy (in supporting the MPLA) was not compatible with the spirit of détente.[60]

In further statements on the crisis a fortnight later Kissinger's warnings became much sharper. He made it clear that Washington 'could not remain indifferent' to Soviet and Cuban military involvement in Africa. Moscow, he pointed out, must exercise restraint, charging that the Soviet Union had 'introduced great-power rivalry into Africa [by supporting the MPLA] for the first time in fifteen years'.[61] Kissinger noted that the consequences for such a situation were grave, and indicated that 'time was running out; continuation of an interventionist policy must inevitably threaten other relationships ... Washington would never permit détente to turn into a subterfuge of unilateral advantage'.[62]

The US Ambassador to the United Nations at this time, Daniel Moynihan, was equally vehement in justifying his country's support for the FNLA-UNITA. He warned in December 1975 that unless appropriate aid was given to the FNLA-UNITA forces, 'the communists would take over Angola and will thereby considerably control the oil shipping lanes from the Persian Gulf to Europe'.[63]

In testimonies to the congressional hearings in January 1976, where he advocated more US aid for the anti-MPLA organisations, Kissinger argued that an MPLA victory would be a 'threat' to Angola's neighbours – Zaïre, Zambia and South Africa.[64] An MPLA victory even had consequences elsewhere in the world, as Kissinger claimed in a statement made to an Israeli delegation that visited Washington after the congressional hearings:

> If the United States failed to halt the Soviet military activities in Angola [sic], the Soviet Union and others might not take American warnings seriously in future ... Such a failure could encourage Arab countries such as Syria to run risks that could lead to a new attack on Israel backed by the Russians.[65]

Other US government officials also advocated a tough stand on Angola, especially in the light of United States negotiations with the Soviet Union on the limitation of strategic weapons. CIA Director Colby and Under-Secretary of State Joseph Sisco in testimonies to a select congressional committee in November 1975, argued that US aid to the FNLA and UNITA, in addition to the regimes in Zaïre, Zambia and Kenya, was needed as 'bargaining chips' in future bilateral talks with the Soviet Union on the relaxation of global tensions.[66]

The two Houses of the US Congress did not, however, share the government's essentially Cold War assessment of the conflict. On 19 December 1975 the Senate voted to halt further US military assistance for both the FNLA and UNITA. The House of Representatives endorsed the Senate ban the following month. These moves were a major disappointment to the Ford presidency. It was quite clear from these votes that US senators and members of the House of Representatives did not want a continuing US involvement in Angola which could escalate into a situation similar to the experience in Vietnam. Furthermore, the congressional attitude was influenced by events in the African Division of the State Department, where its head, Nathaniel Davis, who had been very critical of White House policy, resigned in August 1975. Davis felt that the US should seek a diplomatic alternative to the resolution of the conflict by withdrawing immediate military supplies to the UNITA-FNLA. Davis stressed in a series of confidential dispatches to Kissinger (subsequently leaked to the press[67]) that the MPLA had largely fought the anti-Portuguese war, and could not be effectively undermined by US-supported FNLA-UNITA military actions. Davis declared: 'Neither Savmibi nor Roberto are good fighters – in fact they couldn't fight their way out of a paper bag. It's the wrong game [that is, US support for them] and the players we got are losers'.[68] Davis predicted, with some foresight, that if the US intervention in Angola failed, then those US supporters in Central Africa (particularly President Mobutu of Zaïre), would be isolated, leaving Washington with South Africa as its principal ally in the area.[69]

Impact of US Strategy

What therefore was the effect or the impact of US support for the FNLA-UNITA coalition on the conduct, progress and outcome of the Angolan Civil War? A brief sketch of the military confrontation between the FNLA-UNITA and the MPLA, following the collapse of the Angolan transitional government in July 1975, is now relevant. Widespread fighting erupted in Luanda and the surrounding districts of Cuanza Norte, Malange and Cuanza Sul in mid-July between MPLA troops and the FNLA on the one hand, and MPLA and UNITA on the other. Initially the fighting was low in intensity and relatively balanced between the two sets of forces, but after a few weeks, the military situation had tipped decisively in favour of the MPLA. This was basically for two reasons. The battles were going on within the main arc of MPLA strongholds during the anti-Portuguese war. The MPLA readily reactivated its grass root support for what it termed the 'Second War of National Liberation'.[70] Secondly, heavier Soviet weapons were increasingly reaching the MPLA, and this stepped up its firepower against its rivals.

By the end of July, the MPLA forced its opponents out of Luanda. An MPLA column moved south, and after fierce fighting with UNITA, it captured the ports of Lobito, Mocamedes and Benguela, thereby blocking reinforcements reaching its rivals from the Atlantic or by rail. The MPLA control of Lobito had immediate consequences on Zambia and Zaïre. While vehemently anti-MPLA, these states relied on Lobito as their 'gateway' to the Atlantic (we shall deal further with this when considering the intervention of Angola's neighbours). They both reacted by appealing to the United States to assist them to check the thrust of the MPLA military offensive. Confirming that this request was made, Kissinger later told a congressional committee that there were three reasons why Zambia and Zaïre requested US military aid[71]:

(1) They did not want a Soviet and Cuban-backed liberation movement to impose a political solution on the Angolan people.
(2) They feared that the USSR and Cuba might become

dominant powers in South-Central Africa.
(3) They felt that both the Soviet Union and Cuba were threatening the 'stability' of the region.

Three months after this fighting began, MPLA military superiority over its rivals was almost complete. It was in control of 12 out of the 15 provinces of the country,[72] and with independence less than six weeks away, it looked certain that it would form the first nationalist government. But the political and military situation soon changed radically.

In the meantime, the FNLA-UNITA forces had been reorganising rapidly in safe bases in Huambo, Cunene, Uige and Lunda districts. The United States began flying heavy reinforcements of weapons to these forces using giant C-130 transports from bases in Zaïre.[73] To guarantee South African support for their imminent counter-offensive, the FNLA-UNITA sent a high-powered delegation to Windhoek, Namibia (led by Daniel Chipenda, FNLA Deputy Secretary-General) to meet the Commander of the South African army, General Magnus Malan and Defence Minister Pieter Botha. It was a successful encounter for the Angolans: South Africa promised to intervene militarily on their behalf in the war against the MPLA.[74] As part of the agreement, FNLA-UNITA provided the South Africans with detailed information on SWAPO (the South West African People's Organisation) military bases in southern Angola.[75]

In mid-October the FNLA-UNITA launched their counterattack on the MPLA from positions North, East and South of the capital. On 23 October a 3000-strong South African military column entered Angola by crossing the Namibian border, and began to attack MPLA-held territory. An assorted contingent of mercenaries airlifted from Zaïre by the Central Intelligence Agency joined the anti-MPLA forces in the northern sector.[76] By 26 October the MPLA was forced out of the southwestern capital of Sa da Bandeira. Mocamedes fell two days later and by 3 November Lobito and Benguela were captured from the MPLA. Although the MPLA successfully repulsed the attempted assault on Cabinda, by mid-November it was left in control of only four of the country's provincial capitals, in addition to the capital Luanda.[77] The latter was in fact coming under great threat from the north by a heavily-armed FNLA brigade.

This sudden upturn in the military fortunes of the FNLA-UNITA brought relief to the United States, especially as this was occurring on the eve of Angola's projected independence date – 11 November 1975. But the entry of South Africa into the civil war on the side of these same forces was to cause serious problems for the US government, especially with respect to independent African public opinion (this will be elaborated later).

MPLA Victory and the Collapse of the US Strategy

Finding the MPLA facing serious military pressure from this constellation of forces, the Soviet Union and Cuba began a massive airlift of military supplies, and later personnel, to Angola in support of the MPLA. Using the ports of Porto Amboim and Novo Redondo, which were still controlled by the MPLA, Cuba and the Soviet Union sent in reinforcements which included T-54 and T-34 tanks, mobile 122 mm rocket launchers ('Stalin Organs') and artillery.[78] The intervention from these MPLA allies were intended to help defend the Luanda area and halt the South African drive from the South. This was followed later by the deployment of the first contingent of Cuban infantry units alongside the MPLA forces. As from 7 November Cuba began its dramatic airlift of thousands of combat forces from Havana direct to Luanda (code-named 'Operation Carlota' – see below) in a bid to save the MPLA from defeat.

Cuba's intervention marked a decisive turning point in the war. Cuban and MPLA forces quickly checked the concerted FNLA-UNITA-South African offensive. On 11 November the MPLA was able to proclaim the People's Republic of Angola in Luanda; the FNLA-UNITA in turn announced the formation of the Democratic People's Republic of Angola in Huambo, central Angola. After a series of fiercely fought battles in the following three months, the South African army was forced out of Angola. The FNLA was utterly destroyed as a fighting unit and the survivors of the Zaïrean military units fighting against the MPLA retreated across the northern border in a shambles. Some UNITA units under

Commander Savimbi made their way back to the Ovimbundu highlands where they had originally been based during the anti-Portuguese war. By March 1976 the Angolan Civil War was over with the MPLA victorious. This was a tremendous blow to US policy in the country, and an historic defeat of its age long geo-strategic calculations in central and southwestern Africa.

Other Western Involvement

The involvement of other Western powers (European) in the Angolan Civil War was largely nominal. This was noticeable in contrast to their support for the Portuguese government during the colonial war. France, Britain and the Federal Republic of Germany had consistently supplied arms to Portugal in clear violation of United Nations embargoes. But as soon as the April 1974 coup occurred, the involvement of these powers in the ensuing confrontation within the Angolan independence movements became quite marginal.

France's limited involvement in the war was carried out largely through the Service de Documentation Extérieure et Contre-Espionage (SDECE), the French Secret Service. The SDECE operational bureau in Kinshasa channelled money and arms to the anti-MPLA front. Arms sent included ENTAC anti-tank missiles, 120 mm mortar rounds, Panhard armoured car ammunition and four Allouette missile-firing helicopters.[79] The French operation was in collaboration with the CIA and was generally aimed at buttressing French economic interests in Angola which were located mainly in Cabinda, where the French oil company, Essences et Lubrifiants de France, had exploration rights. France began to supply arms to a Cabindan independence group, the Frente de Libertação do Enclave de Cabinda – the FLEC – which ultimately got into a tactical alliance with the anti-MPLA coalition. But given the MPLA's effective control of Cabinda throughout the war, neither the military activities of the FLEC nor the organisation's Kinshasa-based proclamation of the independence of Cabinda had any long-term effect on the progress or outcome of the civil war.

Among Western European countries, France came closest

to sharing US strategic perception of the likely consequence of an MPLA victory in Angola.[80] With France's long-established political and economic interests in neighbouring Zaïre, and close ties with South Africa, Paris felt that an MPLA regime in Luanda could have a 'destabilising' effect in the region.[81] The French covert support for FLEC secessionist objectives in Cabinda was therefore an attempt to undermine MPLA influence and control in that strategic Angolan principality.

There is no evidence of direct British government support for either of the conflicting parties in Angola. UNITA bought communication equipment in London through private sources. Two British pilots were involved in these purchases and transfers, using planes belonging to Pearl Air (a chartered airline with headquarters in Hong Kong).[82] The consignment were usually transported from London direct to a secret UNITA air base at Silva Porto in the Angolan central highlands. The Callaghan government broadly favoured a policy of non-intervention by all external forces in Angola, and consistently called for a 'government of national unity' (involving the FNLA, MPLA and UNITA) as a solution to the crisis. It did not, however, discourage the recruitment in London of the total number of 200 British mercenaries who were recruited by the CIA to fight against the MPLA.

As for the new Portuguese government (the Armed Forces Movement – MFA), its official position on the civil war was 'neutral'. There were, however, strong indications that certain members of the MFA left wing were sympathetic to the MPLA immediately after the Lisbon coup. When the left strengthened its position in September 1974, with the forced resignation of General Spinola, pro-MPLA orientations became more pronounced. Leading figures of the new MFA, such as Otelo de Carvalho, Melo Antunes, Costa Gomes, Carlos Fabio and Rosa Coutinho, were publicly active Marxists. They reckoned that an MPLA victory in Angola would not only prevent a neocolonial 'take-over' in Luanda, but would help 'consolidate' the Portuguese Revolution itself. Otelo de Carvalho, who later became the commander of the new regime's secret service, COPCON (Continental Operations Command), indirectly helped MPLA propaganda against its rivals after the outbreak of the civil war, when he leaked certain classified documents of the ousted Portuguese government which indicated that UNITA was cooperating with the Portuguese during the liberation war.[83] Robert Moss has shown that during de Carvalho's visit to Havana in July 1975, the Cubans had discussed with him the possibilities of the intervention of their forces in Angola in support of the MPLA.[84]

Despite sympathy for the MPLA among significant sectors of the MFA in Lisbon, the new Portuguese regime gave no active military or diplomatic support to the MPLA during the course of the civil war. In fact the MFA evacuated the remaining personnel of Portuguese citizens in the transitional government in Lisbon as soon as the civil war was underway.

On the whole, the United States' West European allies were less prominently involved in the Angolan conflict. In general terms they shared Washington's position that there was a Soviet 'threat' to subvert Angola, but were not keen to get involved actively on behalf of the anti-MPLA alliance. Instead, it does appear that there was a greater concern at this time in the capitals of Western Europe over what political course the new revolutionary Portugal was going to take.

III THE SOVIET UNION, CUBA AND CHINA

As with the origins of the United States' involvement in Angola, the Soviet Union's support and sympathies for one of the Angolan liberation movements, the MPLA, began in the 1960s. In fact, the first consignment of Soviet arms to the MPLA was dispatched in 1960. In a foreign policy statement in June 1961, the Soviet Communist Party general secretary, Nikita Khrushchev, praised the MPLA-led uprising in Angola earlier on in the year, and expressed confidence in the movement's ultimate victory.[85] The liberation war in Angola fitted in adequately with Khrushchev's general survey of the colonial situation in the Southern World enunciated in his report to the 20th Congress of his party in February 1956.[86]

Soviet scholars and commentators writing on Angola at

this time often stressed the MPLA's marxist orientation and its declared objective to embark on a socialist transformation of Angola after the termination of Portuguese colonialism.[87] Furthermore, Soviet observers noted favourably the good relationship that the MPLA had established both with the Portuguese Communist Party and the Cuban government. It was against this background that the visit to Moscow in 1964 by the MPLA leader, Agostinho Neto, was such a major success for the movement. The Soviet Union pledged more financial and military support for it.

In contrast, Soviet writers were generally critical of the other Angolan liberation movements, particularly the FNLA. FNLA relationships with the West, and especially the United States, were often denounced in the Soviet media. On one occasion a commentary on Radio Moscow accused the FNLA of 'slowing down the Angolan insurgency in response to American pressure'.[88]

The Soviet Union rarely referred to the nature or the extent of its military and financial support for the MPLA during the anti-Portuguese war. In a conference of liberation movements in Rome in June 1970, V. Solodovnikov, the director of the Soviet African Affairs Institute, approached the subject in general terms: 'We [the Soviet Union] have provided the MPLA with considerable quantities of military equipment, various armaments, ammunitions, means of transportation and communication equipment ... We also train MPLA's military personnel and political cadre [in the USSR]'.[89] This has led a Western intelligence study to conclude that the total of military supplies from the Soviet Union sent to the MPLA during the period was worth about £27 million.[90]

The Liberation Movement, External Support and Independence

Colin Legum has argued that the aftermath of the 1960s/1970s Sino-Soviet ideological 'rivalry' was a dominant issue in the Soviet intervention in Angola: 'The animosity between China and Russia exceeded anything either might have felt about US and other Western intervention ... It still remains unclear, how much damage was done to China's influence in Africa as a result of the MPLA's military victory achieved largely through Soviet-Cuban aid'.[91] Legum also notes that 'Russian attacks on the US (intervention in Angola) have throughout been much less harsh than on the Chinese'.[92] He concludes: 'African countries whose links have been closer with China than with the Soviets – especially Tanzania and Mozambique – were awkwardly placed when they found the Russians on their side and the Chinese against them'.[93]

Definitely, Soviet calculations on the Angolan independence struggle must have taken into consideration the Chinese military support for the FNLA (and later the UNITA). It does not, however, seem that this factor was an overriding issue for either the generally consistent Soviet support for the MPLA throughout the years of the anti-Portuguese war, or its decision to substantially increase the level of its arms deliveries to this movement when the civil war broke out in 1975.

Moscow would have been aware that besides the very limited Chinese arms deliveries to the FNLA and UNITA during the anti-Portuguese war, these two movements depended on the US and other Western sources for their military equipment. This trend of arms supplies was unlikely to change if the FNLA-UNITA coalition were to be involved in an intra-nationalist civil war with the opposing MPLA during the process of decolonisation. Furthermore, Soviet analysts were often keen to stress the more sophisticated nature of the MPLA's political and military organisation as against those of its rivals during the struggle against Portugal.[94]

The USSR's denunciation of China's collusion with 'pro-imperialist groupings and organisations, pushing them to take action against the genuine representatives and vanguard of the Angolan people – the MPLA',[95] was no doubt a typical feature of the rhetoric that characterised the Sino-Soviet dispute of the era. Nonetheless, Legum has tended to focus too closely on the texture of the strident polemical exchanges between the two states in his explanation of the motivation and impact of the Soviet intervention in the Angolan conflict.[96] Instead, it is our view that as soon as the Soviet Union evaluated the essentially limited character of

Chinese military support for the FNLA-UNITA, they correctly came to the following conclusions: (1) neither the FNLA nor UNITA, fighting independently or collectively, could have defeated Portuguese imperialism without the support of the MPLA. (2) If, however, either the FNLA or UNITA (or both) were to win, this would be as a result of Western (especially US) military support, and not due to aid from China. (3) China's support for the FNLA-UNITA coalition was pointedly gestural. So, except for condemning the Chinese for lending support to the FNLA and UNITA, who were evidently pro-Western in their general worldview, the Soviet Union did not regard China's involvement as particularly important. This analysis acquires added weight when we recall that the Chinese severed all military links with the FNLA-UNITA coalition in the middle of the civil war, after the South Africans intervened on behalf of the latter.

Other scholars have attached greater emphasis to strategic interests as motives for Soviet intervention in Angola.[97] David Albright is of the opinion that the Soviet Union has consistently sought forms of local support in Africa (and other newly post-independent Southern-World states) aimed at acquiring port facilities in these countries to overcome logistical difficulties associated with its expanding naval forces.[98] Albright refers specifically to Soviet successes in the past in reaching agreement with the governments of Egypt, Somalia and Guinea for Soviet vessels to use local port facilities.

It is Albright's view that similar facilities in the Angolan ports of Luanda and Lobito would be of immense strategic interest to the Soviet Union, considering the positions of these ports on the Atlantic sea lanes used by Western shipping.

So, according to this theory of Soviet intervention in Angola, it was aimed at undermining Western political and economic interests in Africa.[99] Stephen Larrabee is emphatically critical of Soviet intentions in Angola when he writes that the 'volume and openness of Russian intervention in a country far from traditional Soviet interests has raised fundamental questions about Soviet policy goals and particularly Moscow's understanding of détente'.[100] W. Scott Thompson pursues this theme of the dramatic changes in Soviet global

Angola

military abilities in the 1970s and their effect on Africa: 'With such improvements in the USSR's broad strategic capabilities, the Soviets have undoubtedly been reassessing their ability to act regionally. And it is hardly credible that they do not have a clear idea of the degree of Western dependence on the minerals in Africa and on the sea lanes around the continent, along which the amount of oil alone flowing to the West has risen 3,600 per cent since the late 1960s'.[101] Edward Gonzalez agrees: 'Whatever the case may be, the success of the Angolan venture immediately gave Soviet policy in Africa a fresh impetus'.[102]

Equally, it is pointed out by this school of Soviet foreign policy analysts that the Soviet Union has tried to influence African public opinion by increasingly identifying itself with the continent's liberation movements which are waging wars to overthrow the 'solid phalanx of white redoubts' in Southern Africa.[103] The intention of the USSR, it is speculated, is to demonstrate that it has both the capacity and the will to provide effective military assistance to these anti-imperialist forces.[104]

To conclude, writers who propound the 'strategy' thesis as a motive for Soviet intervention in Angola, emphasise that the USSR's policy in the region is targeted at expanding the latter's interest and influence at the expense of the 'traditional' Western presence. This policy is qualified as 'reactive and opportunistic'.[105] It is 'reactive' because Moscow has tended to respond energetically to the changing phases of the internal political situation in post-independent African states.[106] It is on the other hand 'opportunistic' because the Soviet Union has been keen to 'take advantage' of these political changes.[107]

In fact the strategy thesis closely mirrors the explanation presented earlier that the USSR's support for the MPLA was based on shared ideological interests. The critical difference between these two theories is this: while the 'ideological' school stresses the broad consistency of Moscow's support for the MPLA throughout the years of the anti-Portuguese war, and the civil war as a reflection of Soviet-stated foreign policy of support for national liberation movements, the 'strategy' school is more interested in focusing on the range of gains that the Soviet Union could derive from the exercise.

The strategy theory, however, has a major limitation. It has been pointedly Cold War-ist in its enquiry, avoiding the much more important and urgent issues of local forces, interests and *independently-formulated* worldviews. Its primary focus on the effect(s) of local conflicts on the East-West confrontation ensures that analyses end inexorably with zero-sum game conclusions: the victory of a Soviet-supported liberation movement is a defeat for US (Western) interests and influence, or vice-versa. But the evidence of recent or contemporary international relations has not substantiated this kind of simplistic outcome. In Africa, for instance, the left-wing regimes in Mozambique, Ethiopia, Guinea-Bissau, Zimbabwe, Ghana, Congo-Brazzaville *and in fact* Angola, since 1976, have sought and have had good relations with the West. Yet there is another sphere of the preoccupation of the strategy school which underlines the limitation mentioned earlier on. It perpetually alienates the control and appropriation of Africa's crucial resources – human and natural. Implicit, and quite often explicit in its survey, the strategy school categorises these resources as 'Western political and economic interests'.[108] It does not occur to this school that it is precisely the termination of Western control of these resources, so vulturously exploited by its governments and transnational corporations in the past 400 years, that is the definitive objective of many an African liberation movement. While the strategy school conveniently ignores this historical goal of the liberation movement, it is, however, keen to assert that these resources will pass over to the Soviet Union, a Western global ideological rival, if the latter were to support the process of liberation. In the theoretical predilections of the strategy school it does not ever consider that, as one African head of state once put it, 'Africa is not about to throw off one colonial yoke for another'.[109]

On the evidence available, we can state that Soviet support for the MPLA since 1960 was fundamentally motivated by ideological reasons. It was conceivable that Moscow expected to gain some strategic pay-offs in Angola for supporting a victorious MPLA, but there are no indications to support the existence of some Soviet grand or *ad hoc* design to 'subvert' Angola in the process and seize its resources.[110] The escalated Soviet support for the MPLA after the civil war started in July 1976 must be seen as a concerted effort to aid an ideological ally to gain power in the fierce two-tier jockeying for political and military supremacy that developed. The Soviet Union's reaction to the April 1974 Portuguese coup d'état was that of immense appreciation. In December 1974 the 'Committee on Afro-Asian Solidarity', which is generally sympathetic to Soviet foreign policy, declared 1975 the 'year of practical aid to the peoples of the former Portuguese colonies'.[111] The deputy-chairperson of the Committee, Aleksandr Dzasokhov, led a Soviet delegation to Angola in February 1975, followed by a second visit in April, during which he discussed with MPLA leaders the question of continuing Soviet military aid to their forces.[112]

While the USSR did not criticise the outcome of the Alvor conference in January 1975, there was some disappointment in Moscow that the FNLA and UNITA would share power with the favoured MPLA. In respect to the goodwill that prevailed at Alvor, the Soviet Union temporarily ceased its long-term press denounciations of the FNLA and UNITA. Moscow did not relent in its arms supplies to the MPLA while the transitional government was in power, just as the United States continued to send weapons to UNITA and the FNLA. As soon as this government collapsed in July 1975, the USSR stepped up its arms deliveries. Soviet, Yugoslav and East German ships carrying arms for the MPLA started using the Luanda port after the MPLA had forced the FNLA-UNITA out of the capital and surrounding districts by the end of July.[113]

Giant Soviet Antonov-22 transport aircraft flew in more supplies, which included surface-to-surface missiles, SAM-7 anti-aircraft missile, Katyusha rockets, T-34 and T-54 tanks, armoured reconnaisance vehicles (BRDM-2), helicopter gun ships, heavy artillery and light aircraft.[114] Flying direct from the Soviet Union, these planes used airfields in neighbouring Congo-Brazzaville, and Guinea, as staging bases for the Angolan operation. A team of Soviet military advisors helped to direct and coordinate the deployment of these armaments on the ground. After seven months of fighting which led to an MPLA victory, a Western intelligence estimate put total Soviet military expenditure in this conflict at $400 million.[115]

'Operation Carlota'

The background to Cuba's relationship with the MPLA could be traced to August 1965.[116] Then the well-known hero of the Cuban Revolution, Ernesto Che Guevara, had been fighting a guerrilla war in neighbouring Congo-Leopoldville (now Zaïre) against anti-Lumumbist forces. The Congo was the fifth African country Guevara visited during his four-month tour of the continent (December 1964-March 1965), having stopped over in Algeria, Guinea, Ghana and Tanzania. 'Africa', according to Guevara, was 'one of the most important, if not *the* most important, battlefield against all forms of exploitation in the world'.[117]

Following the defeat of the Lumumbist National Council of the Revolution with which Guevara was fighting, the Cuban revolutionary crossed into Congo-Brazzaville with his 200-member Cuban force. There he met the MPLA leader Agostinho Neto, who by then had established guerrilla bases there to fight the Portuguese.

Guevara accepted an MPLA request to help it train its military cadres both in bases in Congo-Brazzaville and in Cuba. In the summer of 1965 more Cuban troops were sent to Brazzaville to follow up the implementation of the Cuban-MPLA training scheme. In January 1966 relations were further strengthened, when Neto paid an official visit to Havana.[118] The success of this visit was such that when the Cubans organised the widely-publicised and immensely successful Southern-World 'Tricontinental Conference' at Havana later in the month, they invited the MPLA as the 'sole and authentic representative of the people of Angola'.

It is relevant to note that Cuban military ties with the MPLA were established a decade before the first Cuban combat troops set foot in Angola. This is because: (1) it will enable us to establish why Cuba decided to send its military forces to the MPLA when the civil war broke out, and (2) it will help us to determine whether the Cubans were acting as a Soviet 'surrogate' in the civil war, as some students of the conflict believe.[119]

After the success of the 1959 Cuban Revolution, the new leaders in Havana were convinced that Latin America was at the threshold of a revolutionary transformation. They reasoned that the revolutionary process which began with the overthrow of the Fulgencio Batista regime would spread throughout Central and South America. But liberation struggles in the region during the following decade did not lead to any concrete victory. Left-wing uprisings in Nicaragua, El Salvador, the Dominican Republic and elsewhere, ended without success. In the case of Bolivia in 1968, Che Guevara himself was killed by the Bolivian military while leading an insurgency of partisans. Moreover, Cuban military support for Latin American revolutionaries was meeting with serious opposition from the Soviet Union which felt that a successful revolution in the region was still highly 'vulnerable' due to the US geo-political presence.[120] These setbacks prompted the Cuban leadership to reassess its support for liberation movements abroad.

Africa of the early and mid-1960s became of growing interest to the Cubans. This was the epoch of rapid decolonisation of the continent and for the Cubans, this process was revolutionary. Castro later contrasted the situation then in Africa and Latin America:

> Africa is the weakest link of imperialism today ... Imperialist domination is not as strong there as in Latin America. Therefore, the possibility for fundamental changes on the African continent is real.[121]

Cuba's African policy was henceforth directed towards establishing close relationships with progressive independent states on the continent, and providing material support to insurgent movements fighting colonial regimes.[122] Havana then established close links with Nkrumah's Ghana, Bella's Algeria (a detachment of Cuban troops fought with the Algerian army against Morocco in the 1963 border war between the two countries), Massemba-Débat's Congo-Brazzaville, Lumumba's Congo-Leopoldville and Touré's Guinea. In all these states, Cuban military advisers trained local militias, and cadres from national liberation movements fighting in colonial-held contiguous territories. When the Cubans started their political and military relationship with the MPLA, they also had similar connections with the FRELIMO in Mozambique, and the PAIGC in Guinea-Bissau. It is significant that these three movements were all fighting in

Africa's Portuguese colonial territories.

For Cuba, the overthrow of the Caetano regime in Portugal in April 1974 was a major setback to fascism and imperialism. Diplomatic ties were renewed with Portugal after the visit to Havana of Colonel Otelo de Carvalho, the leading left-wing member of the Armed Forces Movement (MFA) in July 1975. A communiqué released after the visit expressed hope that the success of Angolan independence could only be guaranteed by 'progressive forces' (read MPLA) in the former Portuguese territory.

The Angolan provisional government fell a few days later. When fighting erupted between the MPLA and its FNLA-UNITA rivals, it requested and received more military supplies from Cuba (and the Soviet Union). As we have already stated, the MPLA used this latest consignment of weaponry with devastating effect during its offensives on the FNLA-UNITA in July-September 1975. Then followed the beginning of the dramatic military reversal of mid-October, compounded later by the South African intervention. By late October an MPLA defeat looked imminent.

Cuba reacted quickly to rescue what it saw as an attempt by hostile forces to destroy a long-term ally. In October three Cuban merchant ships left Cuba for Angola, carrying troops and military supplies for the MPLA. The troops included 480 training experts, who soon set up four training centres in Angola on arrival. Within six months, they built up 16 MPLA infantry battalions, and 25 mortar batteries.[123] A team of field medical doctors and 115 vehicles supplemented this Cuban mission.[124]

While these Cuban forces were on their way to Angola, President Ngouabi of Congo-Brazzaville, a firm supporter of the MPLA, arrived in Havana for a visit. A statement issued after the visit expressed Cuban-Congolese solidarity with 'the heroic (MPLA) combatants' of Angola, who are confronting 'reactionary elements and imperialist interests'.[125] Before Ngouabi returned home, he signed a bilateral agreement with Castro, but the terms of this were not specified. It is, however, relevant to recall that when later in October a Cuban military delegation arrived in Brazzaville, two of the three (Cuban) troopships were moving into Angolan waters. It was then reported from Brazzaville that this delegation had come to 'verify implementation' of the recently-concluded Castro-Ngouabi Havana agreement.[126]

On 7 November 1975 Cuba began the massive airlift of troops and military supplies to the MPLA to supplement the ship consignment. This was the beginning of what the Cubans named 'Operation Carlota'.[127] Some of the planes flew direct from Havana to Brazzaville, while others refuelled in the Cape Verde Islands on their way to Brazzaville. After disembarking in the Congo, the troops and supplies were either taken overland to Cabinda or were transported by small boats to the Angolan ports controlled by the MPLA. They in turn quickly joined the MPLA in combat operations against the FNLA-UNITA coalition. By February 1976 when the MPLA won the war, the estimated number of Cuban troops deployed in Angola was 12 000.[128]

So, as the records show, Cuba had sufficient reasons to send its military forces to support the MPLA after the outbreak of the Angolan civil war, besides those that may have motivated the Soviet Union to intervene in the conflict.[129] This was particularly due to Havana's long-term relationship with the MPLA. As Gabriel Garcia Marquez has aptly described this intervention, 'Cuban aid to Angola resulted not from a passing impulse, but from the constant policy of the (Cuban) revolution towards Africa'.[130] In a recent interview on the unresolved anti-colonial struggles in Southern Africa, Fidel Castro could not have been more forthright in Cuba's continuing optimism and support for Africa's liberation:

> Nothing can stop the course of history. Nothing can prevent Namibia's independence just as nothing can prevent the tens of millions of Africans living in ghettos and Bantustans in their homeland from one day becoming the masters of their own destiny. The concentration camps of Dachau and Auschwitz also came to an end one day.[131]

This analysis is not to suggest that Cuba's intervention in Angola did not serve the interests of the Soviet Union during the period – namely the desire for an eventual victory of the MPLA. But it should be stressed that Havana was a clearly motivated autonomous participant in the circumstance, even though its interests happened to have converged with those of the Soviet Union.[132] It is instructive to restate the views of

John Stockwell, the former Chief of the CIA Angola Task Force on Cuba's intervention: 'After the war we learned that Cuba had not been ordered into action by the Soviet Union. To the contrary, the Cuban leaders felt compelled to intervene for their own ideological reasons'.[133] Elsewhere in Africa, on the Eritrean national liberation struggle, Mohamed Babu has shown that this heritage of Cuban autonomy in international politics *can even diverge* from the express interests of the Soviet Union.[134]

Cuba was therefore not a 'surrogate' of the Soviet Union in its Angolan intervention. The fact is that to focus merely on Soviet interests in this conflict, to the exclusion of Cuba's and indeed *others'*, leads to simplistic conclusions that reinforce Cold War analytical preoccupations.

China

Just like the Cubans and the Soviet Union, China sought to establish ties with progressive or revolutionary independent states in Africa, in addition to supporting liberation movements fighting in existing colonial territories in the 1960s. Peking sent military aid to the Front for National Liberation (FLN) confronting French colonialism in Algeria, and it also established strong relationships with the governments of Ghana, Guinea, Mali, Tanzania and Zambia. When the national liberation war began in the Portuguese-occupied states of Guinea-Bissau, Mozambique and Angola, the Chinese gave support to the PAIGC, the FRELIMO and FNLA (and UNITA) respectively.

China's support for the FNLA, and the Soviet Union's support for the rival MPLA began when the ideological debates between the two communist states were becoming pronounced and strident in the early 1960s. By 1962 these debates had caused an open rift between the two and each tried to seek support abroad for its political position. China's main argument was that the Soviet Union had become a non-revolutionary *status quo* 'hegemonic' power which had similar interests to the United States in seeking to 'dominate' the world. On Africa, this Soviet objective meant the following: 'People have become increasingly aware that in contending for hegemony with the other Super-Power [the US], the Soviet revisionists stoop to anything to frenziedly penetrate and expand in Africa in a vain attempt to replace old colonialism'.[135]

As for the Soviet Union, the Chinese backing for liberation movements abroad was often imbued with 'pseudo-revolutionary tactics ... adventuristic actions [sic] ... and [have] often resulted in dividing and weakening the [liberation] forces'.[136] On the specific case of Angola, the Soviet Union attacked China's 'support to pro-imperialist groupings and organisations, pushing them to take action against the genuine representatives and vanguard of the Angolan people – the MPLA'.[137]

The Chinese were fully aware of the ideological preferences of the FNLA (and UNITA) as against those of the MPLA, but argued that these differences were 'something normal [that] could have been reconciled by them through peaceful consultations under the banner of national unity free from outside interference'.[138] Essentially, China's support for the FNLA/UNITA, despite the apparent contradictions, fitted in well with the tenets of Mao's foreign policy and particularly the theory of Three Worlds which emphasised the primacy of two 'imperialisms' [US, USSR] dominating the world.[139]

China's support for FNLA/UNITA was, however, mainly political, lacking any substantial military aid prior to the collapse of Portuguese colonialism in Angola in 1974.[140] For instance, China's total material support for UNITA between 1966 and 1970 amounted to a paltry £5000.[141] Generally, China's military assistance to the two movements was indirect: it trained some of their military personnel in bases in Tanzania used by the Front for the Liberation of Mozambique. In May 1974, however, following appeals from President Mobutu of Zaïre, China expanded its military support for the anti-MPLA coalition. It agreed to send military instructors to help train a new FNLA regiment of 15 000 troops in bases in Zaïre.[142] Between June and August 1974, 450 tons of Chinese arms, including AK47 rifles and light mortars, were sent to the FNLA.[143] As we have seen, this level of arms delivery was meagre compared to what Cuba and the Soviet Union were sending to the MPLA.

Quite clearly China had calculated that given the distance and its associated logistic problems, in addition to its own resource limitations, it could not match the Soviet Union, and the United States, in the spiral arms race that developed in Angola, leading to the civil war in the summer of 1975. In addition, Peking felt highly isolated in independent Africa in October 1975 when the South Africans joined the war on the side of the FNLA-UNITA. On 27 October China withdrew its military mission in Zaïre.

To sum up, China's impact on either the progress or outcome of the Angolan conflict was minimal. Our interest in its involvement though, was the motive for supporting the anti-MPLA alliance.

IV AFRICA: SOUTH AFRICA AND THE CONTIGUOUS STATES

There were two distinct phases of the military intervention of South Africa in the Angolan conflict. In August 1975 a South African unit crossed the Namibian border and seized the hydroelectric dam project on the Cunene River, southern Angola, then under construction. From there they attacked bases belonging to the Namibian liberation movement, the South West African People's Organisation (SWAPO), and MPLA regiments stationed in the area.

The second phase came on 23 October, when the South Africans launched 'Operation Zulu' which involved a coordinated operation with the FNLA-UNITA forces to challenge the MPLA military control of the country.[144]

The fate of the $216 million Cunene hydroelectric project which was built largely by the South Africans in the last three years of Portuguese colonialism, had been a cause for concern to Pretoria as Portuguese rule came to an abrupt end after April 1974. The huge Cunene project was intended to generate power to work the complex of zinc, copper, uranium, diamond and copper mines just across the frontier in northern Namibia.[145] Precisely, South Africa's concerns were as follows: an unfriendly African government in Angola was liable to cut off the vital supply of power from

Cunene and this would disrupt the mineral exploitations.[146] Secondly, a discontinuation of the Cunene project would jeopardise the new South African settlement schemes in the region which had been intended to encourage more white immigrants to live in the border area so as to enhance security.

There were, however, wider issues which accounted for South Africa's military intervention in Angola. The sudden collapse of Portuguese colonialism in Mozambique, and later Angola, had shattered a critical feature of South Africa's strategic network in the region. This was the security provided for South Africa itself and the territory of Namibia that it controlled, by the presence of friendly Portugal in these contiguous east and west 'flanking' states. These territories were seen as the outer perimeter for the defence of the South African homeland – a sort of *cordon sanitaire*.

The position of Angola for South African defence was a highly contentious issue for military planners in Pretoria. Angola has an extensive common border with the state of Namibia, which until recently was occupied by South Africa, and where partisans of SWAPO had waged a protracted armed struggle for liberation. Furthermore, Angola has two important ports in the southern Atlantic (Luanda and Lobito) and controls the main western terminus of the strategic Benguela railway. This railroute has served as a vital outlet for Zaïrean and Zambian copper exports to the Atlantic coast, and this has been of interest to the South Africans (we shall return to this later).

Economically, Angola's huge natural resources had always been conceived by the South Africans during the Portuguese era as vital in creating an economic constellation of Southern African states.[147] This regional economic grouping was expected to enlarge the existing Southern African Customs Union which incorporated South Africa itself, and Botswana, Lesotho and Swaziland.[148] It was expected to include Zambia, Angola, Malawi, Mozambique and Zimbabwe. South Africa's role in the economic community would be to provide the technological support, while the rest of the member states would, of course, act as a guaranteed consumer market, in addition to providing cheap labour. For South

Africa, the unexpected fall of the Caetano regime in April 1974 was a shattering blow to these conceptions and interests.[149]

Evidence of South African cooperation with the Portuguese during the latter's counter-insurgency war in Angola is overwhelming. Pretoria assigned intelligence officers to its Luanda consulate to work directly with the Portuguese military.[150] Regularly, intelligence information was exchanged among officers of the South African military, the Portuguese and those of Rhodesia.[151]

As from 1966, South Africa began to conduct helicopter patrols over the southern Angolan border regions near Namibia, and in 1968, a Luso-South African treaty authorised Pretoria to operate an air base composed of Allouette III helicopters and Cessna T-85s in eastern Angola.[152] A joint Portuguese-South African command centre was later installed at Cuito Cuanavale in southeast Angola, from where the South African airforce carried out both reconnaissance flights and attacks against both the MPLA and SWAPO.[153] This enhanced South African military involvement in Angolan life during the period also coincided with an increase in South African commercial activities in Angola.[154] Pretoria demonstrated the importance it attached to these commercial ties when the South African Foreign Trade Association staged an extensively publicised trade fair in Luanda in 1969.[155]

With the end of Portuguese colonialism, the immobilisation of the Angolan *cordon sanitaire* was an enormous setback to South Africa. Its decision to intervene in Angola after the fall of the provisional government in Luanda, and the subsequent MPLA military supremacy over its FNLA-UNITA rivals, should therefore be seen partly as an attempt to redress a geo-strategic reversal.

'Operation Zulu'

The speed and decisiveness of the South African invasion column reflected the importance Pretoria attached to the Angolan situation. As soon as the column crossed the Namibian border on 23 October, it stormed all major MPLA fortifications in the region. In quick succession, the column, now reinforced by UNITA and FNLA detachments, attacked and overran the cities of Sa da Bandeira, Mocamedes, Benguela, Lobito and Novo Redondo.[156] The army was well equipped – Alouette helicopters, Mermon-Herrington light tanks, 4.2 in. mortars and Panhard armoured cars – and was constantly reinforced from South African bases in Namibia, as well as from a rearguard base later set up at Sa da Bandeira in southwest Angola.[157] The South Africa-FNLA-UNITA thrust kept the MPLA on continuous retreat northwards. By 10 November (the eve of independence day) it reached the southern bank of the River Nhia, 200 kilometers from Luanda. Meanwhile, from the north across the Zaïrean border, the FNLA attack on the MPLA was also succeeding: a spearhead FNLA brigade had occupied Caxito, just 25 kilometres from Luanda, when the South African-led army was advancing towards the Nhia. It then appeared that 'Operation Zulu' was on the verge of scoring a decisive victory – the only action remaining was the overrun of Luanda.

The reason for the South African intervention was given later by Premier Vorster, couched in the standard anti-communist rhetoric of the Pretoria regime:

> It is obvious that South Africa is concerned over the blatant Russian and Cuban military support for the MPLA in Angola ... We are concerned because we know that the aim is not simply the establishment of a Marxist state in Angola, but to endeavour to create a whole row of Marxist states from Angola to Dar es Salaam and if it is at all possible, to divide Africa into two ... If they achieve their objective, not a single African country will be able to feel safe.[158]

The governments of the neighbouring states of Zambia and Zaïre identified with these anti-communist sentiments to some extent. Zaïre's hostility to the MPLA since it supported the FNLA during the anti-Portuguese war was obvious, and we have already discussed this elsewhere. We need to add at this point that President Mobutu felt very disappointed with the military superiority which the MPLA established over its rivals in Angola after the July 1975 breakdown of the

Luanda provisional government. There was therefore a strong inclination to support 'Operation Zulu' as this afforded a good opportunity to crush the MPLA and thereby install an FNLA-UNITA government in Luanda. As John Stockwell, who commanded 'Zulu' from the Zaïrean front later put it, 'the South Africans had some [international] encouragement to go into Angola. Savimbi invited them, after conferring with Mobutu, Kaunda, Felix Houphouet-Boigny of the Ivory Coast and Leopold Senghor of Senegal, all of whom favoured a moderate, pro-West government in Angola'.[159] Mobutu particularly felt that an MPLA-controlled Angola would be a threat to the Zaïrean use of the vital Benguela rail route to the Atlantic port of Lobito.

The Benguela railway was also a relevant subject in determining the Zambian position, considering that Lusaka had supported UNITA during the anti-colonial war. With the closure of its borders with Rhodesia and the attendant difficulties with the use of Mozambican ports, land-locked Zambia benefitted from the Benguela railway for the export of its copper to the Atlantic. Just as Mobutu, President Kaunda feared that the MPLA might deny Zambia the use of this rail route, but the fact was that there were no indications whatsoever in MPLA political or military circles that such a measure was considered.

While Kaunda openly supported US Western arms support for the UNITA-FNLA, he has persistently denied complicity with the South African intervention. Yet besides the CIA, South African sources have alleged that Kaunda cooperated with 'Zulu'.[160]

Failure of 'Zulu', Triumph of 'Addis Ababa'

South Africa, however, failed in its bid to dislodge the MPLA in Luanda and install its FNLA-UNITA allies. The MPLA was able to hold onto the defensive line north of the River Nhia until the Cubans reinforced them in the third week of November 1975. Renewed attempts by the South Africans to cross the river were thwarted. The Cuba-MPLA military were soon in a position to launch a counterattack on the northern front to repulse the FNLA threat on Luanda, and the oil principality of Cabinda. After three weeks of fighting, the FNLA were driven out of Cabinda, and the FNLA contingent moving towards Luanda was compelled to retreat to Carmona, 300 kilometres to the north. Later, the FNLA lost their strategic air base at Negage, which brought the operations in the northern sector to a decisive conclusion.

The Cuban-MPLA southern counter-offensive, code-named 'Operation Addis Ababa', began with a commando attack on Novo Redondo, one of the important towns to be occupied by their opponents in mid-December 1975. The Cubans and the MPLA were encouraged by the initial gains they made after the attack on Novo Redondo to expand the range of their offensive to include the entire stretch of enemy forward positions running along the River Nhia. A major battle was now underway which went on with varying intensity for the following three months. South Africa and its allies were forced out of town after town in Southern Angola during this period – Cela, Santa Combo, Sa de Bandeira, Mocamedes, and so on. On 27 March 1976 the last contingent of the South African army was forced to retreat across the Namibian border. On 1 April 1976 Cuban-MPLA forces moved into Raucana in triumph and retook the Cunene dam complex. 'Operation Zulu' had at last been defeated.

In the meantime, South Africa's intervention in Angola had had a dramatic effect on the responses of independent Africa to the conflict. In an unexpected development on 27 November 1975, the Nigerian government, which had lately called for the setting up of an FNLA-MPLA-UNITA national government, recognised the MPLA regime in Luanda.[161] Lagos clearly referred to the South African intervention as the reason, and condemned what it described as a US-South African plot to destroy a 'sister African country'.[162] Nigeria contributed $25 million towards the MPLA's post-colonial reconstruction of Angola. Several other African countries, including Ghana, Sudan and Tanzania, announced their recognition of the government of the MPLA, citing the South African intervention as their reason.

OAU Manoeuvres

It was, however, at the Organisation of African Unity that African attitudes and orientations towards the South African intervention, and other features of the Angolan crisis were prominently played out. Prior to the outbreak of the civil war in July 1975, the official African policy to Angola, through the OAU, was the recognition of the four-party transitional government in Luanda which was formed after the January 1975 Alvor conference.

Soon after the June 1975 military clashes in Luanda, which involved units from three Angolan liberation movements, the OAU organised a conference in Nakuru, Kenya, attended by the leaders of the FNLA, UNITA and the MPLA. After five days of negotiations, the Angolan leaders reiterated their support for the provisional government in Luanda. They pledged to order their forces to cease all hostile attacks on other movements.[163] The OAU in response reaffirmed its continued support for the transitional administration until the general elections, which were to be organised before formal independence on 11 November 1975.[164]

The Nakuru Agreement did not, however, stop the fighting among Angola's liberation movements. On the contrary, there was an escalation of the clashes, which led eventually to the generalised civil war in July 1975. Four months later, the OAU could no longer maintain its corporate position in supporting the MPLA, FNLA and UNITA as constituting the Angolan national government. This was as a result of the recognition by Mozambique, Guinea-Bissau, São-Tomé and Principe, Somalia, Algeria, Congo and Guinea of the MPLA as the sole government (the People's Republic of Angola) in Luanda on 11 November.

While leaders of the eight countries just mentioned were among the closest supporters and allies of the MPLA during the anti-Portuguese war, it is, however, significant to stress that each of their decisions to recognise the MPLA government took account of South Africa's intervention in the conflict.

A serious crisis developed in the OAU over these recognitions. Eight other African states – Zaïre, Uganda, Central

African Republic, Burundi, Gabon, Senegal and Mauritania – attacked the recognition of the MPLA. In a joint statement issued in late November, while leaders from these countries were in Kinshasa to attend celebrations marking Zaïrean independence, they accused the pro-MPLA states of violating OAU policy on the Angolan conflict. They then called on the OAU Secretary-General to convene an emergency summit meeting of the organisation to discuss the Angolan crisis.

An OAU summit was duly summoned in Addis Ababa on 10 January 1976 to discuss Angola. By then, a total of 21 member states (out of 46) had recognised the MPLA government. After three days of deliberation, the meeting ended in a stalemate, with exactly 22 states supporting an OAU recognition of the MPLA government, and 22 against.[165] Two other states, Ethiopia and Uganda, abstained because the former was host country and the latter held that years' chairpersonship of the organisation. A few weeks later, especially as the MPLA continued to make further military progress in the war, more African states recognised the People's Republic of Angola, which was admitted officially to the OAU in June 1976.

Quite clearly, the OAU could not play a significant role in the crisis 'management' that resulted from the Angolan conflict. Unlike the Nigerian Civil War, none of the contending power groups in Angola had constituted an internationally-recognised central authority in the country before the outbreak of the civil war. This meant that neither the MPLA nor the FNLA-UNITA could have received the sort of official OAU sympathy that federal Nigeria had from the organisation right from the outset of the crisis. Furthermore, secession was not a feature in the Angolan crisis, and thus made intervention by member states less contentious. The fact that the Angolan crisis was a case where a set of two rival political factions were trying to fill a 'vacuum' created by the absence of a 'legitimate' central authority, meant that OAU members were able to display a greater freedom of action from official policy.

V CONCLUSIONS

The Portuguese colonial control of Angola ended unexpectedly in April 1974 after combatting a three-party African liberation war for 13 years. The new government in Portugal, the Armed Forces Movement (MFA), pledged to dismantle its colonial administration in Angola on 11 November 1975. This was to be preceded by a transitional government made up of the MPLA, FNLA and UNITA, and representatives of the MFA. But six months after its inception, the transitional government collapsed, and a civil war followed.

The reaction of the external powers that were involved in the civil war was generally consistent with their past and existing interests in Angola. The United States' huge economic and financial interests in the country had been effectively preserved by the Portuguese colonial regime. The sudden overthrow of this government propelled Washington to seek the support of an alternative African regime in the country that could maintain the economic status quo. The FNLA-UNITA, which for most of the years of the war of independence had been recipients of US weapons, provided this alternative. The main thrust of United States policy was therefore to eliminate the MPLA from the contest for power that developed among the three liberation movements in the transitional government. Washington considered the politics of the MPLA hostile to its interests, and furthering the geo-political interests of the Soviet Union in central and southwestern Africa.

For the Soviet Union, its military support for the MPLA at the outbreak of the civil conflict was in the first instance due to its long association with a liberation organisation which shared similar ideological orientations. Soviet support during the 13 years of the anti-Portuguese war was vital in helping the MPLA to emerge as the most successful (militarily and politically) of the three liberation movements in the country. By declaring its support for MPLA's military objectives after the fall of the provisional government, the Soviet Union was essentially continuing a process which it expected would eventually lead to this movement's political leadership of Angola. It is conceivable that the USSR would have expected to achieve some strategic gains in this region of Africa if the MPLA were ultimately successful.

Cuba's intervention in Angola on the side of the MPLA had an ideological motivation similar to that of the Soviet Union. Both Moscow and Havana had similar goals in Angola but, as we have stressed in this study, Cuba was not acting as a Soviet 'surrogate' or fighting a 'proxy war' for the Soviet Union. On the contrary, Cuba was an autonomous participant in the conflict, striving to support an ally with which it had had very close ties uninterruptedly since 1963.

The South African government felt that a radical MPLA government in Angola, just after another radical regime (the FRELIMO) had come to power in neighbouring Mozambique, posed enormous threats to its continuing occupation of Namibia, and subsequently its exclusivist control of South Africa for its white minority population. South Africa was also concerned that the projected creation of an economic community of Southern African states, under its hegemony, would suffer a major reversal if the rich resources of Angola were no longer under the control of a friendly or pliant regime in Luanda.

The South African military intervention in Angola which began in October 1975 nearly succeeded in installing such a pliant regime under the aegis of the FNLA-UNITA. Thus the defeat of the South African expeditionary task force, after six months of the war, dealt an irreversible blow to the fortunes of the FNLA-UNITA movement. It also marked decisively the limitations of the capabilities of the South African military, which strategists and writers often tend to exaggerate.

4 Zaïre

I INTRODUCTION

Twice within a 15-month period in 1977–78 Zaïre was a major focus of international news coverage. This publicity activity concerned the cross-border attacks on Zaïre's eastern province of Shaba, formerly Katanga, by Zaïrean insurgents based in northern Angola.

In March 1977 a contingent of 1500–2000 fighters belonging to the National Front for the Liberation of the Congo (FNLC), a leading Zaïrean opposition group opposed to the regime of General Mobutu, invaded the Shaba province (hereafter Shaba I). They only stopped short of capturing the important mining town of Kolwezi due to the timely intervention of Moroccan troops which Mobutu called in. After 80 days of concerted counter-offensive, the Zaïrean-Moroccan allied army forced the FNLC attackers to retreat to their Angolan bases.

But they returned once more in May 1978 (Shaba II). With a larger force of 4500 troops the FNLC attacked and captured Kolwezi. From Kolwezi, they expected to consolidate, receive new reinforcements from their Angolan bases, and mount an all-out guerrilla campaign across the country to press for the overthrow of the Mobutu regime.

We need to shed more light on the identity of these insurgents. The National Front for the Liberation of the Congo constitutes the present generation of the old 'Katanga gendarmes' who fought and lost the Katanga secessionist war in 1963.[1]

In July 1960, two weeks after the independence of Congo-Leopoldville (now Zaïre), Moise Tshombe declared the eastern province of Katanga (presently Shaba) independent. He mobilised thousands of militia from the predominantly Lunda nationality of the province to defend the new republic. This militia became popularly known as the 'Katanga gendarmes',[2] and its resistance to the central government in Leopoldville, and the subsequent United Nations' intervention, which went on till 1963, was independent Africa's first civil war.

Having lost their bid to establish a Katanga Republic in 1963, the gendarmes retreated across the border into (Portuguese) Angola where they sought sanctuary among the Luanda population of Angola's northern provinces. The following year the gendarmes returned to the Congo when, in a sudden turn of events in a fast unfolding political drama, Moise Tshombe became a united Congo's Prime Minister. Tshombe in turn integrated his gendarmes into the country's national army, then commanded by General Mobutu.[3] In 1965, however, the gendarmes were forced out of the Congo to resume their exile in Angola when in another quirk in the drama, Tshombe was overthrown in a coup d'état carried out by Mobutu.

Henceforth, the Portuguese colonial regime in Angola agreed to give the Katangan gendarmes permanent settlement in Angola, provided they assisted the Portuguese counter-insurgency operations against Angolan liberation movements, especially those fighting in the country's northern provinces.[4] It should be recalled that the Angolan liberation movement in the north at this time was the National Front for the Liberation of Angola (the FNLA, led by Holden Roberto), which was receiving substantial political and military support from General Mobutu.

The gendarmes accepted this offer, but were still committed to their political objectives in the Congo as a long-term goal. Indeed it appears that by offering to fight against the FNLA which was clearly allied to Mobutu, the gendarmes felt that they were fighting the Congolese leader by proxy! To reinforce their principal preoccupation with politics in the Congo, the gendarmes formed the National Front for the Liberation of the Congo in July 1968 under General Nathaniel Mbumba.[5]

Following the collapse of Portuguese colonialism in Angola in April 1974 and the civil war that ensued in the country, the FNLC switched their support for the MPLA, thus ensuring that they continued their (local) war against the FNLA. In fact the FNLC played an important role in the capture of the key Benguela railway town of Vila Luso from the FNLA, which they in turn handed over to MPLA partisans.[6]

After the victory of the MPLA in the Angolan Civil War, stronger links were developed between the new Angolan leaders and the FNLC. One of the areas of cooperation was in military affairs. This included the provision of training facilities for FNLC units by MPLA officers. In return, the FNLC helped Angola to police its northern districts, where pockets of defeated FNLA fighters operating from bases in southern Zaïre still posed occasional security threats.

The MPLA's victory in Angola was a major boost to FNLC morale. Henceforth, the FNLC dropped its historical secessionist inclinations. It now saw its future political direction as a struggle to spearhead a 'war of liberation' across Zaïre to topple General Mobutu and establish a democratic People's Republic.[7]

The FNLC strategy for the campaign to overthrow Mobutu, was once again based on its seizure of Zaïre's Shaba province. There were three main reasons for this. The most obvious was the familiarity of Shaba territory. Most of the FNLC are Lunda, and this meant that they were generally familiar with the terrain. Moreover, older members of the movement had been militarily active in the province in the previous decade, as we have said. Secondly, Shaba is contiguous with the FNLC's northern Angolan bases, and this would no doubt lessen the usual logistical difficulties that affect such a campaign. Thirdly, and perhaps most important, the FNLC was aware that Shaba is economically Zaïre's most important province.

'Economic Heart' of Zaïre

Two-thirds of Zaïre's entire mineral wealth lies in Shaba. This includes copper (6 per cent of the world's reserves), which accounts for well over two-thirds of Zaïre's foreign revenue, industrial diamonds (38 per cent of the world's reserves), uranium and cobalt deposits, which are probably the world's largest. Shaba's capital, Kolwezi, was in effect the capital of Zaïre's mining industries and the country's extensive hydro-electric power installations. Essentially, the FNLC strategy in attempting the overthrow of Mobutu was geared towards attacking and seizing Shaba which was in effect the nerve centre of Zaïre's economic life.

The FNLC's other anti-Mobutu initiative during this period was political. It sent off envoys to Zaïrean opposition groups in Europe (principally based in France and Belgium) aimed at forming a broad Zaïrean Patriotic Front to succeed the regime in Kinshasa. Among the groups it contacted were the African Socialist Forces, the People's Revolutionary Party, the National Movement for the Liberation of the Congo, the Action Movement for the Resurrection of the Congo and the Democratic Forces for the Liberation of the Congo.[8]

On both occasions of the Shaba attacks, General Mobutu called for external military assistance to defend his regime. Neither Shaba I nor II entailed the intense military campaigns which characterised the Angolan Civil War, or the earlier Nigerian Civil War. Each of the Shaba confrontations in fact was a brief military event, or what an observer has described as 'this strange little war'.[9] Their importance in our discussion here is to focus on the array of foreign forces and interests which were involved. Given the low level of military operations that occurred, these external forces were disproportionately numerous and extensive. An important factor to note is that the outcome of the civil war in neighbouring Angola in early 1976 greatly influenced the perceptions and calculations of most of the foreign powers who intervened in the Shaba conflicts.

II WESTERN EVALUATIONS AND REACTIONS

Soon after the FNLC launched Shaba I in March 1977, General Mobutu accused the Soviet Union, Cuba and Angola of complicity.[10] Coming about a year after the end of the conflict in neighbouring Angola, the West, but particularly the United States and France took the attack seriously.

Yet while the United States Department of State felt that the attack on Shaba was 'dangerous', and that 'there had of necessity been some level of Angolan complicity', it had no firm evidence to support Mobutu's claims of Soviet and Cuban involvement. The US government therefore decided to limit the extent of its direct military response to the crisis. It supported the decision of Morocco to send troops to Zaïre, using French logistic support, to counterattack the FNLC offensive. For its own part, Washington sent what it described as 'non-lethal' military equipment, worth $15 million, to the Zaïrean army.[11] Later on in the crisis, the US supported a Nigerian diplomatic initiative to mediate in the conflict.[12]

The US response to the Shaba crisis has to be understood within the context of its extensive economic and strategic interests in Zaïre. Apart from South Africa and Nigeria, Zaïre has the highest level of US private investment in Africa.[13] The US imports 95 per cent of its cobalt, 12 000 tons annually,[14] from Zaïre. US transnational corporations have enormous stakes in the exploitation of other sectors of Zaïre's rich metallurgical resources such as iron, tin, copper, nickel, cadmium and colombite, in addition to oil. US interests are also involved in Zaïre's hydro-electric potential, estimated to be one of the most extensive in the world. In addition, it has substantial interests in Zaïre's banking system and financial institutions. In November 1976 the US Citibank led the negotiations between a number of banks and the Mobutu regime aimed at preventing Zaïre from defaulting on its loans.[15] The outcome of these talks was the allocation of more loans to a regime that even a US congressperson has described as 'ostentatious ... [sic], arrogant, egomaniacal and indulgent ... [in the midst of] widespread poverty of [its] people'.[16]

The United States has always regarded Zaïre as its most influential and closest ally in the Central African region. Since General Mobutu came to power in 1965, he has maintained a very good working relationship with successive US governments.[17] US economic and military relations with Kinshasa have generally reflected this goodwill. Between 1962 and 1977 the total US aid package to Zaïre was $400 million, while the total investment amounted to $500 million.[18] Outstanding US private and public loans to the country on the eve of the Shaba I attack amounted to $1 billion.[19] Between 1962 and 1974 the US sent $61 million worth of military equipment to the Zaïrean armed forces. Shortly after the beginning of the Angolan Civil War in

1975, Washington allocated the sums of $19 million for 'military sales credit' and $12 million for 'security supporting assistance' to Zaïre,[20] which later passed over substantial parts of these funds to the FNLA-UNITA coalition in its struggle against the MPLA. As John Stockwell makes very clear in his book, Kinshasa, Zaïre's capital, has emerged as the major centre for the CIA's covert, and overt operations in central and southwestern Africa, since Mobutu took office.[21]

The US and the Shaba Insurrections

Despite the extensive US military and economic interests in Zaïre, Washington was highly restrained in its response to the Shaba attack, as we have already indicated. There were two main reasons for this. Firstly, US military intelligence differed substantially from Mobutu's assessment of both the extent of the FNLC offensive and the threat that this posed to his regime. On both counts the US concluded that Mobutu had exaggerated the impact of the insurrection. The US Ambassador at the United Nations, Andrew Young, was particularly derisive: '[If Mobutu] can't stop a couple of thousand Katangan gendarmes, we shouldn't send the Marines to help him'.[22] As was pointed out earlier, US intelligence had also ruled out any Cuban and Soviet involvement in the Shaba assault, even though it had noted some Angolan approval.

Secondly, the Mobutu regime was the focus of intense criticism in Washington at this time both in the government (part of President Carter's so-called Human Rights Policy) and Congress (especially in the Foreign Relations Subcommittee on Africa). The extent of the Mobutu regime's corruption and incompetence, which had been given wide coverage in Stockwell's accounts and those of other writers, was frequently referred to *by officials in Washington*.[23] Writing on Zaïre during this period, Ghislain Kabwit has observed: 'The trouble is that the Mobutu regime has created a rapacious class of bureaucrats, army officers, and others, who enjoy a modicum of power, and who participate with foreign businessmen through massive corruption in the spoils and exploitation of ordinary city dwellers and rural people ... [The] economy is crumbling, and the army practically lives on the backs of the ordinary people'.[24]

While the US government had no intention of withdrawing its support from the Mobutu regime as a result of the criticisms of Zaïre in Washington and elsewhere at this time, the Carter administration nonetheless chose 'not to be identified' with Kinshasa, and 'quietly urged France to play a more active role in Zaïre'.[25]

Predictably, the Mobutu regime was furious over the United States' seemingly half-hearted support for Zaïre in confronting the emergency created by the Shaba I attack. Mobutu told an American news magazine interview: 'I confess [that] we are bitterly disappointed by America's attitude. Neto [Angolan President] is a pawn of the Cubans and the Russians, but you [the Americans] won't face up to the threat. It is your weakness versus their will power and strength'.[26] He particularly criticised Andrew Young (the US envoy at the UN) for not taking the 'communist menace' in Africa seriously. At the same time, Mobutu was full of praise for France and Belgium for their open and bold support for Zaïre. These two countries (in close collaboration with Moroccan troops and Egyptian military advisers) intervened on behalf of Mobutu to check the FNLC attack. We shall be assessing the overall effect of these interventions later, and at the same time examine critically what real military threats the FNLC posed to the Mobutu regime.

Between Shaba I and II, the US tried to improve relations with Zaïre. It increased its military aid from $30.2 million in FY 1977 (that is, after Shaba I) to $42.5 million for 1978, while economic assistance for the same period was worth $14.6 million.[27] The US government also authorised an estimated $68 million loan package from the Export-Import Bank to Zaïre for the Inga-Shaba power station.[28]

As part of this general improvement in Washington-Kinshasa relations, the US was noticeably more assertive in its criticisms of the FNLC, following the movement's second attack on Shaba in May 1978. As before, the Zaïreans accused the Soviet Union and Cuba of complicity. This time, the United States agreed with the Zaïreans, but only as regards Cuban involvement.[29] The US was particularly worried about the effects of the initial success of the FNLC which had overrun Kolwezi, the Shaba capital, routing the Zaïrean army garrison in the town. The FNLC Commander, General Mbumba, was confident that his troops would consolidate their control of Kolwezi, and initiate a country-wide insurrection to topple the Mobutu regime.[30]

Once again, the US supported a Franco-Belgian military intervention in Shaba. Furthermore, it allocated 18 giant C-141 transport aircraft as logistic back-up for this intervention.

Yet, in a dramatic development one month after the beginning of the Shaba II crisis, the US announced a re-evaluation of some of its strategic assumptions regarding the emergency. It now claimed that there was no 'conclusive evidence' to suggest either Cuban or Soviet involvement with the FNLC insurrection. It further qualified this new position by alleging that Cuba was aware of the plan to attack Shaba but had done nothing to prevent it.[31]

The immediate consequence of this re-evaluation in Washington was a noticeable lessening of the strident anti-Soviet/Cuban rhetoric which had characterised comments made on the crisis by US government officials. Soon, the US withdrew its support from a French proposal (made during the May 1978 Washington summit of NATO heads of state) to set up a so-called Pan-African Defence Force which would intervene in crisis situations in Africa.[32] This rapid-deployment force, which was expected to be trained and armed by the West, was the subject of sharp and unrelenting criticism by a number of African leaders, intellectuals and trade union organisations. Instead, the US supported the 'less contentious' alternative Franco-Belgium programme to limit the Western response, at this time, solely to the events in Zaïre. The focus should be on the retraining of the Zaïrean Armed Forces, concentrating especially on the paratroop regiments stationed in Shaba who had been no match for the more disciplined and tenacious FNLC contingents.

The long-term policy of the United States was that Zaïre needed a major fusion of Western economic and military aid.[33] Washington felt that economic support was particularly crucial because a further deterioration of social conditions in Zaïre would exacerbate domestic dissent, which insurgents such as the FNLC would exploit. As a specific proposal in this direction, the US announced the formation of a Zaïrean Aid Consortium (ZAC, also called 'The Friends of Zaïre').[34] ZAC's first task was to draw up a comprehensive plan for the economic revitalisation of Zaïre. All the Western powers (and Japan), the EEC, as well as the World Bank, and the International Monetary Fund, expressed interest in contributing to the initial fund of $400 million for the project.[35]

On the whole, the US response to the two Shaba insurrections were unusually restrained. While there was no doubt that the US sought to ensure the survival of the Mobutu regime, it nonetheless felt that Zaïre had exaggerated the involvement of external powers, particularly Cuba and the Soviet Union, in the FNLC attacks. In any case, the US was quite content to encourage the interventions of its allies – France, Belgium, Morocco, Egypt and Saudi Arabia – to safeguard the Mobutu government, Nothing more could have suited a government in Washington at this time still traumatised by the United States' defeat in the Vietnam War.

France and Belgium

Unlike the United States, France was more receptive in responding to Zaïre's appeal to the West to intervene during the Shaba attacks. A week after the announcement of the Shaba I insurrection, the French endorsed a Zaïrean-Moroccan agreement for the dispatch of Moroccan troops to the combat zones of Shaba.[36] Paris would provide the military aircraft for the airlift of the Moroccans, and funding for the entire operation would be paid for by Saudi Arabia.[37]

French interests in Zaïre had grown steadily in the 1970s, especially at the expense of the Belgians who had colonised the country until 1960.[38] At the time of the Shaba I crisis, France's direct investment in Zaïre was $20 million, but it had huge stakes worth several million dollars in a number of projects run in cooperation with the Zaïrean government or other interests in the country. These included the equipment for the Voice of Zaïre, which involved a domestic satellite communication facility, short-term loans to both state and private financial institutions and shares in the strategic copper/cobalt international conglomerate, the Société Minière de Tenke Fungurume.[39] Apart from airlifting Moroccan troops and equipment to Shaba, the French also sent their own security advisers from the SDECE, the secret service, to help the Moroccans organise the defence of Kolwezi, the Shaba capital.[40] The French, in effect, directed the Zaïrean-Moroccan counterattack against the FNLC.

With the experience gained during Shaba I, the French expanded further the extent of their intervention in Zaïre when the FNLC led the second insurrection in Shaba in May 1978. This time the French interventionist force was made up of 500 French paratroops, army engineers and technicians. Unlike Shaba I, this French contingent fought the Shabans directly. They succeeded in forcing the FNLC out of Kolwezi and the neighbouring districts within a fortnight of beginning operations. As a result, most of the FNLC fighters once again crossed into Angola to resume their exile.

French interventionism in Zaïre was not restricted to the military sphere. The French government campaigned actively among its Western allies for concerted support for the Mobutu regime. It was largely responsible for organising two special conferences on Zaïre in 1978 – the May meeting in Brussels of a consortium of Western banks, the EEC, the World Bank and the IMF to discuss ways of restructuring the Zaïrean economy, and the June meeting in Paris of officials from the United States, Britain, Belgium, Federal Germany and France to examine 'Africa/Zaïre Security'. As mentioned earlier, Paris had also formulated a proposal during the May 1978 NATO heads of state summit in Washington for the West to set up an African version of a rapid-deployment force to intervene during times of crisis anywhere on the continent. The proposal was only abandoned after US hesitation.

As for Belgium, it had the most extensive interests in Zaïre before the Shaba invasions. These amounted to $700–$1000 million,[41] and as the ex-colonial power in Zaïre, these interests were principally in the form of pre-independence capital. Belgian-Zaïrean relations had, however, been in severe difficulties since 1974 when President Mobutu nationalised several Belgian (and other foreign) businesses under his 'Zaïreanisation' economic policy. Belgian interests suffered greatly from these take-overs.

Yet the Belgians came to Mobutu's support soon after the FNLC attack on Shaba in March 1977. While Brussels rejected Mobutu's request for the dispatch of a thousand Belgian paratroops to repulse the Shabans, it did agree to facilitate the delivery of Belgian weapons including mortars, machine guns and anti-tank rocket launchers. The Belgium military mission in Zaïre was instructed to liaise with the Zaïrean military on matters of security geared towards the defence of Shaba.

As in the US and French examples, the Belgium intervention during Shaba II was much more pronounced. A contingent of 1700 troops was sent out from Belgium into Shaba after a week of the FNLC attack in May 1978. But unlike the French, the Belgians did not engage the FNLC. By the time the Belgians had the opportunity of being deployed, most of the fighting in the Kolwezi sector had been concluded. Apart from evacuating the Belgian mining community in the province, the Belgian expeditionary force was reduced to policing important industrial sites in Shaba to ensure that these were safe from any sabotage from FNLC units retreating from the combat zones into Angola.

The FNLC, Mobutu and the West

An important element that has emerged so far in this study is the compelling keenness with which the US, France and Belgium pursued their intervention in the Shaba insurrections. It remains, however, to assess the specific threats posed to the Mobutu regime by the FNLC attacks.

By March 1977, when the FNLC launched its first attack on Shaba, the Zaïrean economy was going through a major crisis. The continuing fall in the price of copper, the main source of foreign exchange revenue for Zaïre, the sharp rise in the oil bills (particularly since the 1973 Middle East War), the dislocation of the Benguela railway (an export outlet for Shaba's mineral products), due to the Angolan Civil War, and the legendary corruptive features in the workings of the economy all contributed to a serious crisis in the country which was approaching breaking point.[42] Zaïre's costly intervention in the Angolan War had had adverse effects on the economy, especially with respect to the hundreds of thousands of people in the southern provinces bordering Angola who remained displaced. Political instability was also rife in Zaïre during the period. A mass demonstration in early 1978 in the eastern province of Bandundu, near Shaba, over the rising cost of living was brutally suppressed by the military with 2000 civilian deaths.[43] A trial after these disturbances followed, leading to the execution of 14 community leaders accused of organising the demonstrations. The government's harsh measures in its handling of the Bandundu protests were to lead to the further alienation of the Mobutu regime throughout Zaïre.

It was against this deteriorating socio-economic situation in Zaïre that the Congolese Front for National Liberation launched its first attack on Shaba in March 1977. While numerous anti-Mobutu political movements emerged over the years, the FNLC was one of the few that possessed a military wing to confront Mobutu militarily. Furthermore, the FNLC was the only effective Zaïrean opposition organisation based in Africa, as the others were mainly in exile in Europe (France, Belgium, Switzerland). With guerrilla bases in Angola, a contiguous and friendly state, the FNLC had decisive advantages over the other movements.

But the FNLC had serious handicaps in leading the various factions of the Zaïrean opposition nation-wide to topple Mobutu. It still remained fundamentally a Shaba regional organisation, with limited support elsewhere in the country. Its political and ideological orientation was still suspect among other Zaïreans who had not forgotten its secessionist past nor its numerous and often contradictory alliances.[44] Finally, the FNLC's unsuccessful attempt to form an anti-Mobutu patriotic front with the rest of the opposition on the eve of the Shaba I attack may have accounted for the absence of 'spontaneous uprisings' by the people throughout Zaïre, an expectation that was a central feature in its strategy.

In effect, the most concrete military achievement that the FNLC could have hoped to achieve during these insurrections was the seizure of Shaba. It was inconceivable that 3000–4500 lightly-armed forces could have overrun Zaïre, a territory almost twice the size of Western Europe. General Mobutu's regime must surely have been aware of that. Yet the FNLC's past history, and the fact that its bases were in Angola under an MPLA administration which Mobutu had worked strenuously with his Western allies to stop from assuming power in 1975, meant that the Zaïrean government could easily internationalise the crisis as a way of confronting the Shaba insurgency. And this was exactly what it did.

There is also evidence that Mobutu was doubtful of the loyalty and ability of his own military forces to cope with the emergency. Soon after the FNLC began their attack (Shaba I), most of the units of the Zaïrean army deployed in the province deserted without organising any defence. Mobutu himself overruled the deployment of the special paratroop brigade from the Kinshasa military region to Shaba after the units there took flight. He may have thought that these troops would either mutiny or simply defect to the enemy as some contingents of the Shaba regiments had indeed done.[45] Military morale took a further battering in March 1978, one year after Shaba I, when Mobutu dismissed 250 middle-ranking officers on charges of insubordination. Thirteen other officers were later executed after a secret trial during which they were accused of plotting to overthrow the Mobutu regime.[46]

By concentrating primarily on the international links of the FNLC, some of which were deliberately exaggerated, Mobutu succeeded in diverting the attention of most of the world from the multi-faceted crisis that his regime was going through in 1977/78. This also contributed in frustrating any chances internally in Zaïre for the construction of an anti-Mobutu opposition bloc which the FNLC had envisaged.

Mobutu's call on his Western allies to intervene in Zaïre could not have come at a more auspicious time. The Zaïrean government had been under attack in Africa and elsewhere since March 1976 for allowing the Federal Republic of Germany to install a multi-million dollar OTRAG rocket firing base in Shaba.[47] The West had all along connived with the Bonn government over the rocket base deal, even though it was a clear violation of existing United Nations Space Treaty provisions and the 1954 Treaty of Brussels, restricting German rearmament. [48] The West must have been incensed when the FNLC stated openly that it was going to attack the base during its operations in Shaba.[49] Such threats had no doubt ensured Western support for Mobutu whatever were their other considerations. The speed with which the West began to 'restructure' the Zaïrean economy, with stringent fiscal controls supervised by its financial institutions (heralding the fate of most other African economies in the late 1970s/early 1980s) soon after the Shaba insurrections,[50] showed clearly that Washington, Paris and Brussels had merely been spurred on by the oppositional politics of the FNLC to reinforce their socio-economic stranglehold on Zaïre.

III AFRICAN ATTITUDES

In Africa the Shaba conflicts invoked bitter memories of the bloody three-year civil war that took place in Zaïre (then Congo-Leopoldville) immediately after independence from Belgium colonialism in June 1960. This was particularly due to the fact that this fighting had taken place in the same eastern province of Shaba (then called Katanga).

In the 1960 confrontation a secession had been declared by the well-known Shaba politician, Moise Tshombe, to oppose the central government led by Patrice Lumumba. Tshombe had mobilised a military force to defend the Katanga Republic before its collapse in 1963 due to operations carried out by the United Nations and the Congolese central government forces. As indicated earlier, a new generation of Katangese insurgents spearheaded the attacks on Shaba in 1977 and 1978.

Coming soon after the conflict in neighbouring Angola in 1975–76 which involved an extensive range of intervention, particularly by extracontinental powers, the Organisation of African Unity and some of its members, such as Nigeria, expressed a desire to mediate in Zaïre.

Nigeria's Peace Initiatives

Nigeria's Foreign Affairs Minister, Joe Garba went to Kinshasa and Luanda on peace missions soon after the Shabans began their attack in March 1977. Garba asked both governments to exercise restraint in an attempt to de-escalate the growing level of conflict. The Zaïreans maintained that while they supported a diplomatic resolution of the crisis, the FNLC units must be withdrawn unconditionally. They also called for a pan-African condemnation of Angola for giving sanctuaries to a 'rebel movement' in violation of the OAU charter. As for the Angolans, they denied complicity in the Shaba attacks. While they acknowledged allowing the Shabans to establish bases in Angola, they indicated, quite unconvincingly, that they knew nothing of the insurrection. Instead, Angola raised the issue of continuing Zaïrean government military support for surviving units of the rival FNLA, and the FLEC, a Cabinda independence organisation.

Garba called for an immediate cessation of hostilities in Shaba during his mediations. He asked Angola to pressure the FNLC to evacuate their forces from Shaba and promised that Nigeria would undertake to arrange talks to normalise Angolan-Zaïrean bilateral relations. Foremost in this normalisation proposal was a Nigerian plan to disarm all military organisations in both states which were opposed to either of the governments.[51] Nigeria or the OAU would supervise the operation. Nigeria also asked Mobutu to withdraw his invitations to outside powers to intervene in the conflict, so as to enable its mediation to succeed. Mobutu rejected this point out of hand, bringing the Nigerian initiative to an abrupt end. After ten days of shuttling between Luanda and Kinshasa without success, Garba called off his mediating mission.

Zaïre had no regrets over the failure of the Nigerian mediation. On the contrary, its political position on the conflict received a boost in the Organisation of African Unity when a majority of member states meeting in Libreville in July 1977 supported a resolution reiterating full support for the 'inviolability of Zaïre's borders'. In what was seen as an implicit criticism of Angola's role in the Shaba insurrections, the resolution reminded OAU members to 'prohibit the use of their territories as bases for political subversive activities against another African state ...'[52]

Morocco, Egypt, Sudan

During each occasion of the Shaba attacks, Morocco dispatched 1500 troops to Zaïre to help General Mobutu stem the offensives. French planes were responsible for transporting the Moroccans and these operations cost Rabat $70 million, which was paid for by Saudi Arabia.[53]

Why did Morocco send troops to Mobutu during the Shaba emergencies? King Hassan saw a relationship between the uprisings in Shaba and the struggle in Western Sahara by the Polisario Front who are fighting against Morocco's occupation of the territory.[54] Apart from the internal security 'threats' posed by these movements, Hassan accused them of also maintaining links with the Soviet Union and Cuba which encouraged 'communist infiltration' of Africa. Furthermore, by intervening in Zaïre, Hassan felt that Morocco was coming to the aid of an ally which it had helped in the early 1960s to crush a secessionist movement – in the same Shaba province.[55]

Egypt and Sudan employed very similar anti-communist rhetoric in justifying their own support for Mobutu during the Shaba insurrections. Egypt even went as far as making the ludicrous claim that Zaïre was the 'source of the Nile',[56] while announcing the dispatch of a dozen airforce pilots to fight against the FNLC. For its own part, Sudan sent a team of military advisers to help train Zaïrean troops and maintain security after the recapture of Kolwezi from the insurgents.

More support for Zaïre came from 'francophone' Africa. In a meeting of its heads of state in Paris in May 1977, also attended by France, a declaration approving the Franco-Moroccan intervention in Shaba was adopted. As for South Africa, the Western-organised intervention in Zaïre showed that concerned states were 'waking up (at last) to the threat of Marxism in Africa'.[57]

While no African state officially supported the Shaba insurrection, some were, however, highly critical of the extent of foreign intervention. Soon after the outbreak of Shaba II in May 1978, Nigeria severely criticised the US-Franco-Belgian intervention which it saw as a 'case of gunboat diplomacy and neocolonialism'. But the most scathing criticism came from Tanzania. President Julius Nyerere declared:

> We must reject the principle that external powers have the right to maintain in power African governments which are universally recognised to be corrupt, or incompetent, or a bunch of murderers when their people try to make a change. The peoples of an individual African country have as much right to change their corrupt government in the last half of the twentieth century as in the past the British, French and Russian people had to overthrow their own rotten regimes.[58]

Both Tanzania and Nigeria also attacked the conception of the Pan-African Strike Force proposed by France, which they felt was aimed at serving the interests of 'embattled' and 'reactionary' regimes in Africa.[59]

OAU Mediation

In its 1978 annual summit held in Khartoum, Sudan, the OAU offered to mediate in the bilateral crisis between Angola and Zaïre which had been exacerbated by the Shaba conflict. The OAU repeated its support for Zaïrean independence and territorial integrity, but in a departure from its Libreville resolution in 1977, it obliquely attacked President Mobutu when it condemned the 'invitation of foreign forces to intervene in African conflicts by member states'.

Having achieved some 'evenness' in the wording of the Khartoum declaration, the OAU set out to improve Angola-Zaïre ties. Six months of painstaking negotiations finally led to a formal normalisation of relations.[60] According to the accord, Zaïre recognised the MPLA government of Angola and agreed to suspend all support for Angolan opposition groups based in Zaïre. Zaïre promised to rehabilitate its nationals who were then in Angola if they wished to return home. There would be no recriminations of any persons or political organisations.

For its own part, Angola agreed to shut down all FNLC bases in its territory. It also accepted the terms on the treatment of refugees endorsed by Zaïre. Both states also declared their willingness to negotiate for the reopening of the Benguela railway. This implied that the Mobutu regime would have to abandon its support for the UNITA organisation, whose military operations in Angola still kept the railway route severely disrupted.

IV CUBA, THE SOVIET UNION AND CONCLUSIONS

The persistent Zaïrean allegations of Soviet-Cuban involvement in the Shaba conflicts were without foundation. As observed earlier, even the Western countries that intervened on behalf of the Mobutu regime discounted these allegations.

This is not to suggest that either Moscow or Havana would have regretted the fall of General Mobutu from power as a result of the FNLC insurrections. Of course, both the Soviet Union and Cuba had had a very strained relationship with the Zaïrean government, particularly over Angola.

In spite of some association which Cuba had maintained with the FNLC, especially with respect to their mutual support for the MPLA during the Angolan civil strife, there were three reasons why it did not give direct military backing to the insurrections. First, the timing of the insurrections – particularly Shaba I. After the MPLA's victory in the Angolan civil war in 1976, the Cuban forces deployed in Angola were mainly preoccupied with the consolidation of the MPLA control of the country. This entailed the following considerations: (1) to bring to an end continuing UNITA military operations in central and southern Angola; and (2) to increase aid to the Namibian liberation movement, SWAPO. Cuba's calculation to step up its support for SWAPO at this time was aimed at stemming the flow of South African military supplies to UNITA from across the Namibian frontier. Secondly, there was evidence of a general Cuban disenchantment with the FNLC's political and ideological orientation. The Cubans did not think that the FNLC had the fortitude, comparable to the MPLA, to sustain a protracted insurgency that might be required to carry out the sort of political change they advocated for Zaïre.

Lastly, Cuba was aware that the security situation in

Angola's border regions at this time (that is, prior to the Shaba I attack) was generally stable. This had been the case since the 1976 decisive military defeat of the FNLA. So, quite clearly, there was no reason for Cuba to wish to attack Zaïre. On the contrary. As Basil Davidson has put it, in his usual candour, 'As for the Cubans, they didn't appear on the scene except in the imagination of distant Western journalists etc. etc. If they *had* appeared on the scene, what would have happened to Mobutu's forces and their friends in Shaba? Another story, one thinks!'[61]

Nonetheless, Cuba and the Soviet Union were aware each time the Shaba insurrections were underway. The fact that they did not prevent either of the attacks was because they were not inclined to help the Mobutu regime to solve its seemingly intractable crisis.

By way of conclusion, we need to restate that the Shaba conflicts were short-lived military episodes. Very small-scale fighting was involved, and correspondingly few casualties were incurred by both the FNLC and the array of foreign troops and military advisers who intervened on behalf of the Zaïrean central government.

Despite this low-level military activity, the Western response, from the United States, France and Belgium, amounted to an overkill. For the West, the FNLC attacks were a pretext to prop up a regime which oversees one of Africa's economically and strategically most important countries. The West's response was no doubt dictated by the aftermath of the Angolan Civil War of 1975–76. The United States, particularly, was still opposed to the MPLA government, always emphasising the latter's close relationship with Cuba and the Soviet Union. Thus, the Western interventions in neighbouring Zaïre during Shaba I and II were seen as opportunities to regain 'lost' geo-political ground in central Africa.

It should be stressed that the major relevance of the Shaba conflicts was their interrelationship or linkage to the geopolitics associated with the Angolan Civil War. The difference between the 'Shabas' and the Angolan war was, of course, that militarily the former were low key events contrasted to the stormy and dramatic campaign that characterised the latter.

5 The Dynamics of Intervention: A Comparative Survey

As indicated in our discussions so far, especially in chapters 2–4, the following principal themes have emerged as the dominant focus of our enquiry to determine the nature of intervention in the conflicts in Nigeria, Angola and Zaïre: (A) the determinant of the extent of intervention; (B) the type of intervention that contending power groups (in each conflict) are prepared to accept; (C) the motive for intervention; (D) the mode of intervention; and (E) the consequences (or outcome) of intervention. A comparative survey, primarily involving the three conflicts, but also drawing on other continental examples, and based on exploring further the constituent features of the five principal themes now follows. A set of propositions will be derived from the analysis which are expected to illustrate the dynamics of intervention in civil conflicts in contemporary Africa.

A DETERMINANT OF THE EXTENT OF INTERVENTION IN CIVIL WARS (IN AFRICA)

Six groups of participants involved in the civil war may be distinguished:
  (a) *Contending Power Groups* – or the primary parties in the conflict;
  (b) *Contiguous States* – in relation to the state in conflict;
  (c) *The Sub-African State System* – this term is used to identify African regional political, ideological or economic associations such as the Organisation Commune Africaine, Malagasy et Mauritiènne (OCAMM), the Economic Organisation of West African States (ECO-WAS), the Afro-French Summit, the Commonwealth African States, the Southern African Development

Conference, the Southern African Frontline States, the Arab League, and so forth;
(d) *African State System* – principally the Organisation of African Unity (OAU);
(e) *The Ex-Colonial Regime* – used in this study to refer primarily to Britain and France;
(f) *The United States and the Soviet Union.*

A further exposition of each of the six groups of participants is required:

(a) Contending Power Groups

We can isolate two types in this study:
(i) Established (constitutional or *de facto*) Central government versus Insurgent group/groups;
(ii) Contending groups, with absence of Established (constitutional or *de facto*) Central government.

For the purpose of our analysis, type (i) above will be presented schematically as EC-I (where EC represents Established Central government); I is Insurgent group/groups; (-) is versus. Type (ii) is expressed as c(NEC), where lower case c represents 'contending groups in conflict', while NEC means 'No Established Central Government'.

Commentary
1. With reference to our study, the Nigerian and Zaïrean conflicts represent case (i) above.

Nigeria
Central government (Lagos) versus Insurgent power group (Biafra).

Zaïre
Central government (Kinshasa) versus Insurgent power group (FNLC).
2. As for case (ii) above, this is represented by the Angolan conflict.

Angola
Contending power groups – MPLA, UNITA-FNLA.

Other remarks
1. Most civil wars in post-independence Africa are of the (i) type (EC-I), with (ii) c(NEC) being the exception. Civil wars in Ethiopia, Sudan, Chad, Western Sahara and Burundi are all of the EC-I category. After the collapse of the Lumumbist government in Congo-Leopoldville (now Zaïre) in August 1960 and the 'constitutional' crisis which ensued between Premier Patrice Lumumba and President Joseph Kasavubu, the civil war which followed can be categorised as c(NEC): there was no longer an existing central government as rival armies of various political groups contended for control of the power centre in Leopoldville.
2. Out of all the three case studies, only in Nigeria was one of the contending power groups secessionist, namely Biafra (the Insurgent group). Other civil wars in Africa with secessionist political objectives occurred in Sudan and Congo-Leopoldville (in the 1960s). In the Angola and Zaïre cases (studied), none of the contending power groups had secessionist goals. The Burundi Civil War of the 1970s also falls within the latter category, while the conflicts in Ethiopia and Western Sahara are of a different form. In Ethiopia, particularly with respect to Eritrea, the conflict began when the Ethiopians (Central government) annexed Eritrean territory, formerly occupied by Italian imperialism, after the end of the Second World War. The Eritrean Struggle is clearly an anti-colonial conflict, even if the coloniser in this case, Ethiopia, is an African power. The same applies to Western Sahara which the Moroccan Kingdom annexed in 1974 after the formal end of Spanish imperial occupation of the territory.
3. For the underlying reasons for the conflicts examined, discernible differences between the main contending power groups over the management and reconstruction of the post-colonial state characterised the Angolan example, and to some extent the Zaïrean, while the fundamental issues at stake in Nigeria concerned a national minority which wanted to set up an alternative autonomous political entity. In this

regard, Biafra shares some affinity with conflicts in southern Sudan, Eritrea, Tigre, Oromo and Western Sahara.

(b) Contiguous States

1. In the case of Nigeria, these are Cameroon, Chad, Niger and Benin (formerly Dahomey). Contiguous countries with respect to Angola are Zambia, Zaïre, Congo-Brazzaville and Namibia (formerly occupied by South Africa), and for Zaïre the following: Angola, Zambia, Tanzania, Burundi, Rwanda, Uganda, Sudan, Central African Republic and Congo-Brazzaville.

Commentary
1. Contiguous states are obviously deeply concerned with civil war developments in the crisis state. The following reasons explain their concern:
(i) Fears that conflict may spill over to their territory;
(ii) Effects on their internal socio-economic situation in the case of refugees crossing the border from the disturbed state;
(iii) Possibilities of 'hot-pursuit' of retreating forces by more dominant contending power group (especially the Central government in conflicts of the EC-I type);
(iv) Effects on their economy or disruption of essential communication facilities.
2. In addition to the above which are principally defensive factors, a contiguous state may wish to actively influence the politics in the crisis state (see below).

Other Remarks
1. The concern of contiguous states becomes quite serious if they happen to be landlocked in relation to the crisis state. Chad and Niger are examples in the Nigerian War. Both depend on the principal Nigerian ports of Lagos and Port Harcourt (this was part of secessionist Biafra) for their import/export trade. Zambia is distinctly a good case of a concerned landlocked state in reference to both the Angolan and Zaïrean Wars. Due to Zambia's closures of rail and road routes through Rhodesia (now Zimbabwe) to South Africa in

The Dynamics of Intervention: A Comparative Survey

the south, it had depended on the Benguela railway (which runs from Zaïre to the Angolan port of Benguela) for the export of copper. Landlocked Rwanda, Burundi and the Central African Empire (now Central African Republic) had also relied, but to a lesser extent than Zambia, on the Benguela route for their trade.

2. The behaviour of contiguous states in civil war situations:

Proposition I
In civil wars of EC-I type, contiguous states always tend to support the central power faction.

Assessment from Study

(1) *Nigeria*
   – Cameroon: actively pro-central power faction.
   – Chad: actively pro-central power faction.
   – Niger: actively pro-central power faction.
   – Benin (then Dahomey): pro-central power faction.

1. Benin was less active in its pro-federal Nigeria policy two years after the outbreak of the war (summer 1969) compared with other countries that border Nigeria. This was evident when President Emile Zinsou agreed to a controversial International Red Cross plan to fly in relief supplies to Biafra at night using Cotonou (the Benin capital) as a staging base. The Zinsou decision upset Lagos, which had insisted that the Biafrans had always preferred night flights so as to continue to maintain their arms imports uninterrupted from the possibility of intercepting federal fighter aircraft. We need to point out, however, that despite this apparently conciliatory attitude to Biafra, Benin never contemplated recognising the secession. Benin only exercised a greater freedom to act in the circumstances (compared with other neighbouring states) because while contiguous to Nigeria's western border, its territory is not in the crucial eastern frontier which was within the arc of the conflict.

(2) *Zaïre*
   – Burundi: sympathetic to central power faction.
   – Rwanda: sympathetic to central power faction.

- Central African Empire: sympathetic to central power faction.
- Zambia: sympathetic to central power faction.
- Congo-Brazzaville: indifferent, but not hostile.
- Tanzania: indifferent, but not hostile.
- Angola: unsympathetic.

1. In this case, only one contiguous state, Angola, can be regarded as 'unsympathetic', but our study demonstrates that Luanda was not actively involved in the Shaba insurgencies even though the FNLC used Angolan territory for its attacks. Angola's role in this conflict (sympathy for the cause of the FNLC) was influenced by a historically-unresolved crisis with the Zaïrean authorities (that is, the Angolan War). At no time of the Shaba attacks did Angola openly accept responsibility for the action of the FNLC, nor did it endorse the latter's political objectives. It should be recalled that as soon as Luanda resolved its bilateral differences with Kinshasa (three months after Shaba II), the Angolan government effectively neutralised the FNLC hostility towards Zaïre.

2. In a wider African perspective, the position of both Sudan and Somalia on the civil conflicts in Ethiopia can also be understood within the context of an outstanding historical crisis between the central government in the conflict state (in this case, Ethiopia) and the contiguous countries (Somalia, Sudan).

3. On the whole, contiguous states show a greater diplomatic sensitivity in conflicts of this type with evident bias for the established central government. This is indicative of governments' intentions to conform with existing international regulations governing interstate relations. In our case studies (Nigeria, Zaïre), support for the central power faction by the contiguous states was mainly political and diplomatic. There were no military interventions.

Proposition II
In civil wars of c(NEC) type, contiguous states play a considerable interventionist role.

The Dynamics of Intervention: A Comparative Survey 137

Assessment from Study

(1) *Angola*
- Zaïre: activist support for the FNLA-UNITA power group.
- Zambia: support for the FNLA-UNITA.
- South Africa: activist support for the FNLA-UNITA (in this analysis, South African 'contiguity' with Angola is in relation to Namibia which Pretoria controlled until recently).
- Congo-Brazzaville: support for the MPLA power faction.

1. According to our study of Angola, contiguous states play a greater interventionist role in this type of civil war, c(NEC), than in EC-I. This is due to the obvious state of 'power vacuum' created by the absence of central power authority in the crisis state. In the Angolan case, this was clearly the situation after the collapse of the MFA-MPLA-FNLA-UNITA transitional government in Luanda in July 1975.

It follows that with the absence of central power authority in the crisis state, neighbouring countries feel less restrained by existing international law from intervening, especially if their behaviour is construed as a move to restore 'law and order', or to maintain 'regional stability'. Contiguous states can intervene in the following ways[1]:

(i) Sending military advisors and/or combatants. To illustrate with the Angolan example, this was true of Zaïre (for the FNLA-UNITA) and South Africa (FNLA-UNITA).

(ii) Sending weapons and other military supplies. The role of both Zaïre and South Africa was the same in this regard in their support for the FNLA-UNITA alliance.

(iii) Allowing own territory to be used as sanctuaries by favoured power groups in the crisis state. Zaïre allowed the FNLA to use its territory; Zambia similarly offered its territory to UNITA, and South Africa allowed UNITA to use northern Namibia for training purposes. Congo-Brazzaville authorised the use of parts of the country for both training and staging bases, for MPLA attacks on the Cabinda principality.

(iv) Permitting friendly insurgent groups to use logistic facilities in own territory (such as roads, railway, airports,

waterways and other communication facilities) for purposes of military operations in the crisis state. Zaïre gave these facilities to the FNLA-UNITA; Congo-Brazzaville allowed similar facilities for the use of the MPLA, while South Africa gave similar support to the FNLA-UNITA.
(v) Firm diplomatic support for a favoured group. Zaïre, South Africa and Zambia actively championed the political goals of the FNLA-UNITA, while Congo-Brazzaville was a strong political ally of the MPLA.

(c) Sub-Africa State System

In this survey, this is abbreviated to SASS. For the Nigerian Civil War, the relevant SASS we shall be concerned with is the Commonwealth. We should point out that while the Commonwealth is not an exclusive African political organisation, African members of the body often exhibit close relationships in several matters of inter-state interest (we shall further elaborate on this). As for Zaïre, the SASS to be examined is OCAMM (Organisation Commune Africaine, Malagasy et Mauritiènne). In the case of Angola, no SASS is of any importance. In due course, we shall establish that apart from the Arab World where the Arab League is the vital SASS (during periods of conflict), the Commonwealth and OCAMM play important roles in conflict situations in officially English-speaking and 'francophone' Africa (respectively).

(d) African State System (abbreviated here to ASS)

By ASS, we principally mean the Organisation of African Unity (OAU). As a determinant of the extent of foreign intervention in the Nigerian and Zaïrean wars, ASS role was minimal (to be illustrated below); in these cases, the relevant SASS was much more dominant than the ASS (again, to be illustrated below). The role of the ASS was more evident and pronounced in Angola than SASS. The fact that there is no strong SASS linking 'lusophone' Africa, with the added dimension that Portugal no longer has entrenched political and economic ties with states of this category, is highly relevant. It will be of immense importance to our analysis later.

(e) Ex-Colonial Regime (for our purpose, this is abbreviated to Ex-Col)

Ex-Col is used in a very restricted sense in this study to refer to just Britain and/or France. Especially in the case of France, we have used this term to refer to its relationship with Zaïre. It is true that Zaïre was not colonised by France. Rather, we have used this term because France has superseded Belgium (Zaïre's former coloniser) as the dominant Western power with vested interests in the country. Furthermore, Zaïre is officially French-speaking and belongs to the OCAMM. Essentially, Ex-Col in this context refers to a neocolonial power.

(f) The United States and the Soviet Union (the superpower system abbreviated here to SP)

It was only in Angola that the SP system was prominent in determining the depth of foreign intervention. This was not the case in either Nigeria or Zaïre, even though the Soviet Union assisted federal Nigeria's war effort to some extent (see below).

Proposition III
In civil wars in any of the former British or French/Belgian colonies, the three systems that emerge as dominant in determining the extent of intervention and/or the resolution of the conflict are SASS, ASS and Ex-Col.

Assessment from Study
Proposition III is well illustrated in the cases of Nigeria and Zaïre.

(1) *Nigeria*
1. Britain (Ex-Col) played the most crucial role in deter-

mining the depth of external intervention and the resolution of the Nigerian Civil War. London's military and diplomatic support for the federal war effort was instrumental in the latter's victory over the Biafran independence movement. Using its considerable diplomatic weight in the Commonwealth, Britain was also able to limit the range of Biafra's attempts to break its diplomatic isolation in the international community, which was part of the federal war strategy.

2. While it was true that the Soviet Union (SP) intervened in the war (by also supporting the central government), our study demonstrates that given Britain's interests and influence in Nigeria, Moscow's intervention was not deemed 'hostile' as this coincided with the British objective in the war – continuing maintenance of Nigeria's federation.

3. For the United States (SP), the Nigerian War was essentially a 'British responsibility'. In effect, Britain's goal in the conflict (maintenance of the Nigerian federation) was shared by the superpower system.

4. France's support for Biafra does not undermine the validity of Proposition III. From our study, we showed the overall effect of French support for Biafra. While this might have extended the duration of the war (as it increased Biafra's capability to resist), we noted that it could not have ensured the success of the secession.

5. We have already mentioned Britain's close ties with the Commonwealth organisation in implementing its policy on Nigeria. London stressed in Commonwealth circles that the organisation should support a member state (Nigeria) which was threatened by secession. Using the auspices of the Commonwealth Secretariat in London, Britain arranged a Commonwealth peace conference on the war in Kampala in May 1968 which was aimed at seeking 'the peaceful resolution of the Nigeria crisis based on the unity of the country'. Translated into the language of the war, this envisaged objective meant 'the continuation of the Nigerian federation'. And this was the goal of the federal government.

6. The Organisation of African Unity (ASS) was also relevant in determining the depth of foreign intervention in the crisis, but this system played a subsidiary role compared with the Ex-Col and SASS. ASS (except four 'dissenting' members – Gabon, Côte d'Ivoire, Zambia and Tanzania)

The Dynamics of Intervention: A Comparative Survey 141

took the position that the 30-month-old conflict was 'Nigeria's internal affair'. In three summit conferences held during the war, the OAU merely reiterated its concept of the 'indissolubility of member states' territorial frontiers', without an active role either to scale down hostilities or resolve the crisis.

(2) *Zaïre*
1. France (Ex-Col) played the most important role in organising Western military intervention in Zaïre during the two Shaba conflicts. In embarking on these policies, Paris closely sought and received the support of OCAMM (the relevant SASS).
2. The United States' intervention (SP) in the Shaba insurrection (by providing transport aircraft and supplies to the Moroccan and Franco-Belgian forces) came under the dominant French influence in the country.
3. Apart from statements from the OAU Secretariat in Addis Ababa during the conflicts (principally calling for 'restraint from all interested parties'), the continental organisation (ASS) played a noticeably subdued part in either determining the depth of external intervention in Zaïre or resolving the political issues involved.
4. While spokespersons of OCAMM (SASS) such as Leopold Senghor, Felix Houphouet-Boigny, Sangoule Lamizana, Musa Traore and Jean Bokassa openly defended French interventionist policy in Zaïre and in other African conflicts (Mauritania, Chad, Central African Empire, Niger), the OAU (ASS) did not explicitly condemn the action on any occasion. We should add that except for Guinea, Congo-Brazzaville and Benin, all officially French-speaking African states have defence treaties with France.

From both the Nigerian and Zaïrean examples, there is an added important feature of Proposition III: this is the close linkage between the relevant Ex-Col regime (in the conflict) and the SASS, in determining the extent of external intervention in civil conflicts in ex-British and former French territories in Africa. In these cases, the continental system (ASS) plays a subordinate function. This leads us to formulate the next proposition.

Proposition IV
In civil wars in any of the former French or British colonies, the Ex-Col-SASS dyad emerges as the dominant system in determining the extent of intervention and/or the resolution of the conflict, with the ASS playing a subordinate role.

Other Remarks
1. To further stress the validity of Proposition IV, especially in relation to the relative passivity of ASS in conflicts of this category, we can briefly refer to other developments in a conflict other than any of our case studies – Zimbabwe. In July 1979 the OAU at its annual summit (held in Monrovia) declared that the Zimbabwe Patriotic Front was the 'only authentic nationalist organisation' in Rhodesia which member states 'should only maintain ties with'. No contacts, the Monrovia resolution stressed, should be made with the 'puppet Smith-Muzerewa regime' in negotiations over the resolution of the Rhodesian conflict. Yet six weeks later in Lusaka, the African Commonwealth sub-system (SASS), in cooperation with the Southern African Frontline States (another SASS), endorsed the British government Peace Plan on Rhodesia presented to the Commonwealth Conference. This plan expressly called for a conference of 'all parties involved in the Rhodesian crisis' to be held in London from September 1979. The obvious implication of the Lusaka Accord was that the SASS (in this case) had in cooperation with Britain (Ex-Col) reversed the ASS (that is, the OAU) position taken in Monrovia. This was because in the London talks, the discredited Smith-Muzerewa party was entitled to participate. So the Ex-Col-SASS dyad subjected ASS to a secondary functional position. It follows that given the dyad, the Ex-Col regime plays a more important role in determining not only the depth of intervention in civil conflicts in these territories, but also their resolution. The SASS therefore acts as a local (African) support system to the Ex-Col.

Proposition V
In conflicts in former British and/or French colonies, the Ex-Col regime is the most important factor in determining the extent of external intervention and/or resolution of the war.

The Dynamics of Intervention: A Comparative Survey 143

Assessment from Study

(1) *Nigeria*
1. The role of Britain in the 30-months' civil war validates this proposition.

(2) *Zaïre*
1. French interventionist policies in the Shaba conflicts reflect this tendency.

Other Remarks
1. The dominant role of the Ex-Col regime is due largely to the unbroken structure of alliances and cooperations (in economic and military fields) which these former colonial powers have maintained with the African countries. As we have mentioned elsewhere, France has defence treaties with all 'francophone' Africa (except Guinea, Congo and Benin) which enables it to intervene militarily in these states in 'emergency situations'. All senior military officers from these states are trained in French military academies (including especially St. Cyr) and Paris has military bases in most of the states concerned. Economically, France remains dominant in these territories: it is both the major trading partner and investor. All 'francophone' Africa (except Guinea) is within the protected parameter of the French franc financial zone. This financial arrangement authorises the French Central Bank in Paris to set the value of the local CFA currencies in each of the 'francophone' countries.
2. While Britain has no existing military pacts with any of its former colonies, it has interrelated military training programmes and arms transfer deals with them. These programmes include Nigeria, where senior members of the military still attend specialised courses in British military colleges. Economically, Britain continues to be an influential power in the country. Its privileged position in this sector, which started during the colonial era, has been further consolidated in the years of the boom created by the oil industry. Currently, Britain is playing an active role in the formulation of so-called recovery programmes for the Nigerian economy under the auspices of the International

Monetary Fund and other Western-controlled financial institutions.

3. This study has been able to show that despite the political independence which both Britain and France conceded to their former African territories in the 1960s, these two Western countries still maintain strategic positions in the crucial economic structure of these states. Given this important situation, the Ex-Cols are especially sensitive to ongoing political development in these countries.

Proposition VI
When conflicts occur in territories other than ex-British and ex-French, either of the superpowers (SP) emerges as the dominant power in determining the extent of intervention and the resolution of the conflict.

Assessment from study

Angola
1. With the collapse of Portuguese colonial occupation in Angola, and the absence of the exclusivist control of state power by any of the three contending power groups (MPLA, UNITA, FNLA), the United States and the Soviet Union felt freer to act in the circumstances. Here, there was no relevant sub-African State System (SASS). Instead, the continental system (ASS) was 'elevated' to an important status in conflict management. As soon as some leading members of the OAU (Nigeria, Ethiopia, Ghana, Tanzania) recognised the MPLA government (on the eve of the crucial Addis Ababa January 1976 summit on Angola), the Soviet Union could not restrain its delight that its Angolan policy was converging with an emerging African political consensus.

2. The US obviously recognised the importance of the OAU in the diplomatic sphere of the Angolan crisis. On the eve of the Addis summit, President Ford sent a telegram to every African head of state asking them to support a 'national government' (in Angola) which explicitly included the FNLA-UNITA alliance.

3. Finally in this category of civil war, the behaviour of states outside the superpower system (for example, Cuba in its support for the MPLA faction) is generally in confluence

The Dynamics of Intervention: A Comparative Survey

with the political objective of one of the dominant superpowers.

B THE TYPE OF INTERVENTION THE CONTENDING POWER GROUPS (IN EACH CONFLICT) ARE PREPARED TO ACCEPT[2]

Proposition VII
In civil wars of EC-I category, contending power groups (including the anti-central government factions) have focused on the Ex-Col system for their source of support (diplomatic, arms, and so on).

Other Remarks
For obvious reasons, the central power authority (EC) has a greater sympathy from the ex-colonial regime, with the insurgent contending group (I) finding it very difficult to gain access to the international system.

Assessment from Study

(1) *Nigeria*
1. The federal government (EC) directed its main quest for external support to Britain (Ex-Col). While Biafra (the insurgent group) was unlikely to get sympathies from the British government, the Biafran leadership nonetheless continued to seek British goodwill throughout the conflict as it tried elsewhere (France and other West European countries) to break the diplomatic isolation imposed by the federals.
2. Nigeria's (central government) decision to seek Soviet military (and diplomatic) support during this conflict does not prejudice the validity of Proposition VII: it only indicates the freedom of manoeuvrability of the central authority (EC) in the international system. Moreover, in making this move, Lagos had no intention of jeopardising Britain's dominant interests (economic, diplomatic, military) in Nigeria. On the contrary, the fact that the USSR also supported the federal objective of 'One Nigeria' meant that this was not in conflict with Britain's aim. Furthermore, by guaranteeing Soviet

support for its cause, the federals were able to limit the scope (in the international arena) of Biafra's quest for external alliance(s).

(2) Zaïre
1. The central government (EC) basically sought and received overwhelming support from the French government (Ex-Col). In spite of its left-leaning political orientation, the FNLC (I) also sought support from France. It attracted some sympathy from the socialist and communist parties. Predictably, the French government was hostile to the political goal of the FNLC.

Proposition VIII
In conflicts of c(NEC) category, contending power groups have greater latitude to penetrate the international system.

Assessment from Study

Angola
With the absence of an established Ex-Col system in the country, the three contending power groups (MPLA, UNITA, FNLA) had an unlimited freedom to seek support and alliances in the international system.
1. MPLA – USSR, all East European powers, Cuba, Nigeria and others.
2. FNLA-UNITA – USA, South Africa, Zaïre, Zambia and others.

C MOTIVE FOR INTERVENTION

The following are possible reasons for external intervention in the conflicts studied[3]:
(i) Economic benefits due to existing (or ascertainable) interests in the crisis state.
(ii) Military – this could involve the wish of external powers to seek bases in the crisis territory for the purpose of launching future operations against enemy forces or interests. Alternatively, bases could be sought as a denial strategy with reference to potential or known adversaries.

The Dynamics of Intervention: A Comparative Survey

(iii) Seeking diplomatic influence in a crisis state where hitherto none existed (in certain situations, (ii) and (iii) could merge into one broad motive).

Proposition IX
The intervention of Western powers (and South Africa) in the conflicts are aimed at defending existing economic, financial and strategic interests in the crisis state.

Assessment from Study

(1) *Nigeria*
1. British support for the continuation of the Nigerian federation (the political objective of the EC in the conflict) was aimed at protecting its economic and financial interests in the country. It was Britain's calculation that if the federation broke up, the effect would disrupt and threaten the *integrated* features of these interests.
2. French support for Biafra, albeit limited, was a demonstration of France's historical economic rivalry with Britain in this part of West Africa.
3. The United States, another Western power of major economic relevance in Nigeria, provided full diplomatic backing to Britain's intervention in the war.

(2) *Angola*
1. The United States identified the FNLA-UNITA coalition as the contending power group which was prepared to safeguard its huge economic investment in the country after the defeat of Portuguese imperialism. Washington considered the MPLA hostile to its economic interests, especially given the latter's well-known post-independence socialist reconstruction economic programme.
2. South Africa intervened in the Angolan War for similar economic and strategic considerations. Pretoria had several joint economic schemes with the Portuguese in Angola during the colonial era. Portuguese Angola was also the northwestern frontier of the *cordon sanitaire* of states that formed South Africa's outer perimeter security network prior to 1974.

(3) Zaïre
1. French interventions in the Shaba I and II conflicts were clearly intended to safeguard France's economic, industrial and strategic interests in Zaïre.
2. The United States' intervention was also dictated by similar considerations.

Proposition X
The intervention of the Soviet Union in the conflicts is aimed at either seeking or preserving political/diplomatic influence in the crisis state.

Assessment from Study

(1) Nigeria
1. The Soviet Union was principally involved in the civil war in an attempt to seek political influence in a country where the previous civilian government (1960–66) was noticeably hostile to a Soviet presence. Soviet support for the federal cause in Nigeria did not initiate the sort of controversy in the West as did its intervention in Angola. This was because in Nigeria the Soviet Union backed the group (central government) which the dominant Western power (Britain) supported. This 'confluence of interest' meant that no East-West ideological clashes were envisaged, nor indeed developed.

(2) Angola
1. The Soviet support for the MPLA in 1975 was a case of continuing political and military cooperation between Moscow and this political movement which began in 1961.

Other Remarks
1. The position of Cuba – this arises only in the case of the Angolan conflict. As we have already indicated, Cuba's intervention in Angola was significantly successful because it was operating in a c(NEC) civil war category. Furthermore, its objective (MPLA victory) coincided with that of one of the active superpowers (SP) in the conflict (the Soviet Union). Elsewhere, Cuba's opposition to Soviet support of the Ethiopian war against the Eritrean independence movement is less

widely appreciated. This is precisely because this conflict is of the EC-I category.

D MODE OF INTERVENTION

The following modes of intervention by external parties in the conflicts studied were examined[4]:
(i) Active diplomatic support for preferred contending power groups in the crisis state. All external parties behaved in this way except in two cases, namely France's limited diplomatic support for Biafra (Nigeria), and Angola's subdued backing for the FNLC (Zaïre).
(ii) Clandestine activities carried out in the crisis state by an external party on behalf of a favoured contending power group. The United States' CIA activities in Angola (on behalf of the FNLA-UNITA) and the SDECE (French secret service) operations in Shaba province (on behalf of the Zaïrean central government) are prominent in this regard.
(iii) Military intervention. In the Angolan War, this involved the Soviet Union, the United States, Cuba, South Africa and Zaïre. In the Zaïrean conflict, interventions were organised by the United States, France, Belgium, Morocco, Egypt and Sudan, while in the Nigerian War the intervening powers were Britain, the Soviet Union, France and Egypt.

E CONSEQUENCES OF INTERVENTION

Proposition XI
The outcome of civil wars in former British and/or French states is always dependent on the behaviour of the Ex-Col-SASS dyad, with the ASS playing a subordinate role.

Comment
1. This proposition has already been assessed and validated as part of the other dimensions of this study.

Proposition XII
In territories other than former British and/or French col-

onies, the outcome of civil conflicts depends on the behaviour of the SP system.

Comment
1. Just as in Proposition XI, this has been shown to be true in this study.

Proposition XIII
In civil conflicts in Africa, the outcome is dependent on the nature of the response of the extracontinental power(s).

Comment
1. This last proposition underlines the conclusions we reached in the conflicts we studied. It is our contention that in spite of the local origins of each of the three conflicts, the ultimate victory of the respective contending power group (MPLA, federal Nigeria, Zaïre central government) was *critically dependent* on the strength of support (principally military and political) it derived from non-African parties.

6 Conclusions: Conflict, Intervention and the Future

CONFLICTS AND HUMAN RIGHTS

Most African leaders who attended the 22nd regular summit of the Organisation of African Unity in Addis Ababa in July 1986 were startled by the unprecedented frankness in the speech made by President Yoweri Museveni of Uganda on Africa's policy toward Uganda during a decade of tyranny by the Idi Amin, Milton Obote and Bassilio Okello regimes. Museveni, who earlier on in January 1986 led the Uganda National Resistance Movement to power after five years of armed struggle against these dictatorships, condemned the virtual silence of African governments on events in Uganda during which an estimated three-quarters of a million people were killed: 'Ugandans were unhappy and felt a deep sense of betrayal that most of Africa kept silent while tyrants killed them'.[1] Museveni was particularly critical of sections in the OAU charter which emphasise the 'non-interference in (states') internal affairs',[2] noting: '[these] should not be used as a cloak to shield genocide from just censure ... Africa's silence in the face of such abuses tends to undermine our moral authority to condemn the excesses of others, especially South Africa's racist regime ... Tyranny is colour blind and should be no less reprehensible because it is perpetrated by one of our kind ...'[3]

From Tunis to Pretoria, Bissau to Nairobi, a distinct and typical feature of the condition of the average African national is the ease with which his/her life, or its vital supportive social conditions, falls prey to the pervasive forces of the state. Well over six million Africans have died since 1960 as a result of massacres, civil conflicts and adverse social policies perpetrated by various African regimes or their agents on national minorities, or the broad sectors of the people. This figure represents about three times the number of Africans who died confronting (direct) European colonialism in different parts of the continent over the past 30 years including Algeria, Kenya, Mozambique, Angola, Namibia and South Africa.

One of the consequences of the general course of European imperialism in Africa in the past 500 years (the slave trade, conquest, colonialism and neocolonialism) has been the virtual devaluation of African life. Very few African governments have tried seriously to reverse this appalling trend in the post-colonial epoch. On the contrary, African life currently appears 'most dispensable' in comparison with the rest of humanity. It is against this background that Museveni's speech in Addis Ababa acquires an all-time urgency.

Apart from the fact that the silence of African governments to these heinous crimes of two decades amounts to some complicity with the perpetrators, the ironic historical situation has emerged whereby regimes elsewhere, especially in the West and definitely including those whose past and present policies towards Africa have clearly laid the foundation for the crisis, now lecture Africa (and indeed the rest of the world!) on human rights issues. This is a hypocritical gesture for obvious reasons. Moreover, Western 'concern' for human rights violations in Africa is extremely uneven and inconsistent: regimes usually regarded as pro-Western (most) do not often form the focus of criticism in this field. In this regard, it is more likely for orchestrated protests to be made by Western governments if human rights were trampled upon in Burkina Faso and Angola, than say Kenya or the Côte d'Ivoire. Yet, this form of choice process once again underscores the point we made earlier on about the devaluation of African life – *for some reasons*, it appears to have a measure of greater worth in Burkina Faso than in Côte d'Ivoire!

By taking the issue of human rights in Africa to the high profile of OAU summitry, President Museveni has tried to achieve four important objectives. First, he has rescued such an important subject from the hypocritical and distortive treatment that we have just referred to. Second, the emphasis that human rights must be a fundamental concern to an African head of state (because 'Tyranny is colour blind and

Conclusions: Conflict, Intervention and the Future   153

should be no less reprehensible because it is perpetrated by one of our kind.') Third, African states should openly criticise human rights violations anywhere in the continent and give support to the resistance organised by the victims. Fourth, Museveni shows quite clearly that conflicts, of varying features, in contemporary Africa underlie these human rights violations.

CONFLICTS, DEVELOPMENT, PEACE

In a recent study of the interrelated issues of conflicts, peace, human rights and development in Africa, Okwudiba Nnoli advocates two sets of agenda for the future.[4] Firstly, the strategic recommendations. These presuppose a liberated Africa which focuses on the accomplishment of the following tasks as of utmost priority[5]: (1) the reorganisation of the economy in order to optimise the complementarity of skills and occupations, and to strive for an integration between the 'horizontal' and 'vertical' spheres of economic activities; (2) emphasis on food production to eliminate the current scourge of hunger, starvation and scarcity; (3) transformation of the rural economy, the home of the majority of Africans, to provide the three 'basics' – food, shelter and healthcare; (4) transformation of cultural and scientific institutions aimed at providing mass literacy and universal access to primary, secondary, tertiary and leisurely education – this is a new society where the state 'must intervene to eliminate or, at least, ameliorate the effects of those forces which prevent the individual from contributing the maximum to production ... as well as the right to enjoy cultural benefits and freedom of scientific, technical and artistic work',[6] and (5) the reinvestment *internally* of the enormous African capital continuously being transferred to the West. Employing a Cabralian paraphrase, Nnoli asserts: 'Until the African masses are put squarely back into history, the search for peace, development and regional security in Africa can not even begin'.[7]

Nnoli's other agenda for action is designated 'tactical',[8] and is of immediate relevance to our study. Nnoli calls for the demilitarisation of African states, under the aegis of an

OAU-sponsored African summit conference, and action against South Africa. Apart from those states which are on the firing line of the aggression from Pretoria, most African countries do not have a serious *external* security threat. Ninety per cent of African military, police and other security apparatus are therefore directed against sectors of the local population who oppose the prevailing harsh political economy – national minorities, workers, peasants, journalists, academics, and the like. Not surprisingly, an overwhelming number of African regimes annually spend more on their military and security agencies than on total expenditure allocated to health, education and housing for the people.[9] Against this background, it is highly unlikely that an OAU summit will make any headway on a pressing subject such as demilitarisation – leaders whose existential preoccupation is to survive in power at all costs will not be in a hurry to catch a plane to attend a conference aimed at dismantling or reducing the weaponry that bolsters the militarised and repressive institutions that sustain the civil conflicts so endemic in contemporary Africa. Instead, campaigns for continental demilitarisation should be incorporated within existing democratic and popular struggles waged in many an African country. The progressive intelligentsia should be able to organise regional or all-Africa conferences on the subject. Research information exchanged and published thereafter would greatly enhance the objectives of the campaign initiative.

Yet Nnoli's appeal to an OAU initiative on demilitarisation has a strategic relevance towards finding a lasting solution to Africa's conflicts. He is anxious to place on the agenda of Africa's highest supranational assembly a subject which will ultimately force African leaders to discuss seriously the numerous civil conflicts that presently rage in a number of countries on the continent, and which have been responsible for the deaths of thousands of people either through direct combat or through hunger and starvation, as the examples of Ethiopia and Sudan particularly show. In this context, Nnoli is complementing the important move begun by President Museveni in 1986 of wishing an open African discussion on pressing issues that could fundamentally amount to breeching OAU guidelines on 'non-interference in states'

Conclusions: Conflict, Intervention and the Future

internal affairs'. The other point, of course, is that Nnoli is aware that his 'strategic recommendations for action', presented above, cannot be achieved in an Africa still ravaged by civil conflicts.

CONFLICTS, INTERVENTIONS AND THE FUTURE

As we have shown in this study, especially in chapters 2–4, what lies at the centre of continuing civil conflicts in Africa is the alienating imperative of the post-colonial African state. The African state is still essentially the trading post created by European imperialism, and for its peoples, particularly national minorities, the state has no organic essence. It is a 'non-national state',[10] and it hardly makes any difference whether the prevailing or 'official' political economy of the state in question is capitalist (for instance, Nigeria) or 'post'-capitalist (for example, Ethiopia).

It is therefore not surprising that 30 years after Africa's post-colonial independence, the sites of the continent's intellectual and other cultural creativity remain located in the crucibles of its various nations: Yoruba, Wolof, Kikuyu, Igbo, Eritrean, Ashanti, Somali, Baganda, Bakongo, and so on; as for the state, it appears to exist primarily to police the crisis of neocolonialism with such ruthlessness that characterises the present epoch.[11] It is a cruel irony that six million Africans have had to die in the past 20 years in conflicts that centre principally on whether or not one African nation or another should belong to states created strategically by European imperialism to exploit the people and their resources. This European 'scissors and paste job' has indeed caused Africa 'much blood and tears',[12] and it requires a concerted and robust African intellectual and political opinion to prevail on the state authorities in Ethiopia, Sudan, Morocco and elsewhere to come to terms at once with the political aspirations of national liberation movements in their territories, and save the continent the anguish of further loss of precious lives and the waste of scarce resources caused by ongoing civil conflicts. As Nzongola-Ntalaja appropriately notes, '[t]he dogma of the preservation of colonially-inherited boundaries should not become a licence that governments can use to oppress minorities or the screen behind which to hide their incompetence and indifference to the suffering of the peoples'.[13]

Furthermore, such a concerted African opinion, which acknowledges the legitimacy of these national liberation struggles in post-colonial Africa, would be able to build up a momentum to check the external interventionism, discussed in chapter 5, which has been particularly pervasive and overwhelming in African conflicts precisely because the contemporary African state shares with the rest of the 'international' community, especially the superpower system, a spurious consensus that advocates the 'inviolability' of the territorial character of post-colonial Africa. As we have shown, this 'consensus' has prevailed at the expense of millions of African lives in the past two decades and tens of thousands of potential fatalities are envisaged if the present conflicts continue unabated.

It has been demonstrated in this study that for the West, African conflicts have been opportunities to intervene to defend and reinforce age-long economic and strategic interests so entrenched all over the continent. As for the Soviet Union, interventions in African conflicts have acted as essential leverage in expanding its own strategic influence, as part of its global rivalry and competition with the West. In the conflicts in the Horn of Africa presently, Soviet interventionism is inextricably linked to Ethiopia's desperate attempt to destroy the Eritrean national liberation movement where one of Africa's most advanced post-colonial societal reconstructions is being carried out. Mohamed Babu has solemnly observed:

> Quite frankly, the Soviet Union has different priorities, quite often not incorporating the objective goals of Africa. Once in a time the Soviet Union was a revolutionary power and base. Now it is preoccupied with superpower manoeuvering – trying to match US global objectives with its own globalist considerations. It is a shock that the state of the Soviet Union with an admirable revolutionary tradition of Lenin ... would, today ... be spearheading the Ethiopian offensive to destroy the Eritrean revolution – to bombard cities, to bombard villages, to bombard nomads,

to bombard peasants in the fields. Eritrean kids are slaughtered with Soviet napalm. This is unacceptable. This is not associated with what we know of socialist morality.[14]

The March 1988 stunning success of the major Eritrean offensive against the Ethiopian military may not only be a turning point in the 26-year-old conflict,[15] Africa's longest national liberation war, but it could represent a strategic defeat for external interventionism in conflicts in Africa, considering that the Eritreans have had to depend on *internal* resources (Ethiopian weaponry, self-manufactured) for their arms procurement for this attack and the current phase of the defence of their homeland.

African politics in the 1990s, and through the course of the early decades of the next century, will be dominated centrally by the issue of nationality. The 1960s' dogma of the 'sanctity' of the post-colonial state's political boundaries, which was decreed by the continent's political 'establishment', has to be abandoned to ensure that constituent nations and peoples in the existing states should decide democratically on the reconstitution of the state system in Africa, based explicitly on the *domestic* interests of the peoples concerned. African peoples, just like peoples elsewhere in the world, should decide freely to which state, old or new, they wish to belong. Bludgeoning peoples into one state or the other through the ruthless might of the armed forces, and supported lavishly by external interventionism, has caused Africa the death of six million inhabitants since 1960. Surely, this carnage must be brought to a halt.

The African post-colonial state in which 'departing' European imperialists clobbered together nations and principalities of varying political, cultural, religious and ideational heritage 30 years ago, has failed abysmally to create an organic national sensibility within its population, a precondition for the accomplishment of the extensive reconstruction of society in the aftermath of the colonial occupation.

The fact, though, was that the realisation of such a national sensibility in this state, was foreclosed right from the outset, as its European creators were keen to continue to exercise influence in the politics of the area in future, in furtherance of their own historical economic and strategic interests. This European interest ensures presently that while there has been a virtual collapse of socio-economic development in most of Africa, the state nonetheless fulfils its historic role as the agency through which Europe, and countries elsewhere, extract enormous surplus product from the continent, as we have shown clearly in this study. The cost has been devastating – the ever-worsening poverty and deprivation among the peoples.

Notes

1 Conflict and Intervention in Africa

1. For a useful background survey of both theoretical and historical literature on the subject, see especially the following: various contributions in the special edition on 'Intervention' in the *Journal of International Affairs*, 22 (2), 1968, particularly essays by James Rosenau, Andrew Scott, Oran Young and William Zartman; James Rosenau, 'Intervention as a Scientific Concept', *Journal of Conflict Resolution*, 13 (2), 1968, pp. 165–87; C. R. Mitchell, 'Civil Strife and the Involvement of External Parties', *International Studies Quarterly*, 14 (2), 1970, pp. 166–94; F. S. Pearson, 'Geographic Proximity and Foreign Military Intervention', *Journal of Conflict Resolution*, 18 (3), 1974, pp. 432–60; Morton Kaplan, 'Intervention in Internal War: Some Systemic Sources', in James Rosenau (ed.), *International Aspects of Civil Strife* (Princeton: Princeton University Press, 1964), pp. 92–121; K. J. Holsti, *International Politics* (London: Prentice/Hall International, 1974); Richard Little, *Intervention – External Involvement in Civil Wars* (London: Martin Robertson, 1975); Richard J. Barnet, *Intervention and Revolution* (London: Paladin, 1972); V. Kubalkova and A. A. Cruicksank, *Marxism-Leninism and the Theory of International Relations* (London: Routledge & Kegan Paul, 1980); Mohammed Ayoob (ed.), *Conflict and Intervention in the Third World* (London: Croom Helm, 1980); Bereket Habte Selassie, *Conflict and Intervention in the Horn of Africa* (New York and London: Monthly Review Press, 1980); Noam Chomsky, 'The Cold War and the Superpowers', *Monthly Review*, 33 (6), 1981, pp. 1–10; Chomsky, 'The United States: From Greece to El Salvador', in Noam Chomsky, et al., *Superpowers in Collision* (Harmondsworth: Penguin, 1982), pp. 20–42; Chomsky, 'Strategic Arms, the Cold War and the Third World', in *New Left Review* (ed.), *Exterminism and Cold War* (London: Verso, 1982), pp. 223–36; Chomsky, 'Intervention in Vietnam and Central America: Parallels and Differences', *Monthly Review*, 37 (4), 1985, pp. 1–29; Roger Burbach and Patricia Flynn (eds), *The Politics of Intervention: The United States in Central America* (New York and London: Monthly Review Press, 1984); Harry Magdoff and Paul Sweezy, 'Lessons of Vietnam', *Monthly Review*, 37 (2), 1985, pp. 1–13; Magdoff and

Sweezy, 'International Cooperation – A Way Out?', in *Monthly Review*, 39 (6), 1987, pp. 1–19; 'Interview with Paul Sweezy', *Monthly Review*, 38 (11), 1987, pp. 1–28; 'The World Crisis of the 1980s: An Interview with Samir Amin', 33 (2), 1981, pp. 33–43; Fred Halliday, *The Making of the Second Cold War* (London: Verso, 1983), and Halliday, *Beyond Irangate: The Reagan Doctrine and the Third World* (Amsterdam: Transnational Institute, 1987).
2. C. R. Mitchell, 'Civil Strife and the Involvement of External Parties', ibid., pp. 182–94.
3. See Morton Kaplan, 'Intervention in Internal War: Some Systemic Sources', in Rosenau (ed.), op. cit., and Frederic Pearson, 'Geographic Proximity and Foreign Military Intervention', op. cit.
4. See, for instance, K. J. Holsti, *International Politics*, op. cit., p. 279.
5. Mitchell, op. cit., pp. 182–94.
6. Pearson, op. cit.
7. Emmanuel Hansen (ed.), *Africa: Perspectives on Peace and Development* (London and New Jersey: Zed Books, 1987), p. 6.
8. See particularly the following: Latin American Bureau, *The Poverty Brokers: The IMF and Latin America* (London: Latin America Bureau, 1983); Chinweizu, 'Debt Trap Peonage', *Monthly Review*, 37 (6), 1985, pp. 21–36; Harry Magdoff, 'Third World Debt: Past and Present', *Monthly Review*, 37 (9), 1986; Peter Korner, *et al.*, *The IMF and the Debt Crisis: A Guide to the Third World's Dilemmas* (London: Zed Books, 1986); John Clark, *For Richer, For Poorer: An Oxfam Report on Western Connections with World Hunger* (Oxford: Oxfam, 1986); Jacobo Schatan, *World Debt: Who is to Pay?* (London and New Jersey: Zed Books, 1987); Frederick Clairmonte and John Cavanagh, 'Impossible debt on road to global ruin', *Guardian* (London), 9 January 1987; Samir Amin, 'The State and the Question of "Development"', in Peter Anyang' Nyong'o (ed.), *Popular Struggles for Democracy in Africa* (London and New Jersey: Zed Books, 1987), and Susan George, *A Fate Worse Than Debt* (Harmondsworth: Pelican, 1988).
9. Frederick Clairmonte and John Cavanagh, 'Impossible debt on road to global ruin', ibid.
10. Ibid.
11. Ibid.
12. Ibid.
13. See *For Richer, For Poorer: An Oxfam Report on Western Connections with World Hunger*, op. cit.
14. Clairmonte and Cavanagh, op. cit.

Notes

15. Ibid.
16. Ibid.
17. Mitchell, op. cit., and passim.
18. Fred Halliday, *The Making of the Second Cold War*, op. cit., p. 92.
19. Ibid., pp. 105–33; pp. 172–202.
20. S. Neil MacFarlane, *Superpower Rivalry and 3rd World Radicalism: The Idea of National Liberation* (London and Sydney: Croom Helm, 1985), especially ch. 5.
21. 'Thomas Borge on the Nicaraguan Revolution: Interview by Frederic Jameson', *New Left Review*, No. 164, July/August 1987, p. 55.
22. Basil Davidson, 'Precondition For Peace', *West Africa*, 1 February 1988, p. 175.
23. MacFarlane, op. cit., p. 199.
24. Fred Halliday, *Beyond Irangate: The Reagan Doctrine and the Third World*, op. cit.
25. Ibid., pp. 18–21, and 'Interview with Paul Sweezy', op. cit., p. 27.
26. Halliday, *The Making of the Second Cold War*, op. cit., ch. 5; Noam Chomsky, in *Superpowers in Collision*, op. cit., pp. 33–42, and Sweezy, ibid., pp. 26–8.
27. Halliday, *Beyond Irangate*, op. cit., p. 8.
28. See Fidel Castro, *A Pyrrhic Military Victory And A Profound Moral Defeat* (La Habana: Editoria Politica, 1983).

2 Nigeria

1. On the contrary, the January 1966 coup *was not* an Igbo plot to take over the Nigerian political establishment. An April 1966 report on the coup prepared by the Special Branch of the Nigerian Police came to this conclusion. (See, for instance, John de St. Jorre, *The Nigerian Civil War* (London: Hodder & Stoughton, 1972), pp. 31–47). Other literature on the civil war that repudiate the 'Igbo plot' allegation include Olusegun Obasanjo, *Nzeogwu* (Ibadan: Spectrum Books, 1987), Adewale Ademoyega, *Why We Struck: The Story of the First Nigerian Coup* (Ibadan: Evans Brothers, 1981), Ben Gbulie, *Nigeria's Five Majors: Coup D'état of 15th January 1966 – First Inside Account* (Onitsha: African Educational Publisher, 1981), and Alexander A. Madiebo, *The Nigerian Revolution and the Biafran War* (Enugu: Fourth Dimensions Publishers, 1980). Obasanjo's position is particularly important because he was not only

a federal civil war hero, but also a post-war head of state. (See Herbert Ekwe-Ekwe, 'Notes on a Controversy', *West Africa*, 2 March 1987, p. 418).
2. These forces were until then not integrated into the national police force, and were often deployed by local politicians for the intimidation of opponents, and the rigging of elections during the era of the civilian government.
3. See Herbert Ekwe-Ekwe, 'The Nigerian Plight: Shagari to Buhari', *Third World Quarterly*, 7 (3), 1985, p. 619.
4. See de St. Jorre, op. cit., p. 95.
5. Communication with Raph Uwechue, editor-in-chief, *Africa* newsmagazine, 9 November 1979.
6. Cf. John Stremlau, *The International Politics of the Nigerian Civil War* (Princeton, New Jersey: Princeton University Press, 1977), p. 51.
7. Quoted in A. H. M. Kirk-Greene, *Crisis and Conflict in Nigeria*, *Vol. I* (London: Oxford University Press, 1971), p. 413.
8. Ibid., p. 374.
9. Ibid.
10. See, for instance, Billy Dudley, *An Introduction to Nigerian Government and Politics* (London and Basingstoke: Macmillan, 1982), pp. 278–9.
11. Cf. Stemlau, op. cit., p. 10.
12. Ibid.
13. For a recent focus on the background to Britain's strategic control of Nigeria's economy, see Toyin Falola (ed.), *Britain and Nigeria: Exploitation or Development?* (London and New Jersey: Zed Books, 1987).
14. Quoted in Stremlau, op. cit., p. 5.
15. Dudley, op. cit., p. 283.
16. Cf. General Olusegun Obasanjo, *My Command: An account of the Nigerian Civil War, 1967–70* (Ibadan and London: Heinemann, 1980), p. 146.
17. Ibid. See also Suzanne Cronje, *The World and Nigeria: The Diplomatic History of the Biafra War* (London: Sidgwick & Jackson, 1972), p. 17.
18. Cf. Cronje, ibid., p. 20; de St. Jorre, op. cit., p. 295.
19. Cronje, ibid.
20. See Sam Epelle (ed.), *Nigeria Speaks: Speeches of Alhaji Sir Abubakar Tafawa Balewa* (Lagos: Longman, 1964), p. 10.
21. Oye Ogunbadejo, 'Ideology and Pragmatism: The Soviet Role in Nigeria, 1960–1977', *Orbis*, Winter 1978, p. 810.
22. Ibid.
23. Ibid., p. 811.
24. Ibid.

25. For a very informed review of British government thinking at this time, see Cronje, op. cit., especially chapters 1–3. See also de St. Jorre, op. cit., pp. 138–41, and Obasanjo, *My Command*, op. cit., p. 149.
26. Cronje, passim.
27. Obasanjo, op. cit., pp. 149–50.
28. David Hunt, *On the Spot: An Ambassador Remembers* (London: Peter Davies, 1975), p. 194.
29. De St. Jorre, op. cit., p. 295.
30. Quoted in Cronje, op. cit., p. 60.
31. For details of British weapons sent to Nigeria at this early stage of the war, see Cronje, ibid., pp. 33–4.
32. Cronje, ibid., p. 60.
33. 'Nigerian Arms Imports, 1967–1969', in *Nigerian Trade Summary*, The Chief Federal Statistician, Lagos, 1970 (Quoted in Cronje, op. cit., pp. 385–93).
34. A useful discussion of the background to the British exploitation of Nigeria's tin mines, and the multilayered forms of workers' resistance can be found in William Freund, 'Theft and social protest among tin miners of northern Nigeria', Donald Crummey (ed.), *Banditry, Rebellion and Social Protest in Africa* (London/Portsmouth: James Currey/Heinemann, 1986), pp. 49–63.
35. For a detailed discussion of British involvement in Nigeria, see Victor Diejomah, 'The Economics of the Nigerian Conflict', in Joseph Okpaku (ed.), *Nigeria: Dilemma of Nationhood* (New York: Third Press, 1972), pp. 318–63, and Toyin Falola (ed.), op. cit., passim. For an insight into Britain's favourable trade balance with Nigeria during this period, see *Nigeria Trade Summary*, op. cit.
36. Compare with Cronje, op. cit., p. 119. For an account of Unilever's enormous interests in the Nigerian economy, see the excellent study by Ikenna Nzimiro, 'The Political Implications of Multinational Corporations in Nigeria', in Carl Widstrand (ed.), *Multi-National Firms in Africa* (Dakar/Uppsala: African Institute for Economic Development and Planning/ Scandinavian Institute of African Studies, 1975), pp. 210–43. See also Magery Perham, *Mining, Commerce and Finance in Nigeria* (London: Faber & Faber, 1948), Claude Ake (ed.), *Political Economy of Nigeria* (London and Lagos: Longman, 1985), especially chapters 1–4; Robert Shenton, *The Development of Capitalism in Northern Nigeria* (London: James Currey, 1986), and Falola (ed.), op. cit., for an informative appraisal of the evolution of British commercial and business interest groups in Nigeria.

37. Nzimiro, op. cit., p. 212–14.
38. Ibid., p. 217.
39. Cronje, op. cit., p. 23.
40. *The Nigerian Review*, January 1968, cited by Cronje, ibid., p. 164.
41. Quoted in Cronje, ibid., p. 38.
42. Ibid., p. 66.
43. House of Commons Debates, *Hansard*, Vol. 779, 13 March 1969, cols 1571–1696.
44. Ibid.
45. See 'Nigerian Arms Imports 1964–1966', in *Nigerian Trade Summary*, The Chief Statistician, Lagos, 1967 (Quoted in Cronje, op. cit., p. 393).
46. Using Nigerian sources (above), and official information elsewhere, Cronje has constructed a comprehensive survey of Nigeria's arms procurement during this period. See especially her ch. 3.
47. Ibid., p. 393.
48. Published in the *Sunday Telegraph* (London), 11 January 1970 (quoted in Cronje, ibid., p. 61).
49. *Economist*, 24 August 1968 (cited in Stremlau, op. cit., p. 331).
50. Cronje, op. cit., pp. 80–1.
51. Stremlau, op. cit., p. 80.
52. Cronje, op. cit., p. 62.
53. Ibid.
54. Ibid., p. 62–3.
55. *New York Times*, 10 June 1967.
56. *The Times* (London), 4 December 1967.
57. Communication: Uwechue.
58. For a comprehensive report on mercenaries recruited by both sides in the war, see de St. Jorre, op. cit., ch. 12.
59. *The Times*, 17 August 1967.
60. See Cronje, op. cit., p. 56.
61. De St. Jorre, op. cit., p. 315.
62. See Cronje, op. cit., pp. 44–5, 61–2.
63. Ibid., p. 82.
64. Ibid., pp. 99–100.
65. In *Strategic Survey 1967* (London: IISS, 1968), p. 37.
66. See A. H. M. Kirk-Greene, *Crisis and Conflict in Nigeria, Vol. II* (London: Oxford University Press, 1971), pp. 221–33.
67. Cronje, op. cit., p. 72.
68. Ibid.
69. Ibid.
70. Cf. Stremlau, op. cit., p. 227.

Notes   165

71. Cf. de St. Jorre, op. cit., p. 211; General Ojukwu himself observed: '... But our enemies have been so impressed by the moral aid given to us by France that they have savagely stepped up their military operations against Biafra. What we need now is for this moral aid to be matched by military and diplomatic measures'. (Cited in Cronje, op. cit., p. 203.)
72. See, for instance, the following: Margery Perham, 'Reflections on the Nigerian Civil War', *International Affairs*, Vol. 46, April 1970, pp. 240–4; Perham, 'Nigeria's Civil War', in Colin Legum (ed.), *Africa Contemporary Record* (hereinafter, *ACR*), 1968–69 (New York: Africana, 1968), pp. 10–12; Cronje, op. cit., pp. 194–209; Martin Edmonds, 'Civil War and Arms Sales: The Nigerian-Biafran War and Other Cases', in Robin Higham (ed.), *Civil Wars in the Twentieth Century* (Lexington: University Press of Kentucky, 1972), p. 208; de St. Jorre, op. cit., pp. 210–18; Raph Uwechue, *Reflections on the Nigerian Civil War* (Paris: Jeune Afrique, 1971), especially ch. 6, and Stremlau, op. cit., pp. 224–33.
73. Stremlau, ibid., p. 225.
74. See *ACR*, 1968–69, op. cit., p. 570.
75. De St. Jorre, op. cit., p. 213.
76. Communication: Uwechue.
77. Ibid.
78. Ibid.
79. *Reflections on the Nigerian Civil War*, p. 98.
80. *The Nigerian Civil War*, p. 218.
81. Quoted in Stremlau, op. cit., p. 233.
82. Ibid., pp. 230–2.
83. Cronje, ibid., p. 81, and Kennedy Lindsay, 'How Biafra Pays for the War', *Venture*, March 1969, p. 27 (cited in Stremlau, op. cit., p. 231).
84. Cf. Stremlau, ibid., pp. 230–1.
85. Ibid., p. 232.
86. De St. Jorre, op. cit., p. 215.
87. Ibid.
88. Ibid.
89. Cf. Stremlau, op. cit., p. 233.
90. Ibid.
91. See Bernard Odogwu, *No Place to Hide (Crises and Conflicts Inside Biafra)* (Enugu: Fourth Dimension, 1985), especially ch. 10.
92. Communication: Uwechue; de St. Jorre, op. cit., p. 219.
93. Stremlau, op. cit., p. 234.
94. Quoted in Cronje, op. cit., p. 225.

95. For an appraisal of the successful growth of United States' investment in post-independent Nigeria, see Kathleen Langley, 'The External Resource factor in Nigerian Economic Development', *Nigerian Journal of Economic and Social Studies*, 4 (3), 1968, pp. 17–19. See also Oye Ogunbadejo, 'A new turn in US-Nigerian relations', *The World Today*, March 1979, pp. 122–4.
96. Cronje, op. cit., p. 225. See also Obasanjo, *My Command*, p. 149.
97. Cf. Obasanjo, ibid.
98. See de St. Jorre, op. cit., p. 302.
99. Cronje, op. cit., p. 225.
100. Ibid., p. 241; Ogunbadejo, 'Ideology and Pragmatism', p. 813, and Okwudiba Nnoli, 'Realising Peace, Development and Regional Security in Africa: A Plan for Action', in Emmanuel Hansen (ed.), op. cit., p. 222.
101. Quoted in *Crisis and Conflict in Nigeria, Vol. II*, pp. 334–5.
102. Stremlau, op. cit., p. 286.
103. Cronje, op. cit., p. 234.
104. See 'Charter of the Organisation of African Unity', Appendix A, in Okpaku (ed.), op. cit., pp. 281–409.
105. Article II, Ic., ibid., p. 282.
106. Article III, 1–3, ibid., p. 383.
107. Cf. N. Nziramasaga, 'Secession, Federalism and African Unity', in Okpaku (ed.), ibid., p. 229.
108. See 'Why we recognised Biafra', Kirk-Greene, op. cit., p. 211.
109. Ibid., p. 212.
110. During the 1979 OAU conference in Monrovia, President Nyerere found himself defending his country's military involvement in overthrowing the government of a neighbouring state, the Amin regime in Uganda, which was also a member of the OAU. He rejected accusations from some delegates, especially from Nigeria's General Obasanjo, that Tanzania's action amounted to a violation of the OAU charter.
111. Communication: Uwechue.
112. Ibid.
113. Cited in Cronje, op. cit., pp. 297–8.
114. Cf. de St. Jorre, op. cit., p. 196.
115. Ibid.
116. *The World and Nigeria*, p. 300.
117. Ibid., p. 290.
118. See de St. Jorre, op. cit., p. 192.
119. Quoted in Okpaku, op. cit., p. 411.
120. Ibid., p. 412.

Notes

121. Cronje, op. cit., p. 293.
122. Ibid.
123. *ACR*, 1969–70, op. cit., p. C5.
124. *New York Times*, 30 April 1968.
125. *Daily Express* (London, 3 April 1969).
126. De St. Jorre, op. cit., p. 219.
127. See below for details. See also Obasanjo, *My Command*, p. 150.
128. De St. Jorre, op. cit., especially ch. 12.
129. Ibid. See also p. 219.
130. Ibid., ch. 12.
131. Sam Epelle (ed.), op. cit., p. 10.
132. See Ogunbadejo, 'Ideology and Pragmatism', p. 808.
133. Ibid.
134. Ibid.
135. Ibid., p. 810.
136. Ibid.
137. Ibid., p. 811.
138. See Cronje, op. cit., p. 253.
139. Ogunbadejo, op. cit., p. 809.
140. Ibid.
141. Cf. de St. Jorre, op. cit., p. 183.
142. See Cronje, op. cit., p. 253.
143. See, for instance, David Morison, 'Soviet Union and Africa', *ACR*, 1968–69, op. cit., p. 40.
144. See Ogunbadejo, op. cit., p. 813.
145. Ibid.
146. Typical of this anti-Soviet position from the French left is a well-publicised statement issued in November 1968, and signed by a number of scholars, including Jean-Paul Sartre and Simone de Beauvoir, in which the Soviet Union, as well as Britain, Egypt and the OAU are attacked for 'patronising genocide' in Biafra. The statement concludes: 'The struggle in Biafra is today the struggle of the whole Left. If the Left ignores it, if it connives at this genocide ... the Left will inevitably pervert its own actions, and it will cease to exist as a movement'. (Quoted in Stremlau, op. cit., p. 227.)
147. See Ogunbadejo, op. cit., p. 814.
148. Ibid.
149. Ibid.
150. Ibid.
151. Ibid.
152. Cf. de St. Jorre, op. cit., p. 181.
153. Ibid.
154. Quoted in ibid., p. 333.
155. Cf. Stremlau, op. cit., p. 80.

3 Angola

1. For details of the Alvor agreement, see 'The Angola Agreement', *ACR*, pp. C221–C226.
2. Cf. Arslan Humbaraci and Nicole Muchnik, *Portugal's African Wars: Angola, Guinea-Bissao, Mozambique* (New York: The Third Press, 1974), p. 120.
3. Cf. John Marcum, *The Angolan Revolution: Vol. II – Exile Politics and Guerrilla Warfare* (Cambridge, Mass.: MIT Press, 1978), p. 9.
4. See Ernest Harsch and Tony Thomas, *Angola: The Hidden History of Washington's War* (New York: Pathfinder Press, 1976), p. 32.
5. See *Angola: Socialism At Birth* (London: Mozambique, Angola and Guinea Information Centre, 1980), p. 10.
6. Marcum, op. cit., p. 166.
7. Ibid.
8. Harsch and Thomas, op. cit., p. 46.
9. Cf. Marcum, op. cit., pp. 179–240.
10. See National Security Council Interdepartmental Group for Africa, Study in Response to National Security Study Memorandum 39: Southern Africa, AF/NSC – 1969, 15 August 1969, published in Mohamed A. El Khawas and Barry Cohen (ed.), *The Kissinger Study of Southern Africa: National Security Memorandum 39* (Westport, Connecticut: Lawrence Hill, 1976), p. 136.
11. Ibid., p. 105. This is the so-called Option 2 (from five available options) which President Nixon adopted as his policy document for Southern Africa.
12. Ibid., p. 90.
13. See Harsch and Thomas, op. cit., p. 50.
14. Ibid. General Spínola, a former governor and commander-in-chief of the Portuguese armed forces in Guinea Bissau, advocated this 'Commonwealth' or 'Federation' solution to the African-occupied territories on the premise that Portugal could not win the colonial wars. He had discussed these views in his book, *Portugal e o Futuro* (Lisbon: Arcadia, 1974).
15. For full details of the United States' covert activities to ensure the victory of the anti-MPLA liberation movements, see John Stockwell, *In Search of Enemies* (London: Andre Deutsch, 1978). Stockwell was chief of operations of the special CIA Angola Task Force with headquarters in Kinshasa in 1975–76.
16. See Humbaraci and Muchnik, op. cit., p. 187.
17. Cf. United States' reaction to Israel whenever the latter uses

US-supplied weapons for *offensive* military operations against Palestinian refugee settlements in Lebanon and elsewhere (which contravenes existing bilateral agreements). While Washington sometimes condemns such violations publicly, it has always been reluctant to discontinue arms deliveries to Israel as a result.
18. Quoted by Humbaraci and Muchnik, op. cit., p. 189.
19. Ibid., p. 189.
20. Ibid.
21. Ibid.
22. Harsch and Thomas, op. cit., p. 17.
23. Ibid.
24. Quoted in ibid., pp. 16–17.
25. Quoted in ibid., p. 17.
26. Quoted in Marcum, op. cit., p. 127.
27. Ibid.
28. Ibid., p. 235.
29. Ibid.
30. See Harsch and Thomas, op. cit., p. 19.
31. Ibid.
32. Cf. Marcum, op. cit., p. 423.
33. Harsch and Thomas, op. cit., p. 19.
34. Ibid.
35. Ibid., p. 20.
36. Ibid.
37. Mário de Andrade and Marc Ollivier, *The War in Angola: A Socio-Economic Study* (Dar es Salaam: Tanzania Publishing House, 1975), p. 79.
38. Stockwell, op. cit., p. 52.
39. Marcum, op. cit., p. 237.
40. Ibid.
41. Ibid.
42. See, for instance, ibid., p. 392.
43. Quoted in ibid., p. 392.
44. See Harsch and Thomas, op. cit., p. 67.
45. Ibid., pp. 67–8. See also Stockwell's revelations of the extent of the CIA's relationship with Savimbi in his *In Search of Enemies*, pp. 138–56.
46. Quoted by Andrade and Ollivier, op. cit., p. 53.
47. Ibid.
48. Cf. Marcum, op. cit., p. 240.
49. Stockwell, op. cit., p. 55.
50. Ibid., p. 54.
51. Ibid., p. 272.
52. See Marcum, op. cit., p. 263.

53. Cited in ibid., p. 439.
54. See Stockwell, op. cit., pp. 267–8.
55. Harsch and Thomas, op. cit., p. 98.
56. Ibid.
57. Stockwell, op. cit., p. 183.
58. Ibid., p. 223.
59. Cited in Harsch and Thomas, op. cit., p. 101.
60. Ibid.
61. Ibid.
62. Ibid.
63. Ibid.
64. Ibid.
65. Ibid.
66. Ibid., pp. 102–4.
67. Ibid., p. 105; Marcum, op. cit., p. 263.
68. Harsch and Thomas, op. cit., p. 105.
69. Ibid.
70. See Marcum, op. cit., pp. 263–81.
71. Marcum, ibid., pp. 262–3; Stockwell, op. cit., pp. 43–4.
72. Stockwell, ibid., p. 272.
73. Harsch and Thomas, op. cit., p. 100.
74. See Marcum, op. cit., pp. 268–72.
75. Ibid., p. 271.
76. See Stockwell, op. cit., pp. 162–8.
77. Ibid., p. 165.
78. Marcum, op. cit., p. 274.
79. Stockwell, op. cit., p. 192.
80. Cf. French Government Policy in Africa: Statement by M. Pierre-Christian Taittinger, Secretary of State for Foreign Affairs, in the National Assembly, 10 June 1977, in *ACR*, 1977–78, op. cit., pp. C11–C14. See also Alexander Rondos, 'France and Africa: A Widening Role', *Africa Report*, September-October 1979, pp. 4–8.
81. Cf. Rondos, ibid., p. 7.
82. Harsch and Thomas, op. cit., p. 108.
83. See Wilfred Burchett, *Southern Africa Stands Up: The Revolutions in Angola, Mozambique, Rhodesia, Namibia and South Africa* (New York: Urizen Books, 1978), pp. 38–45.
84. Marcum, op. cit., p. 443; Gabriel Garcia, Marquez, 'Operation Carlota', *New Left Review*, Nos. 101–2, March-April 1977, p. 125.
85. See Jiri Valenta, 'Soviet Decision-Making on the Intervention in Angola', in David E. Albright (ed.), *Africa and International Communism* (London: Macmillan Press, 1980), p. 96.
86. See, for instance, S. Neil MacFarlane, op. cit., p. 141.

87. Marcum, op. cit., pp. 171–2.
88. Ibid., p. 171.
89. Cited in Valenta, op. cit., p. 97.
90. See Colin Legum, 'Foreign Intervention in Angola', *ACR*, 1974–75, op. cit., p. A13.
91. Ibid., especially pp. A16–A17.
92. Ibid., p. A13.
93. Ibid., p. A17.
94. See Marcum, op. cit., pp. 171–2.
95. Legum, op. cit., p. A17.
96. See also the following studies by Legum: 'The Soviet Union, China and the West in Southern Africa', *Foreign Affairs*, July 1976, pp. 745–62; 'The USSR and Africa – the African Environment', *Problems of Communism*, January-February 1978, Vol. XXVII, pp. 1–19, and 'African Outlooks toward the USSR', in Albright (ed.), op. cit., pp. 7–34.
97. See, for instance, David Albright, 'The USSR and Africa: Soviet Policy', *Problems of Communism*, ibid., pp. 20–39; Jiri Valenta, in *Africa and International Communism*, pp. 93–117; Edward Gonzalez, 'Cuba, the Soviet Union, and Africa', in *Africa and International Communism*, pp. 145–67, and Valenta, 'The Soviet-Cuban Intervention in Angola, 1975', *Studies in Comparative Communism*, Vol. XI, Nos. 1 and 2, Spring/Summer 1978, pp. 3–33.
98. 'Moscow's African Policy of the 1970s', in *Africa and International Communism*, p. 50.
99. Ibid., p. 54.
100. 'Moscow, Angola and the Dialectics of Détente', *The World Today*, Vol. 32, No. 5, 1977, p. 174.
101. 'The African-American Nexus in Soviet Strategy', in Albright (ed.), op. cit., pp. 216–17.
102. 'Cuba, the Soviet Union, and Africa', ibid., p. 153.
103. Albright, ibid., p. 53.
104. Ibid.
105. Ibid., p. 58.
106. Ibid.
107. Ibid., p. 59.
108. Cf. *Africa and International Communism*, passim.
109. Olusegun Obasanjo, quoted by Legum, ibid., p. 28.
110. Cf. Samir Amin: 'What the Soviet Union is really seeking in the Third World is not exploitation in the classical sense, which it is in any case not really capable of, but a strategic position gained by means of alliances'. See Amin, 'Crisis, Nationalism, And Socialism', in Samir Amin, Giovanni Arrighi, *et al.*, *Dynamics of Global Crisis* (London and Basing-

stoke: Macmillan Press, 1982), p. 212.
111. Valenta, in Albright (ed.), op. cit., p. 100.
112. Ibid.
113. Ibid.
114. See Valenta, 'The Soviet-Cuban Intervention in Angola', p. 27.
115. Stockwell, op. cit., p. 232.
116. Marquez, op. cit., p. 124.
117. Quoted by William J. Durch, 'The Cuban Military in Africa and the Middle East: From Algeria to Angola', *Studies in Comparative Communism*, Vol. XI, Nos. 1 and 2, Spring/Summer 1978, p. 46.
118. Marquez, op. cit., p. 124.
119. For those who have particularly stressed this 'surrogate' thesis, see George Volsky, 'Cuba's Foreign Policies', *Current History*, February 1976, pp. 60–72; Peter Vanneman and Martin James, 'The Soviet Intervention in Angola: Intentions and Implication', *Strategic Review*, Summer 1976, pp. 92–103.
120. Durch, op. cit., pp. 36–9.
121. Quoted in Valenta, 'The Soviet-Cuban Intervention in Angola, 1975', p. 23.
122. Durch, op. cit., p. 43.
123. Marquez, op. cit., p. 124. Cuba never publishes military aid to liberation movements or friendly states as it stresses that such support is part of its 'internationalist' duty. Marquez has had a long-term friendship with members of the Cuban leadership, especially President Fidel Castro. For a recollection of the background to this friendship, see, for instance, Marquez, 'My first trip to Havana', *Granma Weekly Review* (Havana), 24 January 1988. Marquez's account of Cuba's intervention in Angola in 'Operation Carlota' is therefore authoritative.
124. 'Operation Carlota', p. 124.
125. Quoted in Durch, op. cit., p. 65.
126. Ibid.
127. Marquez, 'Operation Carlota', p. 128.
128. Legum, 'Foreign Intervention in Angola', p. A15.
129. Cf. Durch, op. cit., p. 71. See also Fidel Castro, *Angola Giron africano* (La Habana: Editorial De Ciencias Sociales, 1976).
130. Marquez, op. cit., p. 127.
131. Jeffrey M. Elliot and Mervyn M. Dymally, an interview, *Fidel Castro: Nothing Can Stop the Course of History* (London and New York: Pathfinder Press, 1986), p. 180.
132. Cf. Durch, op. cit., p. 71, and Burchett, op. cit., p. 314.
133. See *In Search of Enemies*, p. 172.

Notes

134. See 'In These Times', interview in *Journal of African Marxistes*, No. 10, June 1987, pp. 76–7.
135. Quoted by Legum, 'Foreign Intervention in Angola', p. A17.
136. Quoted in George T. Yu, 'Sino-Soviet Rivalry in Africa', in Albright (ed.), op. cit., p. 179.
137. Quoted by Legum, 'Foreign Intervention in Angola', p. A17.
138. Ibid., p. A16.
139. See *Peking Review*, No. 21, 1971. Further publicity of this new foreign policy line was made in *Peking Review*, Nos. 32 and 35, 1971.
140. Legum, 'Foreign Intervention in Angola', p. A15, and Yu, op. cit., pp. 175–7.
141. See Marcum, op. cit., p. 230.
142. Ibid., p. 246.
143. Ibid.
144. Marcum, op. cit., p. 269.
145. See Harsch and Thomas, op. cit., p. 134.
146. Ibid.
147. See Ruth Weiss, 'South Africa: The Grand African Economic Design', *ACR*, 1970–71, pp. A11–A17.
148. See 'The Southern African Customs Agreement', ibid., pp. C275–C281.
149. The 1 April 1980 Lusaka conference of nine Central and Southern African government leaders (without South Africa) formally rejected this projected Pretoria-led economic community. They instead worked out a long-term programme of lessening the existing economic ties that their countries had with South Africa. This marked the beginning of the Southern African Development Cooperation Conference (SADCC).
150. Marcum, op. cit., p. 266.
151. Ibid.
152. Ibid.
153. Ibid.
154. Ibid.
155. Ibid., p. 440.
156. Ibid., p. 269, and Harsch and Thomas, p. 124.
157. Harsch and Thomas, ibid.
158. Quoted in ibid., p. 126.
159. *In Search of Enemies*, p. 186.
160. See Legum, 'Foreign Intervention in Angola', pp. A31–A32.
161. For a useful discussion of the Nigerian diplomatic recognition of the MPLA government, see Abiodun Sotumbi, *Nigeria's Recognition of the MPLA Government of Angola: A Case-Study in*

Decision-Making and Implementation (Lagos: Nigerian Institute of International Affairs, Monograph Series No. 9, 1981).
162. Cf. Marcum, op. cit., p. 272.
163. For the full text of the Nakuru Agreement (16–21 June 1975), see *ACR*, 1975–76, pp. C80–C86.
164. Ibid.
165. See 'Organisation of African Unity: Extraordinary Session of the Assembly of Heads of State and Government held in Addis Ababa, 10–12 January 1978 – Final Communiqué', *ACR*, 1976–77, p. C5.

4 Zaïre

1. See *ACR*, 1977–78, p. B592.
2. Ibid.
3. Ibid.
4. Marcum, *The Angolan Revolution: Vol. II*, p. 259.
5. *ACR*, 1977–78, p. B592.
6. Ibid., pp. B592–B593.
7. See, for instance, the interview of General Nathaniel Mbumba in *Afrique-Asie*, 31 October 1977, p. 22.
8. It is important to note the continuing retention of the name 'Congo' in the titles of most of the Zaïrean opposition movements. This is no doubt indicative of their critical attitude to the so-called Policy of Authenticity which Mobutu launched in 1971 – this was when he changed Congo-Kinshasa's name to Zaïre (See *ACR*, 1971–72, pp. C181–C182).
9. *ACR*, 1977–78, p. B594.
10. See Ghislain C. Kabwit, 'Zaïre: the Roots of the Continuing Crisis', *The Journal of Modern African Studies*, 17 (3), 1979, p. 281.
11. *ACR*, 1977–78, p. B594.
12. See Kenneth Adelman, 'Zaïre: Old Foes and New Friends', *Africa Report*, January-February 1978, p. 8.
13. Ibid.
14. See Guy Gran, 'Zaïre 1978: The Ethical and Intellectual Bankruptcy of the World System', *Africa Today*, Vol. 25, Pt. 4, October-December 1978, p. 5.
15. Ibid., pp. 18–23.
16. Quoted in Adelman, op. cit., p. 7.
17. For a background analysis of Mobutu's relationship with US governments over the past 23 years, including his connections

with the CIA, see John Stockwell, *In Search of Enemies*, op. cit., especially ch. 6.
18. Ibid., p. 137.
19. Adelman, op. cit., p. 7.
20. Ibid.
21. *In Search of Enemies*, pp. 104–12, and passim.
22. Quoted in Adelman, op. cit., p. 7.
23. See, for instance, Kabwit, op. cit., p. 339.
24. Ibid.
25. See Bruce Oudes, 'The United States Year in Africa: Reinventing the Wheel', *ACR*, 1977–78, op. cit., p. A75.
26. Quoted by Adelman, op. cit., p. 8.
27. Ibid., p. 9.
28. Ibid.
29. See *ACR*, 1977–78, op. cit., p. B590.
30. See Joel Pwol, 'Zaïre: Fourteenth Year of the Second Republic', *Sunday Standard* (Jos), 25 November 1979.
31. Cuba admitted 'foreknowledge of the attack' but insisted that it could not prevent it (see *ACR*, 1977–78, p. B590).
32. For a detailed discussion of the envisaged activities of this force, see *Africa Confidential*, 19 (13), 23 June 1978.
33. *Africa Confidential*, 19 (24), 1 December 1978.
34. Ibid.
35. Ibid.
36. See Galen Hull, 'The French Connection in Africa: Zaïre and South Africa', *Journal of Southern African Studies*, 5 (2), 1979, p. 224, and Claude Wauthier, 'France's Year in Africa', *ACR*, 1977–78, p. A88.
37. Adelman, op. cit., p. 8.
38. Hull, op. cit., p. 226.
39. Ibid., p. 225.
40. Wauthier, op. cit., p. A88.
41. Hull, op. cit., p. 225.
42. See, for instance, Kabwit, op. cit., pp. 397–404.
43. Quoted in ibid., p. 396.
44. *ACR*, 1977–78, op. cit., pp. B593–B597.
45. Ibid., pp. B593–B594.
46. Kabwit, op. cit., p. 396.
47. See particularly Stanley Cohn, 'What's Going Up in Zaïre? OTRAG's Rocket Base in Shaba', *Munger Africana Library Notes*, Issue No. 49, April 1979, p. 15.
48. Ibid., p. 10.
49. See Mbumba, op. cit.
50. Cf. *Africa Confidential*, 19 (13), 23 June 1978.

51. *Africa Report*, July-August 1977, p. 12.
52. *ACR*, 1977–78, op. cit., p. C4.
53. Adelman, op. cit., p. 8.
54. *ACR*, 1977–78, op. cit., p. B594.
55. Ibid.
56. Adelman, op. cit.
57. See *Africa Confidential*, 23 June 1978.
58. Quoted by Kabwit, op. cit., pp. 406–7.
59. See *Africa Confidential*, 23 June 1978.
60. See *Africa Confidential*, 1 December 1978.
61. Communication with Basil Davidson, 13 December 1979.

5 The Dynamics of Intervention: A Comparative Survey

1. Cf. K. J. Holsti, op. cit., p. 279.
2. It should be stressed that a 'linkage of interest' between a contending power group and a prospective external actor is essential in determining the nature of intervention. See C. R. Mitchell, op. cit., pp. 167–70.
3. Cf. Frederic Pearson, op. cit., pp. 432–60.
4. Cf. Holsti, op. cit., p. 279.

6 Conclusions: Conflict, Intervention and the Future

1. See *Guardian*, 30 July 1986.
2. Cf. 'Charter of the Organisation of African Unity', Article III (2), in Joseph Okpaku (ed.), *Nigeria: Dilemma of Nationhood*, op. cit., p. 383.
3. *Guardian*, 30 July 1986.
4. See 'Realising Peace, Development and Regional Security in Africa', in Emmanuel Hansen, op. cit., pp. 215–32.
5. Ibid., pp. 225–9.
6. Ibid., p. 226.
7. Ibid., p. 228.
8. Ibid., pp. 229–32.
9. See Herbert Ekwe-Ekwe, 'Counting the Cost', *West Africa*, 29 June 1987, p. 1250.
10. See 'Crisis, Nationalism, and Socialism', op. cit., p. 199.
11. See Ekwe-Ekwe, 'Africa's Crisis', *West Africa*, 25 May 1987, pp. 1007–9, and Ekwe-Ekwe, 'Remembering Rodney', *West Africa*, 15 June 1987, pp. 1152–4.
12. See Richard Dowden, 'Redrawing the outmoded colonial map of Africa', *Independent* (London), 10 September 1987. Else-

where, Thomas Pakenham has observed: 'One has only to think of the bloody civil wars that followed decolonisation to see the craziness of these lines drawn on maps in Europe by men ignorant of African geography and history'. (See 'The European share-out of the spoils of Africa', *Financial Times* (London), 15 February 1988.)

13. 'The National Question and the Crisis of Instability in Africa', in Hansen (ed.), op. cit., p. 79.
14. 'In These Times', op. cit., p. 76.
15. See Basil Davidson, 'Hope of the Horn', *Guardian*, 1 April 1988.

Select Bibliography

GENERAL

Books

Albright, David E. (ed.), *Africa and International Communism* (London: Macmillan, 1980).
Amin, Samir, Arrighi, Giovanni, Frank, André Gunder and Wallerstein, Immanuel, *Dynamics of Global Crisis* (London and Basingstoke: Macmillan, 1982).
Anyang' Nyong'o, Peter (ed.), *Popular Struggles for Democracy in Africa* (London and New Jersey: Zed Books, 1987).
Ayoob, Mohammed (ed.), *Conflict and Intervention in the Third World* (London: Croom Helm, 1980).
Barnet, Richard J., *Intervention and Revolution* (London: Paladin, 1972).
Bozeman, Adda, *Conflicts in Africa: Concepts and Realities* (Princeton: Princeton University Press, 1976).
Burbach, Roger and Flynn, Patricia (eds), *The Politics of Intervention: The United States in Central America* (New York and London: Monthly Review Press, 1984).
Carter, Gwendolen M. and O'Meara, Patrick (eds), *Southern Africa: The Continuing Crisis* (London and Basingstoke: Macmillan, 1979).
Chomsky, Noam, Steele, Jonathan and Gittings, John, *Superpowers in Collision: The New Cold War* (Harmondsworth: Penguin, 1982).
Clark, John, *For Richer, For Poorer: An Oxfam Report on Western Connections with World Hunger* (Oxford: Oxfam, 1986).
Crummey, Donald (ed.), *Banditry, Rebellion and Social Protest in Africa* (London/Portsmouth: James Currey/Heinemann, 1986).
Elliot, Jeffrey M. and Dymally, Mervyn M., an interview, *Fidel Castro: Nothing Can Stop the Course of History* (London and New York: Pathfinder Press, 1986).
Ferris, W. H., *The Power Capabilities of Nation States: International Conflicts and War* (Lexington, Mass.: Lexington Books, 1973).
Frank, André Gunder, *Crisis: In the Third World* (London: Heinemann, 1981).
Frankel, Joseph, *International Politics – Conflict and Harmony* (Harmondsworth: Penguin, 1969).

Select Bibliography

George, Susan, *A Fate Worse Than Debt* (Harmondsworth: Pelican, 1988).
Halliday, Fred, *The Making of the Second Cold War* (London: Verso, 1983).
Hansen, Emmanuel (ed.), *Africa: Perspectives on Peace and Development* (London and New Jersey: Zed Books, 1987).
Higham, Robin, *Civil Wars in the Twentieth Century* (Lexington: University Press of Kentucky, 1972).
Holsti, K., *International Politics* (London: Prentice/Hall International, 1974).
Hosmer, Stephen T. and Wolfe, Thomas W., *Soviet Policy and Practice Towards Third-World Conflicts* (Lexington, Mass.: D. C. Heath, Lexington Books, 1982).
Korner, Peter, Maass, Gero, Siebold, Thomas and Tetzlaff, Rainer, *The IMF and the Debt Crisis: A Guide to the Third World's Dilemmas* (London and New Jersey: Zed Books, 1986).
Kubalkova, V. and Cruicksank, A. A., *Marxism-Leninism and the Theory of International Relations*, (London: Routledge & Kegan Paul, 1980).
Latin American Bureau, *The Poverty Brokers: The IMF and Latin America* (London: Latin American Bureau, 1983).
Little, Richard, *Intervention – External Involvement in Civil Wars* (London: Martin Robertson, 1975).
Luard, Evan (ed.), *International Regulation of Civil War* (London: Thames & Hudson, 1972).
MacFarlane, S. Neil, *Superpower Rivalry and Third World Radicalism: The Idea of National Liberation* (London and Sidney: Croom Helm, 1985).
Mandaza, Ibbo (ed.), *Zimbabwe: The Political Economy of Transition, 1980–1986* (Dakar: Codesria Book Series, 1986).
Markovitz, Irving Leonard, *Power and Class in Africa: An Introduction to Change and Conflict in African Politics* (Englewood Cliffs, New Jersey: Prentice-Hall, 1977).
Miller, Linda, *World Order and Local Disorder* (Princeton: Princeton University Press, 1967).
Nation, R. Craig and Kauppi, Mark V. (eds), *The Soviet Impact in Africa* (Lexington, Mass.: D. C. Heath, Lexington Books, 1984).
New Left Review, *Exterminism and Cold War* (London: Verso, 1982).
Rosenau, James N. (ed.), *International Aspects of Civil Strife* (Princeton: Princeton University Press, 1964).
Rosenau, James, N. *The Scientific Study of Foreign Policy* (New York: The Free Press, 1971).
Schatan, Jacobo, *World Debt: Who is to Pay?* (London and New Jersey: Zed Books, 1987).

Select Bibliography

Selassie, Bereket Habte, *Conflict and Intervention in the Horn of Africa* (New York and London: Monthly Review Press, 1980).
Shivji, Issa G., (ed.), *The State and the Working People in Tanzania* (Dakar: Codesria Book Series, 1986).
Smith, Clagett, G. (ed.), *Conflict Resolution: Contributions of the Behavioural Sciences* (Notre Dame: University of Notre Dame Press, 1971).
Spiegel, S. L. and Waltz, K. W. (eds), *Conflict in World Politics* (Massachusetts: Winthop Publications, 1971).
Widstrand, Carl (ed.), *Multi-National Firms in Africa* (Dakar/Uppsala: African Institute for Economic Development and Planning/Scandinavian Institute of African Studies, 1975).

MONOGRAPHS/PAMPHLETS

Castro, Fidel, *A Pyrric Military Victory And A Profound Moral Defeat* (La Habana: Editora Politica, 1983).
Castro, Fidel, *Cuba Cannot Export Revolution, Nor Can the United States Prevent It* (La Habana: Editora Politica, 1984).
Frankel, David, *Upsurge in Africa: Cuba, the U.S. and the New Rise of the African Liberation Struggle* (New York: Pathfinder Press, 1978).
Halliday, Fred, *Beyond Irangate: The Reagan Doctrine and the Third World* (Amsterdam: Transnational Institute, 1987).

ARTICLES

Amin, Samir, 'The World Crisis of the 1980s', Interview, *Monthly Review*, 33 (2), 1981.
Babu, Abdulrahaman Mohamed, 'In These Times', Interview, *Journal of African Marxists*, Issue No. 10, June 1987.
Borge, Tomas, 'Nicaraguan Revolution', Interview, *New Left Review*, No. 164, July/August 1987.
Chinweizu, 'Debt Trap Peonage', *Monthly Review*, 37 (6), 1985.
Chinweizu, 'The innocent; if they hang them – A song for the Sharpville Six', *West Africa*, 28 March 1988.
Chomsky, Noam, 'Intervention in Vietnam and Central America: Parallels and Differences', *Monthly Review*, 37 (4), 1985.
Clairmonte, Frederick and Cavanagh, John, 'Impossible debt on road to global ruin', *Guardian* (London), 9 January 1987.
Davidson, Basil, 'Precondition For Peace', *West Africa*, 1 February 1988.
Davidson, Basil, 'Hope of the Horn', *Guardian* (London), 1 April 1988.

Select Bibliography

Ekwe-Ekwe, Herbert, 'Africa and "Devil on the Cross": Revolutionary Themes in the Ngugi Novel', *Monthly Review*, 35 (2), June 1983.

Ekwe-Ekwe, Herbert, 'Perspectives of Underdevelopment', *Third World Affairs 1986*, London: Third World Foundation for Social and Economic Studies, January 1986.

Ekwe-Ekwe, Herbert, 'The Scourge of Hunger', *Third World Quarterly*, 8 (2), April 1986.

Ekwe-Ekwe, Herbert, 'African Literature and Politics', *Red Letters*, No. 20, December 1986.

Ekwe-Ekwe, Herbert, 'Africa's Crisis', *West Africa*, 25 May 1987.

Ekwe-Ekwe, Herbert, 'Remembering Walter Rodney', *West Africa*, 15 June 1987.

Ekwe-Ekwe, Herbert, 'South Africa: Thatcherism and Intervention', *Guardian*, (Lagos), 27 July 1986.

Ekwe-Ekwe, Herbert, 'Who's Afraid of Chinweizu?', *PAL Platform*, Vol. 1, No. 2/3, September 1989.

Ekwe-Ekwe, Herbert, 'C. L. R. James: Scholar, Revolutionary, African', *PAL Platform*, Vol. 1, No. 2/3, September 1989.

Ekwe-Ekwe, Herbert and Owugah, Lemmy, 'Lomé III: What Prospects for Third World States?', *Guardian* (Lagos), 3 June 1984.

Eley, J. W., 'Toward a theory of intervention: the limitations and advantages of a transnational perspective', *International Studies Quarterly*, 16 (2), June 1972.

Forman, Eric, 'Civil War as Source of International Violence', *Journal of Politics*, 34 (2), November 1972.

Girling, G. L. S., 'Pentagon Papers: The Dialectics of Intervention', *World Today*, 28 (2), February 1972.

Mafeje, Archie, 'Culture and Development: The Missing Link', *CODESRIA Bulletin*, No. 1, 1988.

Magdoff, Harry, 'Third World Debt: Past and Present', *Monthly Review*, 37 (9), 1986.

Magdoff, Harry and Sweezy, Paul, 'Lessons of Vietnam', *Monthly Review* 37 (2), June 1985.

Magdoff, Harry and Sweezy, Paul, 'International Cooperation – A Way Out?', *Monthly Review*, 39 (6), 1987.

Mitchell, C. R., 'Civil Strife and the Involvement of External Parties', *International Studies Quarterly*, 14 (2), January 1970.

Paul, R. A., 'Toward a Theory of Intervention', *Orbis*, 16 (1), 1972.

Pearson, F. S., 'Foreign Military Interventions and Domestic Disputes', *International Studies Quarterly*, 18 (3), 1978.

Pearson, F. S., 'Geographic Proximity and Foreign Military Intervention', *Journal of Conflict Resolution*, 18 (3), September 1974.

Rees, David, 'Soviet Strategic Penetration of Africa', *Conflict Studies*, No. 77, November 1976.
Rosenau, James, 'The Concept of Intervention', *Journal of International Affairs*, 22 (2), 1968.
Rosenau, James, 'Intervention as a Scientific Concept', *Journal of Conflict Resolution*, 13 (2), 1969.
Scott, A. M., 'Nonintervention and Conditional Intervention', *Journal of International Affairs*, 22 (2), 1968.
Sweezy, Paul, 'Interview', *Monthly Review*, 38 (11), 1987.
Therborn, Goran, 'From Petrograd to Saigon', *New Left Review*, 48, March–April 1968.
Young, Oran, 'Intervention and International Systems', *Journal of International Affairs*, 22 (2), 1968.
Zartman, I. William, 'Intervention Among Developing States', *Journal of International Affairs*, 22 (2), 1968.

AREA STUDIES

Nigeria

Books
Ademoyega, Adewale, *Why We Struck: The Story of the First Nigerian Coup* (Ibadan: Evans Brothers, 1981).
Africa Research Group, *The Other Side of Nigeria's Civil War* (Cambridge, Mass.: Africa Research Group, 1970).
Ake, Claude (ed.), *Political Economy of Nigeria* (London and Lagos: Longman, 1985).
Akpan, N. U., *The Struggle for Secession, 1966–1970* (London: Frank Cass, 1971).
Cronje, Suzanne, *The World and Nigeria: The Diplomatic History of the Biafra War* (London: Sidgwick & Jackson, 1972).
Crowder, Michael, *West Africa Under Colonial Rule* (London: Hutchinson, 1968).
De St. Jorre, John, *The Nigerian Civil War* (London: Hodder & Stoughton, 1972).
Dudley, Billy, *An Introduction to Nigerian Government and Politics* (London and Basingstoke: Macmillan, 1982).
Epelle, Sam (ed.), *Nigeria Speaks: Speeches of Alhaji Sir Abubakar Tafawa Balewa* (Lagos: Longman, 1964).
Falola, Toyin (ed.), *Britain and Nigeria: Exploitation or Development?* (London and New Jersey: Zed Books, 1987).
Gbulie, Ben, *Nigeria's Five Majors: Coup D'état of 15th January 1966 – First Inside Account* (Onitsha: African Educational Publisher, 1981).

Select Bibliography

Hunt, David, *On the Spot: An Ambassador Remembers* (London: Peter Davies, 1975).
Kirk-Greene, A. H. M., *Crisis and Conflict in Nigeria: A Documentary Sourcebook, 1966–1970*, 2 vols (London: Oxford University Press, 1971).
Madiebo, Alexander, A., *The Nigerian Revolution and the Biafran War* (Enugu: Fourth Dimension Publishers, 1980).
Obasanjo, Olusegun, *My Command: An account of the Nigerian Civil War, 1967–70* (Ibadan and London: Heinemann, 1980).
Obasanjo, Olusegun, *Nzeogwu* (Ibadan: Spectrum Books, 1987).
Odogwu, Bernard, *No Place to Hide (Crises and Conflicts Inside Biafra)* (Enugu: Fourth Dimension Publishers, 1985).
Okpaku, Joseph (ed.), *Nigeria: Dilemma of Nationhood* (New York: Third Press, 1972).
Perham, Margery, *Mining, Commerce and Finance in Nigeria* (London: Faber & Faber, 1948).
Shenton, Robert, *The Development of Capitalism in Northern Nigeria* (London: James Currey, 1986).
Stremlau, John, *The International Politics of the Nigerian Civil War: 1967–1970* (Princeton, New Jersey: Princeton University Press, 1977).
Uwechue, Raph, *Reflections on the Nigerian Civil War: Facing the Future* (Paris: Jeune Afrique, 1971).

Articles
Baker, Ross K., 'The Emergence of Biafra', *Orbis*, XII, Summer 1968.
Baker, Ross K., 'The Role of the Ivory Coast in the Nigeria-Biafra War', *African Scholar*, 1 (4), 1970.
Davis, Morris, 'Negotiating about Biafran Oil', *Issue*, III (2), Summer 1973.
Ekwe-Ekwe, Herbert, 'The Nigerian plight: Shagari to Buhari', *Third World Quarterly*, 8 (2), April 1985.
Ekwe-Ekwe, Herbert, 'Nzeogwu: Notes on a Controversy', *West Africa*, 2 March 1987.
Ekwe-Ekwe, Herbert, 'Religion in Nigeria: Manipulation or Mobilisation?', *West Africa*, 7 December 1987.
Langley, Kathleen, 'The External Resource factor in Nigerian Economic Development', *Nigerian Journal of Economic and Social Studies*, 4 (3), 1968.
Melbourne, Roy M., 'The American Response to the Nigerian Conflict', *Issue*, III (2), Summer 1973.
Ofoegbu, Ray, 'The Relations between Nigeria and its neighbours', *Nigerian Journal of International Studies*, 1 (1), July 1975.
Ogunbadejo, Oye, 'Nigeria and the Great Powers: The Impact of

the Civil War on Nigerian Foreign Relations', *African Affairs*, LXXV (2), January 1976.
Ogunbadejo, Oye, 'Ideology and Pragmatism: The Soviet Role in Nigeria, 1960–1970', *Orbis*, Winter 1978.
Ogunbadejo, Oye, 'A new turn in US-Nigerian relations', *The World Today*, March 1979.
Perham, Margery, 'Reflections on the Nigerian Civil War', *International Affairs*, 46 (2), April 1970.

Angola

Books
Bender, Gerald J., *Angola under the Portuguese – The Myth and the Reality* (London: Heinemann, 1978).
Burchett, Wilfred, *Southern Africa Stands Up: The Revolutions in Angola, Mozambique, Rhodesia, Namibia and South Africa* (New York: Urizen Books, 1978).
Chilcote, Ronald (ed.), *Protest and Resistance in Angola and Brazil* (Berkeley: University of California Press, 1972).
Davidson, Basil, *In the Eye of the Storm: Angola's People* (New York: Doubleday, 1972).
De Andrade, Mário and Ollivier, Marc, *The War in Angola: A Socio-Economic Study* (Dar es Salaam: Tanzania Publishing House, 1975).
El-Khawas, Mohamed A. and Cohen, Barry (eds), *The Kissinger Study of Southern Africa: National Security Memorandum 39* (Westport, Connecticut: Lawrence Hill, 1976).
Harsch, Ernest and Thomas, Tony, *Angola: The Hidden History of Washington's War* (New York: Pathfinder Press, 1976).
Humbaraci, Arslan and Muchnic, Nicole, *Portugal's African Wars: Angola, Guinea-Bissao, Mozambique* (New York: The Third Press, 1974).
Marcum, John, *The Angolan Revolution, Vol. II – Exile Politics and Guerrilla Warfare (1962–1976)* (Massachusetts: MIT Press, 1978).
Spínola, António, *Portugal e o Futuro* (Lisbon: Arcadia, 1974).
Stockwell, John, *In Search of Enemies* (London: André Deutsch, 1978).

Pamphlets/Monographs
Castro, Fidel, *Angola Giron africano* (La Habana: Editorial de ciencias sociales, 1976).
Mozambique, Angola and Guiné Information Centre, London, *Angola: Socialism At Birth* (London: Mozambique, Angola and Guiné Information Centre, 1980).

Sotunmbi, Abiodun Olufemi, *Nigeria's Recognition of the MPLA Government of Angola: A Case-Study in Decision-Making and Implementation* (Lagos: International Institute of International Affairs, 1981).

Articles
Albright, David E., 'The USSR and Africa: Soviet Policy', *Problems of Communism*, XXVII, January-February 1978.
Bender, Gerald J., 'Angola: History, Insurgency and Social Change', *Africa Today*, 19, Winter 1972.
Birmingham, David, 'The Twenty-Seventh of May: An Historical Note on the Abortive '77 Coup in Angola', *African Affairs*, 77 (309), October 1978.
Davidson, Basil, 'Angola since Independence', *Race and Class*, Autumn 1977.
Durch, William J., 'The Cuban Military in Africa and the Middle East: From Algeria to Angola', *Studies in Communism*, XI (1–2), Spring/Summer 1978.
Ebinger, Charles R., 'The External Intervention in Internal War: The Politics and Diplomacy of the Angolan Civil War', *Orbis*, 20 (3), Fall 1976.
Gonzalez, Edward, 'Complexities of Cuban Foreign Policy', *Problems of Communism*, XXVI, November-December 1979.
Henrikson, Thomas, 'People's War in Angola, Mozambique and Guinea-Bissau', *Journal of Modern African Studies*, 14 (3), September 1976.
Larrabee, Stephen, 'Moscow, Angola and the Dialectics of Détente', *The World Today*, 32 (5), 1977.
Legum, Colin, 'The Soviet Union, China and the West in Southern Africa', *Foreign Affairs*, July 1976.
Legum, Colin, 'The USSR and Africa – the African Environment', *Problems of Communism*, January-February 1978.
Marquez, Gabriel Garcia, 'Operation Carlota', *New Left Review*, Nos. 101–2, March-April 1977.
Ponomarev, Boris, 'Invincibility of the Liberation Movement', *Socialism: Theory and Practice*, Moscow: Novosti Press Agency (Supplement), May 1980.
Stevens, Christopher, 'The Soviet Union and Angola', *African Affairs*, 75 (299), April 1976.
Valenta, Jiri, 'The Soviet-Cuban Intervention in Angola, 1975', *Studies in Comparative Communism*, XI (1-2), Spring/Summer 1978.
Vanneman, Peter and James, Martin, 'The Soviet Intervention in Angola: Intentions and Implications', *Strategic Survey*, Summer 1976.

Volsky, George, 'Cuba's Foreign Policies', *Current History*, February 1976.
Yu, George I., 'The USSR and Africa: China's Impact', *Problems of Communism*, XXVII, January-February 1978.

Zaïre

Books
Anstey, R., *King Leopold's Legacy, the Congo under Belgian Rule 1908–1960* (London: Oxford University Press, 1966).
Archer, J., *Congo – the Birth of a New Nation* (Folkestone: Bailey Brothers, 1971).
Brausch, G., *Belgian Administration in the Congo* (London: Institute of Race Relations, 1961).
Massambe-Kamitatu, C., *Zaïre: Le Pouvoir à la Portée du Peuple* (Paris: Editions L'Harmattan, 1977).
Nzongola-Ntalaja, *Class Struggles and National Liberation in Africa: Essays on the Political Economy of Neocolonialism* (Roxbury, Mass.: Omenana, 1982).
Young, Crowford, *Politics in the Congo* (Princeton: Princeton University Press, 1965).

Periodicals
Centre de Recherche et d'Information Socio-Politiques (CRISP), *Zaïre 1976*, Brussels, 1977.
CRISP, *Zaïre 1977*, Brussels, 1978.
CRISP, *Zaïre 1978*, Brussels, 1979.

Articles
Adelman, Kenneth L., 'The Recourse to Authenticity and Negritude in Zaïre', *The Journal of Modern African Studies*, XIII (1), March 1975.
Adelman, Kenneth L., 'The Church-State Conflict in Zaïre: 1969–1974', *African Studies Review*, XVIII (1), April 1975.
Adelman, Kenneth L., 'Zaïre: Old Foes and New Friends', *Africa Report*, January-February 1978.
Bekolo-Ebe, Bruno, 'La dévaluation du franc français et les économies de la zone franc', *Présence Africaine*, 137/138, 1st and 2nd Quarterlies, 1986.
Cohn, Stanley, 'What's Going Up in Zaïre? OTRAG's Rocket Base in Shaba', *Munger Africana Library Notes*, Issue No. 49, April 1979.
De Benoist, Joseph-Roger, 'L'Église catholique et la question de la construction de l'État-nation en Afrique noire francophone', *Présence Africaine*, 127/128, 3rd and 4th Quarterlies, 1983.

Gran, Guy, 'Zaïre 1978: The Ethical and Intellectual Bankruptcy of the World System', *Africa Today*, 25 (Part 4), October-December 1978.

Hull, Galen, 'The French Connection in Africa: Zaïre and South Africa', *Journal of Southern African Studies*, 5 (2), 1979.

Kabwit, Ghislain C., 'Zaïre: The Roots of the Continuing Crisis', *The Journal of Modern African Studies*, 17 (3), September 1979.

Laïdi, Zaki, 'Les rapports internationaux à l'épreuve des conflicts africains: réflexions à partir de l'analyse de la 2me crise du Shaba', *Afrique et Asie Modeme*, 120, 1979.

Lemarchand, René, 'The CIA in Africa: How Central? How Intelligent?', *The Journal of Modern African Studies*, 14 (3), September 1976.

Mbaya, Etiene-Richard, 'La première phase des indépendances africaines: dialétique de contradictions', *Journal of African Marxists*, Issue 6, October 1984.

Mbumba Nathaniel, 'Nous demandons la démission de Mobutu', Interview, *Afrique-Asie*, 31 October 1977.

Nzongola-Ntalaja, 'The State and Class Struggle in Zaïre', *Journal of African Marxists*, Issue 5, February 1984.

Peemans, J. Ph., 'The Social and Economic Development of Zaïre since Independence: an historical outline', *African Affairs*, 74 (259), April 1975.

Pwol, Joel, 'Zaïre: Fourteenth Year of the Second Republic', *Sunday Standard* (Jos), 25 November 1979.

Index

Aba, 29
Abidjan, 14, 44
Aburi, Aburi Accords, 14, 15
Accra, 14
Adekunle, Benjamin, 33–4
Addis Ababa, 55, 56–7
Africa
   Africans, 1, 2, 3, 4, 9, 10, 15, 17, 19, 24, 26, 30, 70, 71, 74, 75, 82, 86, 94, 96, 97 *passim*
   African states, and the Shaba conflicts, 125–9
   African states' responses to the Nigerian Civil War, 51–9
   Central Africa, 67, 78, 83, 85, 100
   conflict, intervention and the future, 151–8
   'conservative' states, 54
   'radical' states, 53, 54
   Southern Africa, 53, 85, 87, 110, 111
   West Africa, 41, 42, 44, 49, 63, 67
African State System, 132, 138, 139, 140–1 *passim*
Aguyi-Ironsi, Johnson, 11–12, 14, 18, 47, 61
Ahidjo, Ahmadu, 13–14, 54, 55
Ahmadu Bello University (Zaria), 28–9
Albright, David, 92
Alexander, Henry, 38
Algeria, 5, 42, 53, 54
   Front for National Liberation, 100
   military aid to federal Nigeria, 96, 97, 108
Alvor, Alvor Accords, 69, 72, 95
Amalgamated Tin Mining (Nigeria) Ltd., 27
Amin, Idi, 5, 151

Angola, 1, 2, 9, 10, 17, 47
   collapse of transitional government, and civil war, 80–90
   Democratic Party of Angola, 71
   Democratic People's Republic of, 86
   FNLA (Frente Nacional de Libertação de Angola, 69, 70–1, 73–4, 78–9 *passim*
   Frente e Libertação do Enclave de Cabinda (FLEC), 87, 88
   GRAE (Govêrno Revolucionário de Angola no Exílo), 71
   'mestico', 70
   Movement for the National Independence of Angola, 70
   Movimento Popular de Libertação de Angola (MPLA), 17, 69–70, 72, 74, 78, 79–80 *passim*
   MPLA establishes relations with Cuba, 96–7
   MPLA's 'Second War of National Liberation', 84
   National Defence Council, 69
   'Operation Addis Ababa', and MPLA's victory in civil war, 107
   People's Republic of, 86, 109
   Union of People of Angola (UPA), 71
   UNITA (National Union for the Total Independence of Angola), 71–2, 73–4, 78, 79 *passim*
   United Struggle of the Angolan African, 69
   US dominant position in the colonial economy of, 76–8
   US support for Portugal in the

Index

anti-colonial war, 74–6
Antunes, Melo, 88
Arab, Arab states, 5, 8, 45, 52, 54, 82
Arikpo, Okoi, 47
Asia, 4
Atlantic alliance, *see* North Atlantic Treaty Organisation (NATO)
Auschwitz, 99
Awolowo, Obafemi, 60

Babu, Abdulrahaman Mohamed, 100, 156–7
Bakongo people, 70
Balewa, Abubakar Tarawa, 11, 17–18, 19, 59–60
Ball, George, 75–6
Bangladesh, 4, 6
Batista, Fulgencio, 97
Belgium, 27, 32, 77
    interests in Zaïre, and intervention in the Shaba conflicts, *see* Zaïre
Bella, Ben, 97
Bello, Ahmadu, 11
Benguela, Benguela railway, 71, 72, 84, 85, 103, 113
Benin (Nigeria), 37
Biafra, 6
    African states, and Biafra, 51–9
    Biafran Organisation of Freedom Fighters (BOFF), 30
Biafra War, ch. 2 *passim*
    contains early Nigerian military operations, 23, 26
    declaration of the Republic of, 12
    France's support for, 40–2
    initial external reaction to independence declaration, 12–21, 22
    major territorial losses to Nigerian offensive (September 1967-March 1968), 29–30
    nature of French arms to, 44
    phases of Biafra War, 21–2, 25–7, 31ff

US policy to Biafra War, 47–51, 63, 64, 65–8
Bie, 71
Bishop, Maurice, 8
Bolivia, 97
Bongo, Albert-Bernard, 55
Bonny, 23, 24–6
Borge, Tomas, 6
Botha, Pieter, 85
Botswana, 57, 103
Britain, 2
    assortment of British businesses and banks operating in Nigeria, 27–8
    Conservative Party, 31
    conquest of Nigeria, 16–17
    Crown Agents, 37
    dominant arms supplier to federal Nigeria's military, 30, 32
    dominant position in the Nigerian economy, 18, 24, 27–9
    intervention in Nigerian Civil War, 25–7
    Labour Party, 31
    non-governmental involvement in the Nigerian Civil War, 36–8
    oil imports from Nigeria, 22–4
    role of British mercenaries in Angolan Civil War, 81
    Royal Air Force, 17, 37, 38
    secret defence pact with Balewa regime, and provision for bases for Royal Air Force, 17, 19
    weapons sent to federal Nigeria after intervention, 26–7, 31–40, 48, 49, 61, 62, 63, 64, 66
Brown, George, 80
Brussels, Treaty of Brussels (1954) on German rearmament, 124–5
Buea, 13
Burkina Faso, 5
Burundi, 109

Cabinda, 70, 85, 107

Index

Cabral, Amilcar, 153
Caetano, Marcello, 98, 104
Calabar, 12–13, 21, 23, 29
Callaghan, James, 88
Cameroon, 13, 42, 54
Cape Verde, 69, 99
Canada, 32
Caribbean, The, 3, 4
Carmona, 107
Carter, Jimmy, 8, 117
Castro, Fidel, 97, 99
Caxito, 105
Cela, 107
Central African Federation, 17
  see also Central African Republic, 109
Central America, 97
Chad, 5, 10, 12–13, 52
China, 5–6
  and Angolan Civil War, 90–2, 100–2
Clark, John, 4
Clement, William, 80
Commonwealth (member countries, organisation), The, 25, 31, 32, 39–40
Contending Power Groups, 131, 132–4
Contiguous States, 131, 134–8
Congo (Congo-Leopoldville; see also Zaïre), 9, 16, 51, 62, 71, 96
  National Council of the Revolution, 96, 97, 112 *passim*
Congo-Brazzaville, 70, 94, 95, 96, 97, 98–9, 108
Côte d'Ivoire (Burkina Faso), 14–15, 44, 52, 54–5
Coutinho, Rosa, 88
Cronje, Suzanne, 55
Cuanza, Norte, 81
Cuanza Sul, 71, 84
Cuba, 2, 5, 6, 82, 84–5, 86
  and the Shaba conflicts, 115, 117, 118 *passim*, 129–30
  'Operation Carlota', 86, 99–100, 105 *passim*
  origins of relations with MPLA, 96–7

'Tricontinental Conference', 96
Cuito Cuanvavale, 104
Cumming-Bruce, Francis, 19, 25, 47
Cunene, 72, 85
  River Cunene, and the hydroelectric facility, 102–3
Czechoslovakia, 37, 64, 65

Dachau, 99
Davidson, Basil, 130
Davis, Nathaniel, 83
De Andrade, Mario, 77
De Carvalho, Otelo, 88–9, 98
De Gaulle, Charles, 14, 40–1, 42, 54
De Spinola, Antonio, 73, 88
De St Jorre, John, 43
Dike, Kenneth, 42, 54
Diori, Hamani, 13, 14, 55
Dodd, Thomas, 50
Dominican Republic, The, 7, 97
Douala, 13
Dudley, Billy, 18
Dzaskhov, Aleksandr, 95

East (bloc), The, 3, 4, 62–3, 92, 94
East Germany, 95
Ebocha, 42
Effiong, Philip, 43
Egypt, 4, 15, 42, 54
  intervention in the Shaba conflicts, 118 *passim*
  military aid, and fighter pilots to federal Nigeria, 57, 65
El-Salvador, 5, 7, 97
Enugu, 19, 20, 21, 23, 29, 61
Eritrea, 5, 7, 54, 64
Ethiopia, 5, 15, 52, 54, 94, 109
European Economic Community, 41
Ex-Col Regime, 132, 139–40, 141 *passim*

Fabio, Carlos, 88
Faulques, R., 45
Favier, Paul, 45
Foccart, Jacques, 42
Ford, Gerald, 83
France, 2, 6, 14, 30

Index

arms to Biafra, 445
arms to federal Nigeria, 45–6
declaration of support for
  Biafran independence, 40–1
economic and financial interests
  in Nigerian federation, 41–2
economic and strategic interests
  in Angola, 87–8
Franco-Nigerian trade during
  Biafra War, 46
interests in Zaïre, and
  intervention in the Shaba
  conflicts, see Zaïre
mercenaries in Angola Civil War, 81
'francophone' Africa, 13, 41, 44
FRELIMO (Frente de Libertação
  de Moçambique), 97, 100
Fritz Werner (arms manufacturing
  company), 32

Gabon, 44
  recognition of Biafran
  independence, 52, 54, 55, 67, 109
Garba, Joe, 125–6
Geldof, Bob, 4
genocide, 12, 49, 65, 151
Germany, The Federal Republic of, 27, 32, 37, 121
  OTRAG project in Zaïre, 124
Ghana, 14, 55, 62, 96, 97, 100, 107
Gomes, Costa, 88
Gonzalez, Edward, 93
Goodluck, Wahab, 60
Gowon, Yakubu, 12, 13, 14, 15–16, 19, 29, 32–3, 49
Grenada, 5, 7, 8–9
Guevara, Ernesto Che, 96, 97
  African travels of, 96
Guinea, The Republic of, 53, 54, 62, 92, 95, 100, 108
Guinea Bissau, 47, 69, 94, 96, 97, 100, 108

Haile Selassie, 55
Halliday, Fred, 6
Hansen, Emmanuel, 3
Hausa-Fulani people, 11, 14
Honduras, 5
Hong Kong, 88
Houphouet-Boigny, Felix, 15, 54–5, 106
Huambo, 71, 85, 86
Huila, 71, 72
Hunt, David, 19, 25–6, 29

Igbo people, 11
  see also eastern Nigeria and
  Biafra; the massacres of, 12, 14, 16, 20, 24, 53, 61
  see also genocide and pogrom; 15, 19, 22, 34, 54
International Monetary Fund (IMF), 120, 121
'IMF' riots, 4
India, 5, 32
Indo-China, 6
International Institute for Strategic
  Studies (IISS), London, 38–9
Iran, 5, 7
Iraq, 5
Islam, Islamic, 55
Israel, 5, 8, 32, 45, 54
Italy, 27, 32

Japan, 120
Jews, 54
Johnson, Lynden, 49

Kabwit, Ghislain, 117–18
Kaduna, 18, 32
Kampuchea (Cambodia), 5
Katanga, 16, 51, 112
  'Katanga gendermes', 112–13
  see also Shaba
Kaunda, Kenneth, 53, 106
Kennedy, Edward, 50
Kenya, 52, 53
Kissinger, Henry, 72–3, 80, 81, 82, 84
Kissinger Study, see NSSM 39
Kolwezi, 112, 114 passim
Korea, 5
Kosygin, Alexie, 63
Khrushchev, Nikita, 89
Kudryavtsev, Vladimir, 63–4

Laos, 5
Larrabee, Stephen, 92
Latin America, 3, 4, 6, 96–7
Leapman, Michael, 65
Lebanon, 7, 8
　Lebanese National Patriotic Forces (LNPF), 8
Legum, Colin, 90–1
Lesotho, 103
Liberia, 15
Libya, 5, 7
　arms sales to federal Nigeria, 57, 76
'Live Aid', 4
Lobito, 84, 85, 92, 105
Lorez, Pierre, 45, 47
Los Angeles Times, The, 81

MacCarthy, Eugene, 50
MacFarlane, S. Neil, 7
MacGovern, George, 50
Makurdi, 37
Malagasy, 54
Malan, Magnus, 85
Malange, 84
Malawi, 103
Mali, 5, 10, 53, 100
Mao Tse-Tung, 101
Marcum, John, 75, 78, 81
Marquez, Gabriel Garcia, 99
Marshall Recovery Plan Programme (Marshall Aid), 5
massacres
　of African peoples in Angola by the Portuguese armed forces, 70, 71
　of civilians in Bandundu, eastern Zaïre, by the Zaïrean armed forces, 151
　of Igbo people in northern Nigeria, 12, 14, 16, 20, 24, 53
Massemba-Debat, Alphonse, 70, 97
Matthews, Elbert, 19, 47
Mauritania, 109
Mbanza, 75
Mbumba, Nathaniel, 113, 119
M'Pangala, 75
Mbundu people, 69

mercenaries, 37, 57, 59, 81
Mexico, 4
Middle East, 4, 8, 22, 54
Mobutu Sese Seko, 55, 56, 73, 78, 81, 83, 105, 112, 113 *passim*
Mocamedes, 72, 84, 105
Morocco, 2, 5, 42, 60, 61, 112
　intervention in Shaba, 118, 120 *passim*
Moss, Robert, 89
Moxico, 70
Moynihan, Daniel, 82
Mozambique, 5, 47, 69, 73, 77, 94, 100, 103, 106, 108
Muhammed, Murtala, 19
Museveni, Yoweri, 151, 152
Muslim, 53, 54 *see also* Islam, Islamic

Nakuru, Nakuru Agreement, 108
Namibia, 5, 10, 73, 85
　SWAPO (South West African People's Organisation), 35, 121
Neto, Agostinho, 80, 96
Netherlands, The, 27, 33, 61
New Jewel Movement (Grenada), 8
Ngouabi, Marien, 98–9
Nicaragua, 6–7, 97
Niger, The Republic of, 12–13, 43, 54, 55
Nigeria, 1, 2, 4, 9, 10
　Action Group, 17, 60
　and the Shaba conflicts, *see* Africa
　civil war in, ch. 2 *passim*
　see also Biafra War
　coup d'état in, 11
　eastern Nigeria's declaration of independence, 12
　see also Republic of Biafra
　federal victory in civil war, 68
　initial foreign reaction to the east's independence, 12–21, 22
　massacres of eastern Nigerians in the northern region, 12
　see also genocide, pogroms
　NAF (Nigerian Air Force), 37, 57
　National Council of Nigerian

Index

Citizens (NCNC), 17, 60
Nigerian Socialist Workers' and Farmers' Party (NSWAFP), 60
Nigerian Youth Congress, 60
Northern People's Congress (NPC), 17
  northern regional response to coup d'état, 11–12
  phases of civil war, 21–3
  'Police Action', 66
  police auxilliaries, 11
  receives initial military support from Britain, 25–7
  steps up military operations in Biafra, 29–30, 31ff
  Soviet intervention in civil war, and military support for federal Nigeria, 63, 65
  the US and civil war in, 47–51, 76, 107, 115
Nhia, River, 105
Nixon, Richard, 49, 50, 72
Nkrumah, Kwame, 62, 94
Nnoli, Okwudiba, 153–5
North America, 3
Novo Redondo, 105
Nsukka, 23, 29, 61
Nyasaland (Malawi), 17
Nyerere, Julius, 53, 54, 128
Nzeogwu, Chukwuma, 11, 18
Nzimiro, Ikenna, 28
Nzongola-Ntalaja, 155–6

Obote, Milton, 151
Obudu, 23
Ogoja, 23
Ogunbadejo, Oye, 21
Ogwaza, 42
Ojukwu, Chukwuemeka Odumegwu, 12, 15, 19, 33, 45, 49, 55
Ojukwu, Louis Odumegwu, 15, 55
Okello, Bassilio, 151
Okpara, Michael, 42
Ollivier, Marc, 77
Onitsha, 23
Onyegbulam, Godwin, 42
Ore, 26, 29

Organisation Commune Africaine et Malgache (OCAM), 13, 14
Organisation for Economic Cooperation and Development (OECD), 18
Organisation of African Unity (OAU), 2, 13, 15, 18
  on Angolan Civil War, 108–9
  response to Nigerian Civil War, 51–2, 53, 54, 55–7, 58, 67–8
Oromo, 64
Ovimbudu people, 71
Ovimbudu highlands, 87
Oxfam (Oxford Committee for Famine Relief), 4

PAIGC (Partido Africano da Independência da Guiné e Cabo Verde), 97, 100
Pakistan, 5, 6
Palestine, 5
Panama, 4
Persian Gulf, 82
Peru, 4
Peters, John, 37
Philippines, The, 7
pogrom, 12, 53
Port Harcourt, 12–13, 23, 24, 29, 30, 41
Portugal, 17
  'Africa Operations Bureau' (Lisbon), 47
  and Biafra's war effort, 46–7, 67
  Armed Forces Movement (MFA), 69, 73, 88, 89
  COPCON (Continental Operations Command), 88
  counter-insurgency in Angola, 69, 70, 71, 72, 73, 74–6, 78, 79–80, 81 *passim*
  'Portuguese Commonwealth' political solution, 73
  Portuguese Communist party, 90

Raucana, 107
Reagan, Ronald, 7–8
  Reagan Doctrine, 7
Rhodesia, Northern (Zambia), 17

Index

Rhodesia, Southern (Zimbabwe), 17, 18
  role in Nigerian Civil War, 58–9, 106
Roberto, Holden, 71, 78–9, 113
Roman Catholic (Christian denomination), 55
Rwanda, 57

Sa da Bandeira, 85, 105, 107
Salazar, Antonio, 75
Sandanista Front for National Liberation (FSLN), 6
Santa Combo, 107
Santo Antonio do Zaïre, 77
Sao Tome (and Principe Islands), 45, 46, 47, 67, 69, 108
Saudi Arabia, 120
Savimbi, Jonas, 79, 81, 83, 106
Scott, Robert, 33, 38
Second World War, 1, 3, 5, 6, 74
Senegal, 4, 106, 109
Senghor, Leopold, 106
Shaba, 6, 114–15
  historical background to Shaba uprisings, 112–14
  Western intervention in the uprisings, 115–25
  Zaïre's economic heartland, 114–15
Shell-BP, 22–4, 27, 48
Shepherd, Lord, 39
Sisco, Joseph, 83
Six-Day War (Arab-Israeli), 22, 45, 54
Smith, Arnold, 39
Smith, Ian, 17–18
Solodovnikov, V., 90
Somalia, 5, 92, 108
Somoza, Anastasio, 6
South Africa, 2, 5, 9, 10, 17, 26, 27
  mercenaries in Angolan Civil War, 81
  intervention in Angolan Civil War – 'Operation Zulu', 102, 104–7, 108, 111, 127
  role in Nigerian Civil War, 58–9, 73, 86
  support for Portuguese counter-insurgency in Angola, 104
Southern World (The South), 1, 3–9
  debt of, 4
  net export capital from, 4, 89
Soviet Union, 2, 6, 7, 19–21, 27, 31, 34–6, 45, 49, 57, 59–66
  and the Shaba conflicts, 115, 118 *passim* 129–30
  arms to federal Nigeria, 65–6
  Asiatic Republics of the, 64
  Baltic States in the, 64
  'Committee on Afro-Asian Solidarity', 95
  Moldavia, in the, 64
  intervention in Angolan Civil War, 90–5
  intervention in Nigerian Civil War, 63
  origins of relations with the MPLA, 89–90
  Ukraine, in the, 64, 82, 83, 84–5, 86, 96, 97, 98, 99, 100, 101, 102
Sri Lanka, 6
Stewart, Michael, 29, 40
Stockwell, John, 78, 80–1, 100, 106, 117
Sub-African State System, 131, 138–9, 140 *passim*
Sudan, 4
  arms sales to federal Nigeria, 57, 107
  intervention in the Shaba conflicts, 127
Suez Canal, 22
Swaziland, 103
Sweden, 32
Switzerland, 32, 37, 123
Syria, 82

Tamil Eelam, 6
Tanzania, 5
  recognition of Biafran independence, 52, 53, 54, 96, 100, 107, 128
Thailand, 5
Thomson, W. Scott, 92–3
Tigray, 64

Times, The (London), 37
Tshombe, Moise, 56, 112, 113
Tubman, William, 55, 56
Tunisia, 4

Uganda, 5, 109
  National Resistance Movement, 151
Uige, 71, 85
United Kingdom, *see* Britain
United Nations, 87, 124, 125
United States (US), 2, 7–8, 17, 19, 27
  Angola Task Force, 78
  arms purchased by Biafra and Nigeria from, 32, 50
  Central Intelligence Agency (CIA), 78, 80, 81, 85, 88, 117
  economic and financial interests in the Nigerian federation, 48
  'Forty Committee', 80
  interests in Zaïre, and intervention in the Shaba conflicts, *see* Zaïre
  National Security Council, 80
  NSSM, 39 (National Security Study Memorandum), 72–3, 80
  responses to Nigerian Civil War, 47–51, 62
  'Security Support Assistance' for Zaïre, as part of intervention in Angola, 81
  support for Portuguese counter-insurgency operations in Angola, 74–6
  support for UNITA-FNLA in civil war against MPLA, 78ff, 88, 89
  US Military Assistance Advisory Group, 75
United States and the Soviet Union, 132, 139, 140, 141 *passim*
USSR (Union of Soviet Socialist Republics), *see* Soviet Union
Uwechue, Raph, 37, 43

Vietnam, 5, 7, 49, 75, 83

Vila Luso, 113
Vorster, John, 105

Walston, Lord, 28
West (bloc), The, 3, 4, 6, 17, 62–3, 68, 90, 92, 93, 94, 95
  interests in Zaïre, and interventions in the Shaba conflicts, *see* Zaïre
Western Sahara, 5
Wicks, Alistaire, 37
Wilson, Harold, 18, 25, 26, 30–2, 36, 50
World Bank, 120, 121

Young, Andrew, 117, 118
Yugoslavia, 95

Zaïre (northern Angola district), 71
Zaïre, The Republic of, 1, 2, 6, 9, 10, 51, 56
  and anti-MPLA forces in Angolan Civil War, 81, 82, 84–5, 103, 105, 108, 109
  insurrections in eastern province of Shaba, 122
  see also Shaba
  'Katanga gendarmes', 112–14
  National Front for the Liberation of the Congo (FNLC), 112 *passim*
  other anti-Mobutu opposition forces, 115
  President Mobutu calls for Western assistance to fight Shaba insurgents, 115ff
  'The Friends of Zaïre', *see* ZAC
  Western interests in Zaïre, and interventions in the Shaba conflicts, 115–25
Zaïrean Aid Consortium (ZAC), 120
Zambia, 4
  recognition of Biafran independence, 52, 53, 54, 83, 84–5, 100, 103, 105
Zanzibar, 53
Zimbabwe, 5, 94, 103